MAKE PEACE BEFORE THE SUN GOES DOWN

From a book coinscribed by Thomas Merton and Dom James Fox to Dom Pacôme Gaboury, abbot of Notre-Dame du Lac des Deux-Montagnes (Canada). Collection of Peter Harrington Rare Books (London).

MAKE PEACE BEFORE THE SUN GOES DOWN

The Long Encounter of Thomas Merton and His Abbot, James Fox

Roger Lipsey

Shambhala
BOSTON & LONDON
2015

Shambhala Publications, Inc.
Horticultural Hall
300 Massachusetts Avenue
Boston, Massachusetts 02115
www.shambhala.com

9 8 7 6 5 4 3 2 1

First Edition
Printed in the United States of America

♾ This edition is printed on acid-free paper that meets the American National Standards Institute z39.48 Standard.
♻ This book is printed on 30% postconsumer recycled paper. For more information please visit www.shambhala.com.

Distributed in the United States by Penguin Random House LLC and in Canada by Random House of Canada Ltd

Designed by Dean Bornstein

Library of Congress Cataloging-in-Publication Data

Lipsey, Roger, 1942–

Make peace before the sun goes down: the long encounter of Thomas Merton and his abbot, James Fox / Roger Lipsey.
—First edition.

pages cm

ISBN 978-1-61180-225-2 (paperback)

1. Trappists—United States—Biography. 2. Merton, Thomas, 1915–1968. 3. Fox, James, Abbot of Gethsemani, 1896–1987. 4. Abbey of Our Lady of Gethsemani (Trappist, Ky.)—History. I. Title.

BX4155.L57 2015

271'.125022—dc23

2014033078

For generous friends in the Cistercian Order

Hospes fui et suscepistis me

Your Reality, O God, speaks to my life as to an intimate.

—THOMAS MERTON, *The Sign of Jonas*, 1953

There is no one who hasn't been influenced by you, Tom.

—DOM JEAN LECLERCQ, letter of 1 June 1968

CONTENTS

CONTENTS

ILLUSTRATIONS

ACKNOWLEDGMENTS

I cannot say that the monastic community at the Abbey of Gethsemani willed this book into existence, but so many members of the community shared their unique knowledge when I was preparing to write that it felt as if a common will had set to work. Fr. Elias Dietz, abbot, kindly consented to my use of the abbey's archives and offered meticulous comments on the manuscript. In light of his review, I was able to correct various errors of fact and perception. I am utterly grateful for his support. I must declare at once that neither the abbot nor any early reader is responsible for errors of fact or interpretation that may remain. New findings drawn from unfamiliar archives need time to settle in the minds of those who care for the legacies of both Thomas Merton and Dom James. We have not agreed on every point; we have conversed in rich and memorable ways.

Not for the first time, Br. Paul Quenon of Gethsemani was my shepherd throughout the research process. As well, he has contributed exquisite photographs to this volume. He cooks in the morning. He helps people in the afternoon and evening. I am so fortunate to be one of those he helps. Br. Lawrence Morey, the abbey archivist, knows my debt to him. Morning after morning it was a joy to see him wheeling carts of boxed documents toward my worktable. Apart from my laptop, we inhabited a timeless monastic atmosphere: which century was it? I thank members of the Gethsemani community who joined me for interviews, many of whom later thoughtfully commented on an early draft: Fr. Michael Casagram, Br. Frederic Collins, Fr. James Conner, Br. Conrad Fleischmann, Fr. Alan Gilmore, Br. Patrick Hart, and Br. Giuseppe Nazionale. Without your knowledge and warmth, what would this book be? A former abbot of Gethsemani, Fr. Timothy Kelly, kindly took time to speak with me from Rome, where he serves as procurator general of the Cistercian Order. I also had the privilege of interviewing Fr. John Eudes Bamberger, friend to both Merton and Dom James, at the Abbey of the Genesee in the Finger Lakes region of New York State. Like his Gethsemani peers, he is elderly now. May he and they live long. I want also to acknowledge the judicious comments and friendship of Fr. Mark Scott, whom I first met at Gethsemani some years ago; he is now abbot of New Melleray Abbey, a Cistercian house in Iowa.

Dr. Paul Pearson, director of the Thomas Merton Center to which all Merton scholars turn, offered a close reading of the book in draft. I am most grateful to him—not for the first time. His immensely able assistant director, Mark Meade, supported my research both at the center and from afar when I needed additional materials. What a remarkable team. Morgan Atkinson, the Louisville-based filmmaker who has done exceptional work on Merton, kindly shared transcripts of his interviews with Fr. John Eudes and Fr. Daniel Berrigan. Invaluable—and so generous on his part.

It was a privilege to exchange by e-mail with Dr. Caroline Zilboorg, Gregory Zilboorg's daughter and literary executor. Her generous permission to cite her father's correspondence has allowed me to clarify a key episode in the shared lives of Thomas Merton and Dom James.

In the publishing world, I am permanently grateful to my literary agent and friend Tracy Cochran. What good fortune to have such an ally. Dave O'Neal, senior editor at Shambhala Publications, had no doubt from the beginning that he wanted to publish this book. I am most grateful to him and his colleagues. Lauren Manoy brought her expert copyediting skills to bear on the notes and bibliography.

My wife, Susan, the first reader of this book, welcomed its chapters with steady interest and encouragement. This too not for the first time: grateful thanks to you.

MAKE PEACE BEFORE THE SUN GOES DOWN

. . .

This book tells the tale of a brilliant writer and man of faith, Thomas Merton, in his relations with an immensely capable abbot, Dom James Fox, at the Abbey of Gethsemani in central Kentucky. They were in many respects a mismatch, fated to struggle with each other for nearly twenty years. To tell their story honestly has been the only option, although it is not without pain and wonder. The plentiful documents that allow the story to be told demand obedience: this book says what they say, sometimes intriguing, sometimes excruciating, sometimes deep, sometimes warm. The story belongs to its time and place and persons, never to be repeated, but it may speak to spiritual communities of our time in which men and women strive, despite the difficulties they face, to acknowledge both the ideals they share and one another.

[1]
Nuance

One of the first and endless lessons of spiritual community is to find one's way somehow—perhaps brilliantly and with friendship, perhaps awkwardly or scarcely at all—with those who, like you, have arrived from points unknown and show no sign of going elsewhere. People of different kinds seek the same light. Unlike in temperament, background, and experience, in gifts and blanks, in willingness and fears, they reach one and the same destination: a spiritual community that called from the distance and drew them in. Whatever the focus may be—a traditional faith, a teaching or way of life—it makes urgent sense to those who respond. They may know a great deal about the community's concerns but are unlikely to know many of those whom they will meet and with whom they may associate for years, even a lifetime.

There is a second endless lesson: one must find one's way with the local human population because of a loyalty to the teaching or faith that surpasses other concerns without exception. Many dramas ensue from these two premises: loyalty to the teaching, human differences. The loyalty pins you in place. The differences, when serious and seemingly without remedy, fling you apart. "Make peace before the sun goes down" is a potent injunction in the sixth-century Rule of Saint Benedict, which to this day governs Cistercian communities. The words are from Paul's Letter to the Ephesians; their authority and challenge are ageless.

As he matured in the monastic life, Thomas Merton became a Cistercian through and through (fig. 1). He was "the next chapter"—our chapter—in the luminous spiritual and intellectual life

FIG. 1. Thomas Merton, 1960s, at the hermitage.

rooted in the example and writings of Saint Bernard of Clairvaux and the generations surrounding him. James Fox, abbot of Gethsemani from 1948 to his retirement in 1967, was by temperament

FIG. 2. Dom James Fox, 1949, soon after becoming abbot of the Abbey of Gethsemani.

and conviction a Trappist (fig. 2). There should be no great difference between these two callings; after all, Dom James would typically close letters with the promise that his correspondents would be remembered "in the daily round of our Trappist-Cistercian life of prayer and sacrifice here at Gethsemani."[1] Notre-Dame de La

Trappe is the monastery in Normandy renewed in practice and rigor by its famed seventeenth-century abbot, Armand Jean le Bouthillier de Rancé. It was a new edition of Cistercian life, rescued from the laxity, financial exploitation, and adversities of prior centuries. But it was a new edition with a difference. "As monastic life is but a school of penitence, humility, and abjection, nothing suits it better than humiliations," wrote Rancé. "Religious congregations are collections of criminals and public penitents who, lacking the fidelity they owed God, and having irritated him by their disobedience, can no longer aspire to receive any goodness from him until they have satisfied his justice through punishments worthy of their sins. . . . The cloister is a prison."[2] The words are from a nearly one-hundred-page exposition—surely the longest of its kind in Christian or any other literature—on the central importance of deliberate humiliation and mortification in the monastic life. Rancé was by no means only a prison warden; he possessed charm, generosity, worldly sophistication, a sure way with words. In his lifetime La Trappe was a magnet for serious religious. But he was also a prison warden.

By the mid-twentieth century the distinction between Cistercian and Trappist was a shade of difference, a wrinkle in a continuous fabric.[3] Dom James was, of course, a Cistercian who cared very much about sustaining a cheerful and cheerfully resolute spirit in the community. But in certain respects—his personal spirituality and the severity of restrictions imposed on Merton—he nonetheless recalls Rancé. We'll look more closely in later pages. On his side, Merton was not a permanently sunny soul. He lived in a state of inquiry, a kind of uneasy joy; he suffered periods of personal agony; and he valued the moderate austerities of monastic life, which for the most part he found natural and helpful. Yet his mature spirituality recalls the warmth, breadth, and depth of the early Christian desert fathers and the first Cistercian generations. "Are you saying," I questioned Fr. John Eudes Bamberger, a man ancient and wise who knew them both well, "that in writing about Thomas Merton and Dom James, nuance is needed everywhere?" "Amen!" he replied.[4] We must carry that amen with us.

This book concerns a long relationship periodically and excruciatingly difficult. It was a relation that would founder in abysses of disagreement, misunderstanding, imposition, and resentment, yet reemerge into the light as a willing partnership, only to founder again. Willingness and profound disagreement would often coexist; each had its days of the week. It was also a relation with secrecies: in the later years neither man was wholly frank with the other. And each was a crucial fact in the other's life; they could not lose sight of each other. For Dom James, Father Louis (as Merton was known in the community) was his principal and recurrent dilemma, his unsolved koan. How many people and issues and needs Dom James approached deftly, often with kindness and practical foresight. But as he wrote to the abbot general of the order in May 1955, "Nothing . . . causes me more anxiety than [the] chronic emotional crises of our good author, Father Louis. They weigh on my conscience, and I certainly do not handle them lightly or arbitrarily."[5] Even in these few words there is a trace of self-justification; he would have had difficulty acknowledging that his policies rather than Merton's character deficiencies gave rise to some of the good author's wilder emotions. For Thomas Merton, Dom James was typically, though not always, an impassable obstacle to freedoms he felt he deserved within the accepted and shared context of Cistercian monastic life. "I am apparently a lifetime property of this corporation,"[6] he wrote to his friend and publisher, James Laughlin, in 1967. Dom James was *his* unsolved koan. These brief passages from correspondence are deliberately mild; each man had much more to say of the other.

Even when harshest, the long encounter between Thomas Merton and Dom James can and should be understood—partially, with nuance—in light of a truth recorded somewhere in the writings of Saint John of the Cross: "If you are going to be a saint, the brothers must make you one."[7] Merton's spiritual and intellectual scope, and his restless nature ever seeking more light and depth of experience, confronted Dom James with a brilliant alien, a creature unlike himself though identically committed to monastic life. To some unquantifiable degree the abbot learned from the encounter, shared with ease some aspects of community life, and toward the end of their association took his lead from Merton in an important respect. On Merton's side, the abbot's restrictions generated immense discomfort but plunged him into sustained reflection about the nature of monastic life in the modern era, the scope and demands of his vocations as a contemplative and author, the struggle for willing obedience and intelligent self-sacrifice, and much else—themes memorably explored in his journal and in correspondence with trusted others. His legacy would be much the poorer had he not encountered Dom James. Up to a point, they were each other's soul maker. I don't know whether they made each other saints; there can be no doubt that they added to each other's resourcefulness and understanding of life.

Their relation as it matured was an agon. This nearly obsolete term fits through its suggestions of competition, ritual, and pain. Every Merton biographer has noticed the difficulty they had with each other. Elderly members of the Gethsemani community have memories, if not always about the difficulty, which tended to be invisible, then about the character of the one or the other. Scholars and religious frequently take the view that, after all, Merton exaggerated his problems with Dom James and often recanted the next day. Some have written that it was a special kind of friendship—and Dom James himself said as much. There is a detectable desire to soften the focus of the vintage photograph, to make it a prayer card. All of this to say that we are on well-trod ground: others have been here before us, others will come later.[8]

If we are to make new sense of this situation and learn from it, we need documents capable of grounding inquiry in what factually occurred, attitudes factually recorded. What was the unfiltered sound of this relationship? What were its events, not only the obvious ones but the hidden ones, the dark matter? For Merton, documentation is no problem owing to the immense holdings of the Thomas Merton Center and publication of his journals and much correspondence; the record is clear and large. But Dom James has remained difficult to know. To view him solely through the lens of Merton's writings is to adopt too readily Merton's perspective. Where, then, to find Dom James *in se,* as he would sometimes embellish with Latin his letters to monastic superiors—in himself, free of Merton's interpretations? Merton was often enough put off by Dom James's homilies and circular letters; his journals make that clear. But where are the texts of those homilies and letters? We should read them to understand for ourselves. Further, it stands to reason that Dom James would have had extensive correspondence about troublesome though good Father Louis with prominent churchmen, with his superiors in the order, and no doubt with others. We should read that correspondence. Private and presumably candid, it is the hidden counterpart to Merton's journals, also largely hidden in his lifetime.

While many documents written by Dom James are preserved in the Thomas Merton Center at Bellarmine University (Louisville), on which all Merton interpreters gratefully rely, others and among the most important survive—rarely read, it seems—in the archives of the Abbey of Gethsemani. Thanks to the generosity and trust of the current abbot and to the good-hearted labors of the abbey archivist, we can draw here on that resource to shape an interpretive history closely based on documents written by each man. As well, interviews with members of the Gethsemani community who witnessed those years have proved to be a unique resource. This is a fortunate time to raise the topic of Thomas Merton and Dom James with these men of religion. Dressed identically, and elegantly, in the traditional white Cistercian robe and black scapular held in place by a rugged leather belt, they are wholly distinct from one another, with individual perspectives and experiences to share, more than enough humor and seriousness, and more than enough love for Merton, Dom James, and the Cistercian way of life that brought them all together.

[2]

With Great Reluctance, an Autobiography

ON THE EVE OF HIS RETIREMENT as abbot of Gethsemani, November 1967, Dom James had reason to tell something of his life story to his superior, Dom Ignace Gillet, the Cistercian abbot general in Rome. "It is with great reluctance that I have to be so autobiographical," he wrote, but he was quite sure that his request to the abbot general needed context. We'll return much later to the substance of that request; for now we can patch elements from this revealing document into a broader view of his life. "It is not without sentiments of sorrow and reluctance," he continued, "—speaking on the human level only—that I write to you this letter. I have some faint idea at least of the many problems that must come across your desk as the Abbot General of a Cloistered Contemplative Order."[1] Communications among senior figures in the Cistercian Order—and surely throughout the Church in that era—obeyed an unwritten code. Expressions of personal humility were frequent; recollections of the conjoined divine and human contexts were both a pious habit and a discreet request to evaluate issues objectively rather than by personal preference. Dom James had well more than a "faint idea" about the issues current in the order and the complexities of monastic administration, but he knew the code. However, niceties never prevented Dom James and his highly placed correspondents from addressing issues with very considerable candor.

We know from sources other than this letter that Dom James was born Harry Vincent Fox on December 10, 1896, in the Boston suburban town of Dedham, to a pious Irish Catholic family with numerous children, all of them destined to join religious communities (his brother Bernard was a familiar presence for years at Gethsemani as the community's driver, though he never chose to become a monk). Throughout life Dom James retained the Boston accent of his youth; he spoke like a Kennedy, or they spoke like him. The children were first generation; their parents had emigrated from County Monaghan on the northern border of today's Republic of Ireland. Young Harry attended Dedham High School. He must have been brilliant: he received annual scholarships to attend Harvard College, the first granted by the Harvard Club of Boston, and graduated in three years with a Phi Beta Kappa key. He pursued a varied course of liberal arts studies focused on history and fully participated in a campus organization, Saint Paul's Catholic Club, for which he served as treasurer in his second year and president in the third. Harking back to those years in the letter to Dom Ignace, he wrote:

> As a young boy and as a youth—I, when going to High School, always felt that our Lord was really calling me to a life of closer union with Him. But strange as it may seem, I did all I could to escape from Him. I never went to a Catholic school in all my life. And when it came time to choose a university for undergraduate work, I chose a non-sectarian university. I finished the four year undergraduate Liberal Arts course in three years and graduated when twenty years old. Then I went to the graduate school of Business Administration, also there at Harvard. . . . I was making plans to become a man of power and influence in the great business world of the United States.

Like many another Harvard man to this day, Dom James had some difficulty referring straightforwardly to the great institution, as if pronouncing its name were boastful; he first writes of it generically as "a non-sectarian university," but he had better reason than most: in that era a young Catholic needed a bishop's permission to attend a non-Catholic institution of higher learning. That must have left a trace. Speaking of those years, long after, with a member of the Gethsemani community, Dom James made clear that he had wanted very much to "get ahead," and among other things to show that a Catholic could do as well as or better than his non-Catholic classmates.[2] It should also be added that, like many another Harvard man, he made friends at college and at the famed B School who could be helpful to him in later life.

The Harvard College yearbook for the class of 1918 reveals that Harry and many of his classmates were enlisted in the armed forces. It was surely a legitimate point of pride to be photographed in uniform. Harry's class photo shows a slender, intense young man in the uniform of a Yeoman Second Class, U. S. Naval Reserve. Joining in February 1918 and formally graduating that spring, he didn't see action or serve for long. He took advantage of his early completion of undergraduate course work to attend business school for a semester at the end of 1917, where he studied disciplines that would prove in part useful later: marketing, accounting, contracts, factory management, military supply. When the war ended in November 1918, he resigned from the navy and spent two years working for the Internal Revenue Service as an auditor of corporate returns.

The religious life was unforgotten. "When I was in the Navy," he wrote to Dom Ignace, "I had made a retreat at the Passionist Monastery in Boston. After the War, something made me go back there for another retreat. It was on this second retreat that Grace overcame Nature and I at last surrendered to our dear Lord. I was then 24 years old. . . . Once I had entered religious life—the inexorable logic of my mind was now concentrated on things spiritual and eternal." One stumbles momentarily over his assertion of "inexorable logic"—it breaks the code of humility. But no matter: he wants to remind the abbot general that he is a clear thinker.

Founded in the early seventeenth century by a cleric now known as Saint Paul of the Cross, the Passionist Congregation is dedicated to the remembrance of Christ's sufferings on the cross and to carrying a message of love and salvation through "preaching the Gospel of the Passion" and leading retreats.[3] Saint Paul of the Cross defined the new community's mission as teaching how to pray. Its members wear dark robes with a striking embroidered emblem representing the Heart of Jesus surmounted by the abbreviated Latin inscription JESU XPI PASSIO: the Passion of Jesus Christ. For non-Catholics and liberal Catholics the Passionists' focus may seem a somber inheritance from another era, but there is every reason to believe that the two thousand members of today's congregation, divided into male and female houses, serve good purposes with good hearts.

The community was not well suited to the young man who became Dom James. "A desire for even greater silence, solitude and seclusion," he wrote to Dom Ignace, "took more and more possession of my heart and of my mind." He applied for and received a "transitus," a formal permission to move to another order and community within the Church. "It seemed to be God's Will," as he reported the judgment of his Passionist superiors, "to pass over to an Order where more silence and solitude would be the regular and normal milieu. The only Order in the U. S. A. at that time, which was 1927—was our Trappist Cistercian order. One of the principal monasteries was here at Gethsemani. The reason I chose Gethsemani was that it was furthest away from Boston." Years later young Thomas Merton would similarly value the distance between Gethsemani and everything else. James entered Gethsemani in January 1927, took solemn vows in the spring of 1929, and was ordained to the priesthood in April 1930.

He took much of the inner teaching of the Passionists with him. Throughout his life he remained devoted to the suffering Son of God and as abbot urged the members of the Gethsemani community to keep the limitless love and sacrifice of Jesus in mind and heart, to make an intimate inner relation with him. His personal notepaper with his abbatial coat of arms at the top displayed a

Celtic cross (the traditional cross with circular nimbus) and, in medieval Irish font, the words DEUS CRUCIFIXUS. In his mideighties in 1979, retired as abbot for more than a decade but living at Gethsemani, Dom James gave a nostalgic talk to the community on the fiftieth anniversary of his solemn vows. Entering Gethsemani for the first time in winter 1927, he recalled, he heard a bell strike as he passed from cloister to church. He felt addressed, he said, "as if HE were saying: 'Your life from now on, will be closely associated with ME in MY sufferings and Crucifixion.'"[4] The capitalizations are his own, the punctuation also. The notes he used to deliver talks drew on all the resources of the era's typewriter to guide verbal emphasis as he spoke: capitalizations, red ink, underlines. He urged the community:

> Your aim should be to keep trying to grow in more and more continuous—conscious—communing with JESUS—one to ONE—Pal to Pal—Person to PERSON. . . . Sometime—in quiet silence and solitude, take out your crucifix—Look right into JESUS' eyes—see HIS eyes looking right into yours—let your glances meet—Rest in that mutual glance—HE is saying silently, to YOU: "This is how much YOU cost ME. . . . This is how much I LOVE YOU. . . . LOVE is measured—not by self-gratification—but by self-immolation. How much will you GIVE UP for JESUS—50%— 57—95—99½—or 100%??? . . . and this is most encouraging—LOVE is nourished, by SELF DENIAL. . . . This growth in Love of JESUS, costs self-love awful—but so what!!!

"Pal to Pal"? As we'll see more thoroughly later, Dom James's spirituality blended simple, heartfelt faith with the ascetic teachings of Rancé and, closer to home, the Passionist openness to God Crucified. A natural question: does this talk of James's old age, more than a decade after Merton's death, reflect his spirituality in the years when Merton regularly heard him speak in chapter? The answer is yes, beyond doubt. Merton had heard some of these very words twenty years earlier, as he noted rather deadpan in his journal: "Rev. Father closed the Chapter with 'Yes, Jesus must be our real pal, our most intimate buddy.'"[5] The monks, now elderly, who knew Dom James are unanimous on the point. One of them, a priest educated as a young man in an elite seminary in Rome, was altogether candid with me. "Dom James had a plethora of clichés," he recalled. "It used to just drive me batty. When I was a student in Rome, I would talk sometimes with Fr. Basil, who was master of students over there, and so he knew all of my complaints about Dom James's clichés. When James came to Rome and gave a talk to the students, I noticed Fr. Basil watching me for my reaction the whole time, to see how I would respond." "Was the talk full of clichés?" I asked. "Oh, yes. That was the thing with Dom James: he was very one-track."[6] Another impeccable witness, Fr. John Eudes, once heard Merton say that "Dom James has too few ideas, but he lives them."[7] This is kind; it is live and let live.

In the 1940s, Fr. James Fox stood out in the American Cistercian community. His New England sturdiness of character; his rock-solid commitment to monasticism under the Rule of Saint Benedict; his noticeable potential to ensure the economic welfare of a prayerful community; and no doubt his personal charm, to which many attested in later years—all of these traits led to his appointment as superior of Our Lady of the Holy Spirit, a daughter house of Gethsemani founded in 1944 on farmland in Georgia. The superior in a Cistercian foundation is second in command, reporting to the founding abbot. Less than two years later, James was elected abbot of Holy Spirit. A touching photograph shows him receiving the abbatial blessing in December 1946 from the Bishop of Charleston: he kneels amid a crowd of monks and clergy; the bishop's hands rest on his tonsured head; he is scarcely visible in the close pack of people, as if the Old Man, whoever he may have been, is being squeezed out of existence to make way for the New Man, the abbot.[8]

His time in office lasted little more than two years. The sudden death of the aged, vastly respected abbot of Gethsemani, Dom Frederic Dunne, who had founded both the daughter abbey in Georgia and another in Utah, led to a call to return to Gethsemani, where Dom James was elected abbot on August 23, 1948. For the occasion, Merton—just thirty-three years old, soon to be acclaimed as the best-selling author of *The Seven Storey Mountain*—served in a minor official role as a scrutator, a compiler and examiner of ballots. A day earlier he had noted in his journal:

> Tomorrow is the abbatial election. . . . Some expect Dom James to be elected on the first ballot. He arrived today with Fr. Ephrem and Fr. Mary from Georgia as witnesses. . . . Tomorrow we choose the one who is to lead us for a certain time to God, to make saints of us. . . . I am not, I think, voting on any natural motive—food and what not. Writing doesn't enter into it. Our Lady will manage everything.[9]

On the following day, our humble scrutator took careful notice of all things—he was a born scrutator—and later made further notes in his journal:

> The election lasted from 7:45 to 12:25—and this included confirmation and installation of Dom James who, of course, was elected. It is easy to see from this end of the affair that he was the Holy Ghost's candidate—in more senses than one. . . . When the voting was over, the result was announced in Latin at the Chapter door, the doors of the church, and the monastery gate. The cloister was unlocked and the novices, young professed, and lay brothers came in. . . . We went in disorder to church singing the Te Deum. Then everyone went back to the Chapter Room and the ones who hadn't voted sat there in silence and waited, rather confused, for the long business of installation, while all the professed made their promise of obedience to Dom James.
>
> It was very moving. Big room packed with people, all silent. A

long file of monks moving up to Dom James's throne. . . . When it was all over we had an abbot. And a holy one too. . . . Dom James is quiet and humble.

That afternoon, when he was in Louisville at the Archbishop's, I got a check for nine hundred dollars on *The Seven Storey Mountain,* so I gave it to him the next morning and he told me to go on writing.[10]

[3]

All for Jesus thru Mary with a Smile

THE RESULT OF THE ELECTION was announced in Latin at three thresholds; the liturgy also was in Latin: ancient usage was respected. Gethsemani at the time, and well into the 1950s, belonged far more to the long history of the Cistercian Order than to the postwar world of torrid economic progress, crowds of newborn Baby Boomers toddling toward life, and rock and roll. The abbot reigned. Under the Rule of Saint Benedict, to this day, he is the representative of Jesus Christ in the community. Though there are limited checks and balances, he wields great power and carries proportionately great responsibility for the spiritual progress and overall well-being of community members and the institution itself. Dom James's style as abbot, through much of his abbacy, blended unquestioned and unquestionable hierarchy with qualities of paternal warmth that endeared him to many in the community, particularly the lay brothers who were responsible for physical upkeep and farming operations. "He was very gentle and very warm and very open with me," a community member recently recalled. "Of course, I was Irish and he was Irish. I think that was a factor."[1]

The Gethsemani community was large and growing larger. The end of World War II had left many young Catholic veterans longing for . . . something. Something that might be found in monastic life. In 1949, the community numbered 165 monks, and there were more to come. As Merton's widely read book *The Seven Storey Mountain* made its rapid way in the world after publication in 1948, Cistercian communities at Gethsemani and elsewhere attracted novices who hoped for new lives and perceptions at least a little like his. Reaching its largest size at some point in the 1950s, Gethsemani numbered well over 250 community members, some living in a tent city that had been thrown together in the *préau,* the central space enclosed by the cloister.

The monastic way of life at the beginning of Dom James's tenure was medieval, with the addition of a few motor vehicles. It was a life of silence—Cistercian sign language, a quite fully developed medieval skill, remained in use; one could speak with one's superiors on suitable occasions, but peers in the community exchanged only in sign. Merton was an advanced practitioner: he is said to have been capable of joking in sign.[2] In 1949, when he was working on a commemorative book we'll soon examine, *Gethsemani Magnificat* celebrating the first century of life at the abbey, Merton transcribed into his journal a characteristic exchange: "Brother Charles comes up and asks me by signs, 'When hundred year big day book come?' And I signal back to him 'plenty late, plenty late.' He says, 'How full pages? Two hundred?' I say, 'Yeah.' He goes away not sad but not altogether happy."[3] It is a bit lumbering, wouldn't you agree, though Merton obviously enjoyed the challenge of transcription. Somehow the members of the community felt they came to know one another.

Relations with Dom James were traditionally ordered. When passing him in a hallway, one bowed deeply; to others, less deeply. Entering his office, the monk would kneel beside his desk, kiss his abbatial ring—an act thought by some to reduce one's stay in purgatory by fifty days—and then take a seat for whatever conversation was needed. I have heard that James didn't especially like the ring practice, but custom prevailed. When a candidate novice came to him for an interview, at conversation's end Dom James apparently had the custom of placing his hand on the individual's head—a normal and lovely benediction—but then squeezing, as if to mime the penitential life that lay ahead. One recipient of this gesture, as a very young man seeking admission to the community, recalled that "the fingers got tighter, and tighter and tighter—and then I found out on the way into town the next day that he did the same thing to another young man who had an interview with him. I guess that was to make you remember, to give an impression."[4]

It wasn't the only penitential reminder. Following long tradition, Dom James kept a skull on his desk, as there had been on the desk of Rancé at La Trappe and many an abbot before and since. However, Dom James's companion skull had a fate of its own. Some years into his abbacy, he received a visit from the movie star Don Ameche, accompanied by the two young sons of another star, Loretta Young. While abbot and star conversed, the boys seized the skull and chased each other around the room, clacking its jaw. What a chaotic moment. The adults somehow retrieved the memento mori from this lively game, and Dom James slipped it into a desk drawer—never to appear again. Perhaps he had perceived some time earlier that the spirit of the community was changing.[5]

There was another sign of changing sensibility, likely at much the same period. The chapter of faults was a famous monastic and Cistercian institution, enacted weekly at Gethsemani through the earlier 1960s, when the reforming influence of Vatican II began to make itself felt. The community would gather in the chapter room, and Dom James would pronounce the traditional opening—"Let us speak of our order," in response to which community members would proclaim their infractions of the rules and regulations by prostrating themselves on the floor or respond to another's proclamation by falling prostrate. It was a dramatic custom. When no one came forward on his own, Dom James would say, "All saints then, all saints?" That tended to set the process in motion. One of the commonest revelations, seemingly trivial to the vanishing point, was "Br. X spoke aloud with his signs." Slow though it was to change, Gethsemani read the signs of the times more quickly than many Cistercian houses. There came a chapter of faults at which no one proclaimed self or other. The next week the same. And the week following. Whereupon the custom was silently set aside. It must have gone into a drawer. Was this an organized protest or an unanticipated, collective sigh?[6]

While the abbot reigned supreme, the respect he enjoyed was not irrefragable. An elderly brother recalls an incident that hints at an undercurrent of independence. "Dom James would walk around in the evening after compline with a flashlight. One of the brothers was opening the walk-in cooler to get something to eat after hours when James came around with his flashlight, and the brother said, 'Reverend Father, if you're looking for trouble, you're going to find it.'"[7]

The state of the monastery and Dom James's vision in the early years are brilliantly evident in two documents, of 1949 and 1952: *Gethsemani Magnificat,* a large-format book richly illustrated with photographs, and a carefully prepared talk he gave at what must have been a gathering of highly placed Cistercians and others who knew less of Cistercian life. The book is a period piece both for Gethsemani and for immediate postwar America, much like an old and fascinating postage stamp, but Dom James's preface conveys a view that changed only somewhat with the years, never beyond recognition. Young Merton wrote most of the book; here and there his individual touch is evident, though much of the text is cleanly written piety, an evocation of the abbey's current life, spirituality, and history.[8] Dom James opens with the question of whether Cistercian life, "this highest form of monastic life of prayer and sacrifice, could be lived and loved by American boys. Could red-blooded American boys, accustomed as they are to freedom, action, and independence, ever measure up to the high heroic requirements of the Trappist ideal?" He responds—naturally—that there is no need for doubt in that regard. "Gethsemani . . . has seventy novices," he continues.

> Many of these boys have distinguished themselves in the Air Force, Paratroopers, Navy and Marines of World War II. During 1941–

> 45 they were ready to give all for their God and Country in the natural order; now at Gethsemani they are giving all for God and Country in the supernatural order, because it will be powerhouses of prayer and penance such as Gethsemani which will be the prime bulwarks of defense of our beloved Homeland and American way of life against the rising tides of atheism and terrorism.... At Gethsemani, boys give—not fifty percent, seventy percent, ninety percent, nor even ninety-five percent—but one hundred percent for God and Country. The spirit of Gethsemani may be summed up in its favorite expression—"ALL FOR JESUS—THROUGH MARY—WITH A SMILE."[9]

Over time, this favorite expression at Gethsemani would wear on its inhabitants and on some of Dom James's correspondents, who reacted ironically to it; it was favored, and overused, by one person only. James had a rubber stamp with these words—"through" truncated to "thru"—to add the motto conveniently to documents (see the frontispiece to this book). Within two months of Dom James's accession, Merton had already wearied of the formula: "I have been going around *toujours avec un sourire,*" he recorded in his journal.[10] You won't have failed to notice that James's percentage rhetoric, perhaps making its debut here in 1949, still seemed apt to him thirty years later in his nostalgic talk to the community. But his preface makes clear that in one respect at least, Gethsemani in the immediate postwar period was not wholly removed from its time: the Church, and Gethsemani within it, perceived a role for itself in the defense of democracy and the United States against Communism. It was to be a powerhouse of prayer in the Cold War. In his preface to *Gethsemani Magnificat* on an earlier page, the archbishop of Philadelphia had already set the tone: "Today the Church of Christ," wrote the archbishop, "is challenged by the organized forces of Anti-Christ, as Atheistic Communism goes on its way triumphant. . . . In these dark days, the Church needs an army on its knees to strengthen those who are fighting the battles of the Lord."

Merton's pages (of course, anonymously written) are lighter, though he echoes in places Dom James's perspective about American boys and heroism. It is good to hear from him about each of the abbots who led Gethsemani and to read his captions for the many photographs. Sometimes he is discreetly impish, as for example in his caption for a vintage photo of the abbey library showing high shelves of books, chairs and such, and a table with stuffed birds: "Gethsemani's library housed fewer books then than now. The stuffed birds have disappeared." His timing was always good.

Dom James's 1952 lecture "The Contemplative Life in the United States"[11] is notable for its emphasis not so much on the contemplative life as on the community and its members. James was at heart a community builder and a man of prayer, not a contemplative. Contemplation did not mean for him, either in 1952 or later, what it came to mean through the mature writings of his brother in religion, Thomas Merton. James does devote some early pages of his lecture to the meaning of contemplation, but what he writes is conventionally pious and superficial, assertion rather than exploration. "Surely it is to be conceded," he writes, "that souls living in ideal conditions of silence, solitude and seclusion, which obtain in a well regulated cloister, other things being equal, ought to attain to a state of special friendship with Jesus, with special power over His Sacred Heart, and therefore a special efficacy for their prayer and penance in obtaining graces for the whole Church. . . . The justification of cloistered contemplatives . . . is not in their agricultural production, nor in their intellectual production, nor in their prayer and penance as such. The justification of cloistered contemplatives is God Himself. Because God alone is—'I am Who I am.' God alone is supreme. All else is secondary. A cloistered contemplative . . . is a living witness, a supreme testimony to the absolute transcendence, absolute sovereignty of Almighty God." Well, yes . . . and no. The notion of achieving special power over the Sacred Heart of Jesus seems unfair both to Jesus and to monks.

But no matter. What deeply interested Dom James was something else: monastic community. He tells numerous stories of young men entering as novices, facing the life, finding their way. He recounts his conversations with some of them, his dire warnings that the life would be hard. To an ex-marine fighter pilot with a good job on Wall Street he made a litany of the deprivations to be expected: "There will never be again any baseball, tennis, swimming, pool or bowling, or cards. There will never be any meat, fish or eggs, unless you are sick. There will never be newspapers, stock-tickers, magazines. . . . There will never be vacations in Florida, Atlantic City or Maine, or permission to visit home again even at the death of father or mother. . . . There will be nothing but relentless regularity." Some of these objects of desire must be the very things he himself had liked as a young man. Along the way he also refers obliquely to *The Seven Storey Mountain:* "Some say it is the books which come from Gethsemani that account for the increase of Trappist vocations in this Country, but I usually answer them that a book may bring a young man here but it takes more than a book to keep a man here. There is no explanation other than the work of Jesus in souls and the correlative cooperation they give."

This was Dom James, both then and later. He loved Jesus Christ with an intimate, childlike love often awkwardly expressed. The great mystery for him was not the mind and its movements toward and away from truth, or the heart and its movements toward and away from goodness, but the Holy Mass, the daily offices, the formal life of prayer and praise. He valued and practiced what he more than once called "self-immolation" for the sake of openness to God and the birth of something other and holy in oneself. It was good monastic tradition; he lived it in his own way. And above all he cared to build and safeguard the community dedicated to these things. All for Jesus thru Mary with a smile.

[4]

The Wall Street Journal *in a Cubbyhole*

UPON HIS ACCESSION AS ABBOT, Dom James discovered that the abbey's financial situation was disastrously weak, and everyone knew that some of its core buildings and outbuildings were firetraps in desperate need of renovation or replacement. As well, the community's size exceeded its housing capacity. In those early years the abbey was overreliant on donations, apart from a small artisanal cheese business that generated a modest income and the kitchen garden that supplied a share of the community's food. The age-old Cistercian injunction *ora et labora*—pray and work—was respected. The abbey, like all other Cistercian houses, was intended to be economically self-sufficient, and the monks did a great deal of work tending pasture and cow herd, gardening, gathering firewood, making a tasty Port du Salut cheese for local sale, and much else. But it was subsistence farming in support of a subsistence monastic economy inadequate to current needs. What to do?

One doesn't have to believe in Providence to recognize the hand of Providence here: the man behind the desk with its time-telling skull was a seasoned financial manager who had received the best entrepreneurial training of his era. He was capable of assessing the situation and responding. We can know how he responded, and in what spirit, largely thanks to the generosity of Br. Frederic Collins, a unique eyewitness who served as treasurer for decades under Dom James and later abbots. Reaching the abbey in 1954 after starting a career at the Ford Motor Company and with a degree in business from Kansas University, Br. Frederic received an extremely summary initial interview: "Do you know Latin?" "No."

"Can you sing?" "No." "Then you're a lay brother." The distinction at the time (now abandoned) between choir monks and lay brothers was quite rigid: lay brothers had a separate novitiate, they looked after practical necessities from cooking and gardening to shoeing horses, they did not attend the daily cycle of offices—and they were by and large delighted to be just what they were, men of religion bound into a community of prayer but with fewer formal requirements than the choir monks, who were either priests or preparing for the priesthood. While the choir monks had recurrent manual work assignments, their lives were far more given to study, prayer, and chant. Caste divisions were built into the community: lay brothers were not even permitted to address a choir monk except under specified circumstances. Let us note once more that Dom James was abbot—father—of the entire community, and not a few lay brothers spoke of him as "Papa"; they appreciated his paternal warmth and unfeigned concern for their welfare and spiritual lives. Nostalgia for Dom James has lasted to this day among some who knew him. His working-class background and sophisticated education gave him span.[1]

Br. Frederic had been drawn to the abbey by his reading of *The Seven Storey Mountain*. After two and a half years in the novitiate, he may have been readying himself for a job on the farm, but Dom James had become aware of his business qualifications. "Shortly after I left the novitiate," Frederic remembers,

> he asked me to start a direct mail business. Dom James had a feel for business, he was a natural businessman, a natural financial man—that was more important than his Harvard degree. He had figured out that the cheese business had potential, and somebody had told him that direct mail was a good way for monks to make a living because we could stay right here inside the enclosure. At the post office we could pick up the mail, and we had the cheese here. We were already selling cheese in the retreat house and a little elsewhere.

I knew nothing about direct mail, but I started making inquiries, and as happens quite frequently with monks of Gethsemani, people were willing to help out. I developed contacts with a couple of direct mail cheese companies in Wisconsin, and they volunteered to tell us how the business works. I even went up there a time or two.

Over the next ten years I managed that business. Started out just cheese, but eventually we added fruitcake—one of our monks had a secret recipe from his family. We also tried to incorporate meat from the farm; the more products you have in direct mail, the easier it is to sell, but shipping meat was tricky, and in the end that business didn't work out. Through those years I was cooperating with Br. Clement, a key person who in turn was constantly checking with Dom James Fox, who wanted the business to grow and had confidence in us both. Whatever major decisions we had to make, the abbot would go along with us.

Merton was not too excited about the business. Our advertising drove him nuts: "Many porkers are called, few are chosen." He used to post little notes on the bulletin board, even wrote notes to me—things like "Cheeses for Jesus." He was entitled to his opinions, but one day I had the chance to speak openly with him. As the manager of the business, I had permission to speak to people who came to help, but they were to remain silent. During our busy season—shipping time, November and December—Merton came with a big group of novices to help out. That was my chance. I could speak but Merton couldn't, he had to listen, where ordinarily *he* was giving talks. I said, "Look, Father Louis, this is what Dom James wants. He wants the business to make enough money to support the monks. You have your opinions about it. You think the farm is still a good thing—you would probably like to be out there with horses and carts, but those days are past." In the end Fr. Louis said, "Okay, okay." He didn't like it.

None of the monks ever saw a financial report, none was ever printed out. But as Dom James had more and more confidence in me, and wanted me to do a good job running that business, he called me over to the accounting office and started showing me financial reports so that I would have the big picture. None of the monks was ever aware of it, but he had a little cubbyhole in the accounting office, and in it was the *Wall Street Journal*. Whenever you have some free time, he told me, come in to this little cubby and read the *Journal*, it will give you a feel for business. For the next fifty years in my job as treasurer, I was reading the *Journal*—a little unusual for a monk.

After ten years, I asked Dom James whether he still wanted me to continue expanding the cheese and fruitcake business. He said yes. Well, I had seen the books: in today's figures it cost a million dollars for the monks to live, and by that time the business was making enough to cover that expense, and we had other income. Dom James said, "I have these daughter houses, six daughter houses in all, and other expenses. We need to make more money." I wasn't too sympathetic to that. But he's the abbot.[2]

And then there were Merton's books, generating annual royalties by Br. Frederic's reckoning in what today would be six figures. Though Merton didn't know the numbers over the years—payments soon went directly to the abbey—he could be quite sure that his literary output supported the community to a substantial degree. Curious, isn't it, that the cheese and fruitcake business and his earnings were, together, mainstays of the community. Curious, too, that it was in part—no small part—the appeal of Merton's writings that enlarged the community and made a nontrivial business operation necessary. As we witness Merton and Dom James entangle, repel, and work with each other in later pages, we should expect discussions of whether and what Merton should write. Some authors have asked whether Dom James viewed Merton's writings as a captive source of income to be retained within the monastery at all cost, even against Merton's best interest as a religious. When I reminded Fr. John Eudes of that charge, he immediately and sharply replied, "Calumny! James had other ways of making money."[3] It is true, as we'll see, that there were years when Dom James persuaded Merton to write and publish very little. Here, too, there are nuances, but the record is indisputable.

Dom James was a marvelously successful fund-raiser for the abbey, with a circle of generous friends in many parts of the country and nearby. One of the monks tells a charming story about a fund-raising visit by James to a well-known Catholic donor in Minnesota. The regional bishop caught wind of his visit and wondered aloud why he had come so far north—why didn't he stay where he belonged? James was friendly with some of the great families and individual donors of his time: the Kennedys, the Skakels, Loretta Young, Peter Grace (chairman and CEO of W. R. Grace and Company), and still others. One of the most storied and generous was a figure, somewhat mysterious then, more mysterious now: Captain Kinnarney of Louisville. He appears to have been the vice president of a private detective agency bearing his family name; he was reputed to be a major shareholder in Churchill Downs, the racetrack famous for its annual Kentucky Derby. However all that may be, he was often visible at the abbey in Dom James's years and earlier, and he was known to be a major donor. He makes cameo appearances in Merton's journals.

James is said to have been a shrewd negotiator; "shrewd" is a word that recurs in conversations with those who knew him, and he didn't mind: in a video made toward the end of his life, Dom James admiringly described a Cistercian abbot whom he knew in younger years as "a shrewd businessman."[4] A "pro at manipulation" is another description, always for what James regarded as the best interests of the abbey and the order.[5] A telling story in that connection is his acquisition of land and buildings for a new foundation, a daughter house, in Vina, California. Receiving an offer of land from the Leland Stanford family, founders of the great university, James went out to have a look. It happened that the land on offer adjoined a choicer parcel with an old vineyard, sturdy buildings, and warehouses, remnants of a failed winery project of many years earlier. That choicer parcel became the home of the Abbey of New Clairvaux, a flourishing monastery to this day.

One further touch is needed in this portrait of Dom James as an entrepreneur. Over the years he was able to accumulate a securities portfolio for the abbey worth, in Br. Frederic's estimation, some two million dollars at today's values when James retired in 1967. After his retirement he would often tease Br. Frederic: "You know, I went to a lot of trouble to build that portfolio. I hope you guys aren't spending it!" James could not have been more satisfied that he had amassed an endowment for the abbey. It was factually a fine and lasting achievement, and the "guys" have looked after it properly. Fr. Timothy Kelly, former abbot at Gethsemani and now procurator general of the order (second in command), is responsible today for understanding and insofar as possible helping the entire family of Cistercian houses worldwide, and he knows their finances. "Gethsemani should be grateful to Dom James for its financial stability," he said recently. "Not all of our houses are in anything like that position."[6]

And yet . . . The level of activity at Gethsemani for years and years, the endless hard noise of construction and farm machinery, the reworking of fields and water resources—none of this was what Merton had in mind when he joined a wonderfully backward, all but medieval monastery in 1941. As he matured into the formidable writer and searching contemplative we admire, he recoiled from the scene shaped by Dom James's will. He needed peaceful hiding places simply to be, to think and feel, to write, to move into the depth of his life. He was a Christian seeker, and he was more: he was evolving into a man of faith, conscience, and inner experience who could speak to the world, and the world listened. Dom James had done brilliantly well in so many respects. Yet he and Merton looked at each other from an increasing distance. We read some pages ago James's assessment of the cloistered contemplative life: "other things being equal," he said, silence, seclusion, and so on were the norm. But other things were not equal.

[5]
His Mind Is So Electrical

MERTON LOVED DOM FREDERIC DUNNE, abbot at Gethsemani at the time of Merton's arrival in 1941 to the old man's sudden death in 1948. Dom Frederic had the traditional Trappist severity —he didn't spare himself and expected the same of others—but he also had the warmth and attentiveness of those who have set fear aside.[1] "Dom Frederic . . . formed and shaped my whole monastic destiny," Merton wrote in *The Sign of Jonas* (1953).

> It was he, together with my novice master, Dom Robert, who decided that I should write books. It was he who firmly and kindly encouraged me and indeed ordered me to continue, in spite of my own misgivings. . . . I really think Dom Frederic was more interested in *The Seven Storey Mountain* than I was. . . . He was glad that the book might find a way to convince men of the reality of God's love for us. . . . He seemed to sense, in a way that I did not, something of the effect the book might have. . . . I shall never forget the simplicity and affection with which he put the first copy of the book in my hand. He did not say anything. . . . But I knew that he was happier about it than I could ever be. A few days later he was telling me to go on writing, to love God, to be a man of prayer and humility, a monk and a contemplative, and to help other men to penetrate the mystery of the love of God. It was the last time I ever spoke to him. . . . His sympathy was deep and real. . . . I don't know who was ever kinder to me.[2]

Merton surely found in Dom Frederic the good-hearted, understanding father he had missed in his own father, who died when

FIG. 3. Thomas Merton on the day of his ordination, 1949.

he was fifteen and hadn't been a steady presence. It was with this background, and possibly this expectation, that he came to know Dom James.

In the first years there was more sweet than sour by far. A newly ordained priest (fig. 3) and still quite young, Merton had every reason to extend to Dom James the trust—and vowed obedience—he had had toward Dom Frederic. Within a few months he realized that Dom James would not be an amazing theologian or a source of compelling ideas about monastic practice. Hearing that a talk by James in French had been well received in a general chapter meeting in France, Merton speculated in the privacy of his journal "that it was his personality that went over rather than his message or his language."[3] Overall, the written record between the two men, who had so many opportunities to speak directly, is much richer than one would predict. Dom James often traveled to daughter houses, to the general chapter, to develop relations with donors and other well-wishers. Merton's letters would pursue him. Pressing matters came up from time to time, issues that Merton preferred to define on the page for clarity's sake and dropped in the abbot's mailbox. He often gave the abbot a written account of personal days of recollection and periodic retreats. There are many such intensely private communications from Merton to abbot, and for years Merton was stringently, even devastatingly honest with Dom James about his struggles, his self-doubt, his sometimes enigmatic, punishing miseries. "Dear Reverend Father, things are pretty dark. I feel as if I had a hole burnt out of my heart. My soul is empty. . . . Please pray for me and bless me."[4] The misfortune associated with these notes is that Dom James could come to view them as the confessions of a disturbed individual; Merton's eloquent self-reflection, searching sincerity, and traditional monastic commitment not to show himself any quarter shaped to some degree his abbot's view of him, and in turn the view shared by his abbot with influential others. This is one of a number of ironies in their developing relation.

A few months after publication of his runaway best seller *The Seven Storey Mountain,* Merton assured Dom James that he cared more for traditional Cistercian values than for publicity. This is still Merton young, and contending with himself. "The fruit of this retreat," he began,

> seems to be . . . that the way to sanctity for me is simply marked out by our Rule and Usages. Keep them with a totally supernatural spirit, not seeking for things to be interesting or rewarding or exciting to myself personally. . . . My resolution is to be perfectly content to amount to nothing, so long as I generously do Jesus' will. . . . I don't want to shine in any way. The only reason why Jesus allows me to get publicity is probably that He sees I haven't enough virtue to be a complete nonentity. Please give me a big blessing and ask our Lady to keep me straight. All for Jesus—[5]

"Simply marked out" . . . it wasn't quite so and would never be quite so. At this early moment in their relation, Merton had already made clear to Dom James that he longed for greater solitude. Perhaps the best, he thought, would be a transitus—an official permission—to exit the Cistercian Order and become a Carthusian, a monk of the order celebrated in recent years by a beautiful film, *Into Great Silence.*[6] Carthusian life puts all the emphasis on solitude, silence, and prayer. Apart from certain stipulated gatherings—three community offices daily, a recreational walk and chat once weekly, and a bit more—Carthusian monks are hermits living side by side. Only in 1951 was a Carthusian monastery founded in the United States in a remote part of southern Vermont—it is there to this day—but Merton would have been content to return to Europe, where he started life. In a journal entry written less than two weeks after publication of *The Seven Storey Mountain,* he wrote in almost childlike language: "I have begun to tell [Dom James] all about the Carthusians and everything, and he says he doesn't see why things can't be fixed up right here."[7]

It is surprising in these years to find Merton occasionally expressing himself in language that seems better suited to Holden Caulfield, that special young man in *The Catcher in the Rye,* published four years after this entry; J. D. Salinger converted to eloquence a youthful lingua franca known also to Merton, though little used by him. Writing to Dom James in summer 1949, for example, Merton described a few hours he had spent in the woods outside the monastic enclosure—he was there only because James had permitted it—and interrupted his reflections to write, "Gee, it was perfect."[8] He was surely experimenting with attitudes and language in his budding relation with Dom James. What reached the abbot? What touched him? If the abbot was the father of the community, then Merton and all were his children, formally speaking, his "subjects." But need they be childlike? Merton received in these early years a letter from the abbot general of the order, addressing him as "mon cher petit Père Louis"—my dear little Father.[9] But Merton was not "petit"; he was a celebrated author with a growing world audience, a vital voice of the Church at midcentury and later. There were margins to be negotiated at Gethsemani between filial obedience and personal integrity. Merton was finding his way. In a note to Dom James written during the 1949 centenary celebration, another Merton declared his existence. Titled by its author "Why doesn't Frater Louis mind his own business?," the note offered "a few idiotic suggestions for the greater glory of God and for the spiritual welfare and happiness of Rev. Father"—suggestions having to do with the overwhelming mass of quotidian details addressed by Dom James that might well be delegated to others, and ending with unsolicited spiritual counsel: "Have an absolute inviolable time when Rev. Father cannot be seen or disturbed by anyone, and let that be a time for prayer and spiritual reading, not for work. At least one hour a day."[10] This would be a theme in their relation over the years as Merton witnessed the life of the master of Gethsemani and its daughter houses.

At the end of 1948 Merton recorded in his journal that "Dom James got me to declare formally I didn't intend to run off and be a Carthusian . . . unless he would let me."[11] But it was by no means settled. This is an apt moment to recognize that, like many honest participants in spiritual communities, Merton was making the most thorough possible use of the ideas and images, worldview and practices, and favored psychology of the community to which he belonged. The materials available within any community are unlikely to be exhaustive; much of value lies outside the designated boundary. But to make thorough use of the materials at hand is the first good thing to do, and he did so. Merton's initial treasure before Gethsemani was literature. His intimate contact with it made him a writer; he knew that he belonged. In the early Gethsemani years he was devoutly, intelligently, rather avidly Roman Catholic and monastic; this was his cultural environment, this is what he cared for and put to work in himself. Again he knew that he belonged. "I do not aim at the heights," he wrote to Dom James in spring 1949, "I aim at the depths. Not at what is exalted and spectacular but what is humble and unenviable and unattractive and blank. I aspire to become a nonentity and to be forgotten."[12] "When I am alone," he wrote again some months later to James, "Jesus is with me at once."[13] In years to come, as Merton read deeply in Christian tradition and made it his own, explored contemplative practice experientially, and encountered Asian teachings and teachers, his frame of reference widened and enriched. The ideas and images and spiritual psychologies progressively available to put to work in himself represented nearly everything there is: what really did he miss? But he remained honest, as at the beginning, and remained a monk, touched for a lifetime by the grandeur of Jesus and the beautiful rigor of Roman Catholic faith and worship. It is moving to witness him at every stage making exhaustively thorough use of the materials at hand and sweeping still more in.

Dom James understood that Merton needed conditions that

other members of the community would neither value nor particularly wish for themselves. He needed hiding places, quiet places. The first was the woods around the monastery—more than two thousand acres of fields, streams, and forest, rising to wooded conical knobs that offered steep, short climbs, sometimes to grand views down toward the abbey and across to other knobs and fields. "You can guess," Merton wrote to Dom James after an early wilderness session, likely the very first, "that the two hours between 2 and 4 p.m. Sunday afternoon, when you let me go out into the woods, were two of the happiest hours I have ever spent in my life. . . . In those two hours I understood things I have never known before about Gethsemani and about my own vocation."[14] The vast landscape around the abbey was nearly terra incognita in those years—a buffer zone filled with creatures. Today it is an extension of the abbey, a nearly limitless ungardened garden with a few paths and sacred spots crafted by the next generation of monks. Merton very much helped toward this change of status.

The second hiding place authorized by Dom James was indoors: the rare-book vault, almost perfect for writing and reflection. "I am locked up in the rare book vault," he wrote to Jacques Maritain, a friend for life and one of the other great voices of twentieth-century Catholicism. "All by myself, in one of the few places in the monastery where you do not hear a couple of tractors and other machines roaring at each other—but I correct myself: I can hear the new diesel monster we just bought, through the open window. It is devouring the earth where our vineyard used to be."[15] At much the same time he recorded in his journal that "the place has two steel doors and is as nearly soundproof as any corner of this noisy Trappist monastery. I have permission to take some of my intervals in there to work on the manuscripts, and Dom James said with a spark of encouragement, 'Maybe this is the solution to your vocation problem,' i.e., the Carthusians."[16]

On what must have been a happy day in June 1949, during the

abbot general's visitation at Gethsemani, Merton had discussed with the lofty and respected Dom Dominique Nogues his wish to write a life of Saint Bernard and asked for his approval of a research visit to a French Cistercian monastery with a strong library. Dom Dominique approved at once and further suggested that Merton come to the order's headquarters in Rome to write. "He explained," Merton recorded in his journal, "how I would have a great deal of time to myself and peace and solitude and what not and it sounded very nice." We know Merton well enough now to know how much this would have meant to him. "But when I spoke to Reverend Father about it," he continued, "he said NO several times with considerable emphasis and in a big hurry and went on to explain that 'there is nothing so distracting as new scenery.' Then the General spoke to him about it and Dom James said, 'If I let him (i.e., me) go to Rome, he will never come back.' He told him I was likely to become a Carthusian at the drop of a hat, which is still true and perhaps truer than ever."[17] Dom James's no, recorded in capital letters, marks an audibly important moment in the long journey ahead.

Monk and abbot were both discreetly campaigning—Merton to secure hours or a life of solitude, Dom James to keep Merton at Gethsemani while responding to his very evident needs without compromising the Rule of Saint Benedict and Cistercian usages as he understood them, strictly but for the good of souls. Merton's tendency to go "a bridge too far" became evident in a letter to Dom James, September 1949, advocating the creation of a new sanctuary in the woods. It could be a small chapel twenty minutes or so on foot from the monastery; it could be a slightly larger chapel where five or six monks could spend the day; it could be "a regular little *grange* in the woods with a chapel, dormitory, refectory, kitchen and scriptorium, all very small and simple, with a monk permanently in residence (guess who??). . . . It will bear thinking and praying over, anyway."[18] Can you hear Dom James sigh? True, James had expressed to Merton his wish "to make Gethsemani . . .

a sort of West Point or Annapolis for Cistercians,"[19] an idea reflecting his military background. But good Father Louis had conjured up instead a miniature Gethsemani out of earshot of machines, out of earshot of the abbot.

Be that as it may, they were cooperating smoothly with each other in an important zone of monastic life: education. In 1950, after his ordination to the priesthood in May a year earlier, Merton had become a teaching assistant subordinate to the master of novices, the redoubtable Fr. M., as Merton identifies him in the journals as published. Merton was responsible for an orientation course on Cistercian spirituality and its origins in earlier Christian sources. This was the beginning of his decades-long effort, well received at the monastery, to share the fruits of his reading and experience. But not well received by all: Fr. M., displeased, had frostily cited a point of Cistercian legislation to argue that Merton shouldn't be including spirituality in the orientation course and really shouldn't be there at all. The underlying issues seem to have been that the novices were enjoying Merton's lectures and raised questions about his material with Fr. M., who found the whole business irritating. Merton wrote to Dom James for advice and a decision. "It is evident," he wrote, "that if the orientation course is to continue at all, for the novices, I must leave the spiritual life almost out of the picture. But if that is the case, I cannot continue the course, as the spiritual life is the only thing I seem to be able to get interested in and I think you will agree that a purely academic course in monastic history, without any reference to monastic ideals, would be for us a waste of time."[20] The issue was pragmatically resolved in 1951, when Merton became master of scholastics, that is, the primary educator not of novices but of the young choir monks studying for the priesthood. In that role he could teach what he loved and knew to be central.

For many years to come, Merton was a recurrent topic in Dom James's correspondence with his superiors in Europe; the superiors changed as time went on, the topic persisted. In January 1950, months after his resounding NO, James reported to Dom Dominique that Merton had again raised the topic of a research visit. "Perhaps later on," he confided to the abbot general, "meaning in five or ten years. At the present time it would upset his whole spiritual life." He feared that "flattery" and "praise" would turn Merton's head. "He might never recover from such a trip at this stage. . . . But he admitted, himself, to me that he was too nervous at the present time."[21] Here enters a leitmotif that recurs in Dom James's correspondence at nearly every stage entrance by Merton: his nervousness. In any case, James was determined to protect Merton from adoring gazes, and with that in mind, in February he asked Merton no longer to say Mass in the church where ordinary folk were welcome. "It used to be a great joy for me to give Communion to a dozen strangers," Merton recorded in his journal. "You feel a profound interest in these faces, these overcoats, the old ones and the young ones. You wonder what their troubles are, their joys and their sorrows. You love them and you want them to be happy."[22]

In March of that year, Dom James again wrote to Dom Dominique. He had heard through Merton's publisher and lifelong friend, Robert Giroux, that Dom Dominique was still keen on Merton's coming to Rome. Speaking of such things with others would inevitably get back to Merton and cause difficulties; please be careful about what you say and to whom. "If [Merton] is allowed to remain at Gethsemani without anyone trying to entice him away," James continued in his letter to Dominique,

> he has good hopes of becoming settled definite as a Trappist Cistercian. But if he starts wandering around now, even to Rome and other Trappist Monasteries under the pretext of further research and studies, he is going to keep on roaming and he will roam out of the Order. He needs a strong hand over him for some ten years yet. Even then I am fully convinced that it is for his best eternal spiritual interests, if he is going to attain any degree of intimacy and union with Jesus, that he live and die here in this monastery.

> His mind is so electrical, it will go jumping here and there in pursuit of good things indeed but yet things which will keep him distracted from the eternal.
>
> His writings, however wonderful, are only temporary things and if he devotes his whole soul's energy to just writing books and not increasing the immolation of himself and union with Jesus, why his life will be a failure, supernaturally speaking.[23]

There are further enduring leitmotifs here: the fear that, given the chance, Merton will roam and roam out of sight; the distrust of his restless creativity; the inability to perceive a living, necessary link between Thomas Merton, author, and Father Louis, monk; the assertion that only stability—living and dying at Gethsemani—will fulfill Merton's spiritual life; the certainty that he, Dom James, knows the way. There is sometimes touching creativity in Dom James's efforts, now and later, to characterize Merton: "His mind is so electrical." He seems to be reaching past what he knows, past his own experience of identity, to describe a person built to a different pattern.

It will sometimes interest us to look across from a Dom James letter to Merton's journal: what was Merton thinking about, that day? As it happens, in late March nearly everyone in the monastery was succumbing to severe flu; one actually heard monks collapsing in the distance or on another floor. Merton also was ill but well enough on March 25 to sit out in an abandoned carriage in the sun—at Dom James's suggestion. A little later he recorded his inner life at the time: "I wondered if I ought to try to begin my Cistercian life over again from the beginning. O my God, what does it mean to love You? What does it mean to believe in You? What does it mean that You have brought us all here?"[24] The exemplary thoughts and feelings of an exemplary monk, if I'm not mistaken—a questioner, a seeker wrestling with the layered reality to which he belonged.

[6]
Saint Anne's, a Toolshed

In the course of 1951, Merton had a number of works in progress, notably for our purposes the revision of his journal published in 1953 as *The Sign of Jonas.* Like any personal journal, it is autobiographical, but as Merton's readers know, it is large—the autobiography of a mind and heart, of a spiritual search that listened for signals, of a perspective undergoing trial and change. As well, in concluding pages newly written for the book, it offers one of the most moving prose poems of twentieth-century literature. Dom James was of two minds about the manuscript. As it made its way through the multinational labyrinth of Church and order censors, who at the time could prevent or demand changes in publications, he ran interference for the book. He thought it worth publishing, if only as a prelude to better and weightier books to come from Merton, and he played a firm middle role between its critics and the willing but occasionally bruised author. On the other hand, as Dom James wrote to one of Merton's monastic correspondents, Sr. Thérèse Lentfoehr, a Salvatorian sister and collector of all things Merton, "I was wondering about your personal reaction to Father Louis publishing a journal while he is still living. . . . There is so much, necessarily and unavoidably of the I, I, I."[1]

This is a theme to which we should return after looking at an equally important way in which Dom James protected Merton from the abstractions of his superiors. We know that in summer 1949 James began permitting Merton solitary hours, scant but meaningful, in the woods. Versed in the decision process of the order, James wrote to the abbot general in April 1951 to recommend that Merton be granted greater access to the woods. Did he see storm clouds on the horizon—or with the best of intentions did his letter soon summon them? "Sunday afternoons and feast day afternoons," he wrote, "I give [Fr. Louis] permission to walk up in our woods. . . . He enjoys it very much. It helps his nerves quiet down. He likes to study hard and type and write." Somewhere in journal or correspondence, Merton irritably noticed that Dom James separated typing from writing; the first activity was satisfyingly visible, the rest wasn't. James continued,

> The other day he came in and said he had another proposition in regard to solitude in the woods. He suggested to spend one day a month. . . . He made the remark, with a knowing look, that such a day of solitude would keep him from going to the Carthusians. I know that is always in his mind. . . . It pops up every so often. Personally, Most Reverend General, I have no objections. . . . I have recognized that he has a different constitution than the others, more highly sensitized perhaps, and that for reasons of health he really has a legitimate reason that others do not have. Of course, such a procedure, strictly speaking, is outside the Rule. But from the point of view of mental and nervous health it comes within the Rule of taking care of the sick. . . . To tell you the truth, I wish I could do the same thing myself.[2]

Just one month later all access to the woods beyond the wall was abruptly withdrawn by a visiting authority, Dom Louis de Gonzague Le Pennuen, father immediate of Gethsemani and current abbot of the French monastery from which a few brave monks had set off for Kentucky in 1848. Such lines of responsibility are preserved in the Cistercian way of life. "Dom Louis decided," Merton noted in his journal, "that he did not want me going off into the woods by myself any more for fear that it might introduce a kind of 'Carthusian spirit' into the house."[3] Through an awkward, forced reasoning he embraced the decision, but Dom James must have realized that the prohibition was more than Merton should be asked to bear. He sent a note to Dom Louis to describe a provisional solution: "Father Louis seems to have accepted the restriction on his solitary intervals in the woods. There is a patch of woods which borders on the east wall of the enclosure. This does very well since it is absolutely isolated and enclosed with a fence. Also it is within sight of the house."[4] Cloistered wilderness. I have found no record of Merton's response to this kindly offer, but that fall Dom James may well have exercised the discreet spirit of independence that persisted at Gethsemani when he authorized Merton to make a seven-day private retreat including afternoons in the woods—which woods, cloistered or wild, I don't know, but Merton felt himself to be at a healing distance. "This usually gave me three and a half hours of solid prayer in solitude," Merton told him in a most grateful retreat report.[5] "At least for me," he continued, "'the community life' is not the absolute and infallible solution for all problems since seven days of relative solitude have apparently done a great deal to dispose of attachments and problems that the community had in large part created and fostered." And he returned to the community far more receptive to the goodness of its people and regimen.

Dom James didn't stop there in his effort to give Merton his one thing needful. The abbey was a considerable consumer of firewood gathered by the monks, and good practice required replanting: ergo, the need for a forester. James wrote in February 1952 to Dom Louis that Father Louis "has charge of forestation now, that is, marking trees to be cut and arranging for replanting. He gets out into his beloved woods during the worktime, and that is sufficient for him. I believe his nervous nature needs a job like that."[6] In the same letter he affirmed that Merton's service as master of the scholasticate—the group of young monks studying for the priesthood—was excellent for all concerned: "Being occupied now with the students and their trials, some of which are like his own, and giving advice to them, he finds himself giving himself advice. And too, the scholasticate takes much off my shoulders and problems off my conscience." Dom James was still Dom James; he was not above obsequiousness toward his superior, and he was managing ever more closely the monastery's finances. In April he wrote to Dom Louis that "our good secretaries are perfecting their accounting system of income and expenses and inventories. They are trying to get the system to take care of every last cent. I am sure you will be pleased with it when you come back."[7]

In the summer of 1952, James went still further in his concern to provide Merton with conditions that would suit him well enough. A disused toolshed was dragged into the woods for him—dragged by the colossal farm machine Merton most loathed, the basilisk-like Traxcavator. The shed wasn't in superb condition, but Merton could not have been more delighted with his protohermitage: "All it needs," he said in a note to James, "is some homasote on the outside, some insulation board on the inside, the door needs to be straightened, and we need a window. Br Clement has offered Br de Montfort for this work."[8] All it needed was nearly everything, but he was satisfied. "I have the will of a monk in the community," he noted in a late-summer entry in his journal. "But I have the *prayer* of a monk in the silence of the woods and the toolshed. To begin with: the place is simple, and really poor with the bare poverty I need worse than any other medicine and which I never seem to get. And silent. And inactive—materially. Therefore the Spirit is busy here. . . . I must really lead a solitary life. . . . Whether it is to be the Carthusians, Camaldolese or somewhere else remains to be seen."[9] At the new solitary refuge, he yearned for greater solitude. The Camaldolese Order had entered his thoughts as a possibility alongside the Carthusians; they were quite similar. That fall he had been in touch by letter with the abbot of the central Camaldolese monastery in Italy. "Very simply," Merton again noted in his journal, "[he] said I could come if I wished and start right out as a hermit. . . . And yet—I cannot do anything right at the moment. Reverend Father would do anything to prevent me from moving one step further in the affair. If God wills me to go to Camaldoli, He will show me when to take the next step and how. So I remain both certain and uncertain."[10]

Merton had another enterprise that fall: coaxing Dom James yet again to live a more authentically spiritual life. James often enough asked his superiors to exert their influence on Merton by letter or during visitations. Less frequently Merton made the same request with regard to James. In a letter of early September to the recently elected Cistercian abbot general, Dom Gabriel Sortais, Merton noted that James had asked him not to accept election as abbot at any future time. He had agreed (and later formalized his agreement as a signed vow[11]—monastic administration was not his way). But Merton then added a plea "on behalf of several religious in the community," as he put it:

> Concerning Dom James himself, . . . I beg you to be willing to tell him with some authority to set aside a little time for his own spiritual life. He never engages in spiritual reading, he has scarcely a minute for himself, he is working all the time, he loses sleep to the point that he was working instead of sleeping and slept only five and a half hours in 24 this summer. He is going to ruin his health. We counsel him here to take a little time for his own spiritual needs—he doesn't pay much attention to that. Were you to speak with him, that would do a little more good.[12]

There was a unique distribution of powers between abbot and monk, such that Merton could reasonably make this request of the abbot general. Dom James possessed institutional power, and Merton was his vowed "subject," concerning whom his decisions were binding with limited recourse. On the other hand, Merton was now a famous author with an ever-growing circle of well-wishers and influential correspondents; he had already been invited to Rome (permission denied) and to Camaldoli (permission not even sought), and there were many more invitations to come. James's power was largely external, real, and fixed—it didn't change very much as time went on. Merton's power was internal, real, and developing as he matured.

As autumn 1952 continued, Merton was coming apart. Still trusting Dom James with his deepest self-perceptions and doubts, he wrote in early November that "my body, nerves, sensibility, emotions, etc. are in complete chaos sometimes. . . . In the depths . . . below all this, I seem to be convinced that God is still there. On the surface everything is confusion and anxiety."[13] He was unable to explain his inner state, but he recognized two external causes: excessive activity in the monastic community, especially in his teaching role, and then, the incessant noise. "Much as I try to abandon myself and accept the cross, the amount of noise and machine-racket (which is *unceasing* wherever I go, during the day hours) is having an effect on me. . . . It does seem to me more than possible that there is, in all this, something radically wrong." In this communication and another in December he admitted to "nervous trouble" and interpreted it, with guidance from a spiritual adviser outside the monastery whom he trusted, as "proceeding from frustration of a truly solitary vocation. . . . I am living for nothing on earth except the hope of living as a hermit. . . . Any other life will be only a stultification of the spirit and a frustration of my whole being."[14] In the December letter he proposed a further three years in his current community roles, followed by "true solitude, either here or elsewhere, depending on what mode of solitude may be deemed fit for me."

That fall Merton also wrote to the abbot general, Gabriel Sortais, and elicited a remarkable response by return mail. "I have no need to make a long journey to find the desert," Merton wrote, originally in French, "I am the desert [*le désert, c'est moi-même*]."[15] Dom Gabriel responded in kind by recounting in a handwritten letter his own experience of desolation at an earlier moment in his monastic life. "The things that until then had seemed beautiful lost their charm, and everything appeared to me divested of beauty, and ugly, and repulsive. . . . God Himself seemed to be playing with me, to reject my wishes, to hold my love in contempt. And the worst was that this seemed to me just."[16] The abbot general's warmly thoughtful response must have helped; by January 1953, Merton was quite all right again. A bluff, forward-looking note to Dom James bears witness to his renewed balance. "It seems that 1953 is going to be a pretty busy year for the Master of Students," he wrote, no longer haunted by grave inner turmoil.[17] Yet he never forgot his call to solitude and neglected no opportunity, however slight, to remind Dom James of it. "The ordinary crosses of the life have never bothered me much," he reported to James after the August 1953 day of recollection. "What gets me is the apparent frustration of all my ideals."[18] A month later, when James was on his way to Europe via what must have been a fueling stop in Iceland, Merton sent a sweet note to meet him at his destination, with an entertaining but intended irony at the end: "May Jesus be with you everywhere in peace, and may Our Lady hold up the wings of those planes. (Iceland is another place I would like to go and make a 'foundation' in. A one-man foundation)."[19]

The refurbished toolshed in the woods brought light to Merton's life in January 1953, typically a cold month in that part of Kentucky, but he seemed to be doing fine. He wrote jubilantly to Dom James from the new venue: "I thought we ought to have a name for the new 'refuge,'" he began,

> and I chose the name *St. Anne's,* if you approve. Having been out here almost all day for two days, I find time goes by much too fast. . . . It is the first time in my life—37 years—that I have had a real conviction of doing what I am really called by God to do. It is the first time I have ever felt that I have "arrived"—like a river that has been running through a deep canyon and now has come out

FIG. 4. Saint Anne's, Merton's first retreat house at the abbey, in 2011.

> in the plains—and is within sight of the ocean. . . . I am glad Our Lord did not let me die before I could taste something of this: it is the real thing, at least for me. . . . Thank you again for allowing me this privilege of being so close to Jesus, even if only for a little while.[20]

In his journal at that time he wrote much the same: "It seems to me that St. Anne's is what I have been waiting for and looking for all my life. . . . Now, for the first time, I am aware of what happens to a man who has really found his place in the scheme of things. . . . I do not have to buy St. Anne's. I do not have to sell myself to myself here. Everything that was ever real in me has come back to life in this doorway wide open to the sky!"[21] Saint Anne's today has returned to its derelict state; the photo in figure 4 dates to 2011. But looking even at this image, one glimpses what it was for Merton: a humble counterpoint to the crowded monastery, a tea hut with no tea.

"Solitude, for you, is medicine," Dom James had told him.[22]

He put it rather differently in a letter to Dom Louis, his superior and father immediate, in which he both protected Merton yet again and subtly condescended. "As I look upon it," he wrote, "this opportunity to be alone from time to time is nothing more than medicine for his nerves and one should be broadminded enough, as long as the Rule is kept intact."[23]

[7]
The Journaling Seminar

"Father Louis is as jumpy as ever," James wrote in mid-June to Dom Louis.[1] He had reason to be jumpy: his superiors, both Dom James and the abbot general, Dom Gabriel Sortais, had spent the winter persuading him on spiritual grounds to give up keeping a journal or publishing on that basis. In mid-February, James informed Dom Gabriel that Merton's "friends"—whom did he have in mind?—were advising him to continue journaling because *The Sign of Jonas* (published in February) was a success, and further books of its kind would be welcome to his readers. With undisguised resentment, James asked Dom Gabriel to intervene by letter. "This is the time to stop him from getting started on another journal," he wrote,

> because if he ever gets started on one . . . , it will grow into a book. . . . There is no need of my talking to him, because he would go over my head to you, or Dom Louis, and my prohibition will not amount to anything. But if you write to him in a nice way, but in a firm and definitive way, it may have results. . . . He is a strange contradiction, although he would not admit it. He is all for solitude and anonymity, and yet he keeps on writing with a view of books to be published someday, etc. Although he is, in his own way, quite humble, docile and congenial.[2]

Dom James's discomfort with Merton could not be more evident. There was too much diversity packed into one human being: headstrong and docile, a solitary with a public . . . Just a day earlier, Merton had sent him a day-of-recollection report that may have reminded him of their differences. Merton started off with characteristically raffish humor: "This is a Mardi Gras pre-Lent official manifestation of conscience, plus resolutions. I start up the engine with a deep groan, and proceed."[3] The report is warm toward Dom James while drawing a sharp distinction between peace at Saint Anne's, discomfort in community. At Saint Anne's, he reports, "I feel like the Magi when they came out of Jerusalem and saw their star." Where the abbey is concerned,

> It is a great help for me to be in the community and look at what goes on without having to pretend that liturgy, exercises, ceremonies, chant, etc. etc. are the ideal answer to my desire for contemplation when they manifestly are not and never have been. . . . In community life I have always had to "pretend" by sheer force of violence that there was "no conflict" between work, prayer, contemplation, activity etc. for me. . . . Anyway, I promise Our Lord that I will stop pretending and be myself.

Dom James could not have been pleased: the great structure of liturgy, chant, and all the rest is the very life of the Rule of Saint Benedict, the life he was vowed to nurture and perpetuate.

Dom Gabriel accepted the challenge of writing to Merton about journaling. He expressed sympathy for Merton's need of solitude: "Sometimes I ask myself if you have been given at Gethsemani the requisite conditions to benefit from that beloved solitude." But he used this point of entry to question whether Merton's activities as a writer thrust him into inappropriate contact with the world. "When one writes a book intended for the general public, one has to think of it frequently, ponder its substance but also refine its form. Doesn't its author's mind also risk being preoccupied by questions of publishing and commercial success? In that there is danger for a Cistercian monk who feels a particular attraction to solitude and who is aware that his inner life will not develop without it." This was only the beginning. Dom Gabriel went on to point to "a more subtle danger if you continue to write and publish your journal. You note down the minor events of each day but also, on occasion, your most intimate feelings, even your most secret relations with God, and you note them down to deliver them to the public, not just a restricted, chosen public . . . but a mixed public of believers and non-believers. . . . I find in this a danger to the interior life. . . . Is it not to be feared that, entirely involuntarily, and as if unknowingly, this thought for the reader, the wish to interest and edify him, will alter the simplicity and spontaneity of your responses as a child of God?"

This last theme he exhaustively pursued. In moments of spiritual weakness or when facing "a duty that crucifies our will," isn't it to be feared that the journal keeper will have in mind to note everything down later in the day and in time share it with the public? "I know, dear Father, that you are too loyal to knowingly permit a lack of sincerity to slip in. But without our knowledge our intimate feelings can be affected." He wrote much the same about the inclusion of vivid detail. He had read enough in *The Sign of Jonas* to have the "slightly disagreeable impression" that Merton's choice of detail was sometimes governed by the desire to captivate his readers. Whereas the genuine charm and loyalty of a journal is that it is written only for oneself. "You see, dear Son," he concluded amiably, "that my feelings for you haven't changed, since I continue to share my reflections with simplicity. My affection for you guides me."[4]

Recognizing his responsibility for this letter, Dom James promptly informed its author about its impact on Merton. "Father Louis . . . took all that you said in very good spirit and said to me that if that is the General's wish, not to write journals or spiritual diaries, well then he will not. He was under the impression that perhaps he did not wish him to write any more at all."[5] This was a misunderstanding, expressed also in a letter (which I've not seen) from Merton to Dom Gabriel. The latter was quick to remedy the misunderstanding. He made clear to Merton that he had no objection to journaling "for your own benefit and personal use" and no objection whatever to future Merton publications. "Each one has received from God his particular talent. Without any doubt yours is to write with ease and to attract the public. Therefore, I believe that this talent must be brought to fruition according to God's thought for you. Now God has willed you to be a Cistercian. This will of God indicates that a certain number of literary genres should no longer tempt your talent. . . . I would see only advantages, were you to explore in greater and greater depth the principles of the interior life and share your findings with the public. In this genre I believe that God has given you the necessary means to do much good."[6]

Merton's journal breaks off at March 10, 1953, and resumes more than three years later in July 1956. In that first entry after such a long gap, he summarizes how he now wishes to proceed. He was already reading Zen literature, though he hadn't yet begun corresponding with D. T. Suzuki; there are qualities of spare Zen declaration and antinomy in his words. As well, his language is not unlike that of his friend the New York painter Ad Reinhardt. The circle of reference, the enriching circle of thought and sensibility, has widened.

> It is necessary to write a book in which there will be a little less of first-person singular, a little less dramatizing, and fewer resolutions.
>
> Or rather, it is not necessary to write a book. Or anything else.
> One is free to keep a notebook. This is sufficient.
> One may write or not write. Therefore one may write.[7]

[8]
Piety and Thunder

MERTON'S JOURNAL WAS THE ENGINE of his authorship. In its pages he explored his vocation and his person, recorded prayers that made themselves known in the gap between what one is and what can be said, responded to his vast reading, kept an inquiring eye on the life of the monastery and its abbot, chronicled his longing for solitude and his search for it, praised God through poetic perceptions of nature. The journal established and enriched his privacy; it was his cloister. It was his great "to whom it may concern." It had no readers, though *The Sign of Jonas* had taught him how to convert journal into book, but he needed to explore and share his life with *someone,* some phantom readership that he knew to be there despite appearances. Though decades passed before its publication, one feels immediately addressed by it. As Dom James feared, the journal centers on "I, I, I." What he failed to recognize is that it is one of the most universal "I's" to be encountered in modern literature, an "I" coordinating the fundamentals of human experience as if on mission for other "I's," yours and mine. Like Merton's growing correspondence, which reached out across the world and across worlds—religious, literary, artistic, and in time the world of peace activists—his journal was a world alongside that he built nearly from day to day. To sacrifice it for more than three years was a comprehensive, rather extreme response to the request of his abbot and the abbot general, a Trappist gesture of self-immolation.

A friend who knows the Merton canon well once commented that Merton is interesting early and late but not so interesting in the middle years. I believe this to be true of his published writings between *The Sign of Jonas* (1953) and some books of the early 1960s—I promptly choose the perfectly wonderful *Wisdom of the Desert* (1960), his homage to the desert fathers, although others might choose others. But his journal in the middle years is utterly, unceasingly interesting; no gap there, as if something in him sagged or retreated. The same is true of his correspondence: no gap, no sag. However, his books and articles in the middle years tend to be pious, edifying, somewhat restrictively Roman Catholic, all but empty of his grand voice. Of course, this is not always so, but from his first book on the Psalms (*Bread in the Wilderness*, 1953) to the essays in *No Man Is an Island* (1955) and his exploration of the Eucharist (*The Living Bread,* 1956), one loses touch with the representative "I" evoked just above, the seeker and discoverer rooted in Catholicism but, in his words, "wide open to the sky." Unquestionably he wished to give full due to his responsibilities as teacher and counselor to the scholastics and, from 1955, to the novices; his superiors asked this of him, and it made sense to do so. There is nonetheless detectable chill and restraint, reflecting, I believe, a sincere wish to serve Church, order, and abbey along channels defined by Dom James and the abbot general. He gave it a long try. Meanwhile his correspondence remained lively and unpredictable.

Extremely lively and unpredictable . . . In April 1954, Merton put in Dom James's mailbox a letter worthy of its date, Passion Sunday. It was an expression of utmost misery, boiling out of a day of recollection. Surely it took James by surprise. We should read it nearly in full. "This has been a good Lent, so far," Merton wrote.

> I am glad to be able to get up with the community and make the morning meditation. I have been needing it. . . .
>
> I am beginning to face some facts about myself. Yes, need for more of a life of prayer, greater fidelity, greater sincerity and simplicity in doing what God wants of me. Easy to say all that.
>
> It depends on getting rid of something very deep and very fundamental in myself. A fault that has been basic for the last twelve

> years—all my life. Continual, uninterrupted resentment. I resent and even hate Gethsemani. I fight against the place constantly. I do not openly allow myself—not consciously—to sin in this regard. But I am in the habit of letting my resentment find every possible outlet and it is such a habit that I do not even pay attention to it. I am not kidding about how deep it is. It is DEEP. Too deep to be fixed with a couple of good resolutions.
>
> It means getting to the root of the whole thing, and I haven't any idea what that root is. But I cannot fully and simply and efficaciously give myself to God's will without removing the real obstacle. By removing the obstacle I do not mean merely making a few acts of abandonment and pure intention, renewing my vows, etc. It takes a whole lot more than that.
>
> Since the resentment pervades everything about the place and every feature of the life, there is no possibility of running away from it or dodging it here. It is a problem that has to be solved, not glossed over.
>
> I am asking Jesus to plant His Cross deep in my heart and clean out all the bitterness that is there. Please pray that I may do what I am supposed to do in this regard. I really want to do the will of God. Please give me your blessing, Rev. Father. I hope I can from now on stop bluffing and get down to business.[1]

It may have been this letter and the direct conversations no doubt surrounding it that first prompted Dom James to feel out of his depth. If Merton so vigorously declared that the traditional monastic remedies for soul sickness could be of no benefit whatever, what remained? In the past, Dom James had relied on the authority and warmth of his own superiors—Dom Louis, Dom Gabriel—when he needed help to bring Merton around to his point of view. But now that resource appeared to be superseded. Did good Father Louis need psychotherapy? If the thought did not occur to Dom James at this point, it would occur in time.

In the same month, April 1954, Merton had received a letter

from one of his most distinguished and loyal correspondents, the Benedictine monk and scholar Jean Leclercq. It raised in the most forthright way a question Leclercq approached by contrasting his own scholarly writings, which earned practically nothing in material terms, with Merton's writings, which found a wide public. "It would be a good thing," Leclercq wrote,

> if at least once you could write just for the glory of God, with no money involved. And that would have the advantage of reacting to a fairly widespread idea in Europe: T. Merton brings in money, so his Superiors exploit him as much as possible, because of the income. I think that is a wrong idea, and I say so every time I have a chance; but it would be a good thing for the practical demonstration to come for once from you and your Superiors. Forgive me for saying frankly things that so many people think. Take it as a proof of friendship. And go on writing books which do good, since you have found a style which our contemporaries like.[2]

I am not suggesting that this was Merton's grave problem, but the letter points to the uneasiness and ambiguities of his situation. In any case, Merton had in effect agreed with his friend: his books and articles for some years to come would appeal to a narrower, predominantly Catholic audience.

By the month of June, Dom James was under the impression that the April crisis had passed. "Father Louis improves much as the days go by," he wrote to Dom Louis. "He is getting more settled. He sees that it is God's Will for him more and more, to become a saint right here at Gethsemani."[3] There is a whiff of smugness in these remarks. In later years James would say more than once, where discernment is concerned, that "God does not send telegrams"; a hardworking abbot needs somehow to uncover what is right and for the best without that telegram. Yet he was often immovably confident.

There was a second lightning strike and roll of thunder in late

September, again stemming from a day of recollection in which Merton seems to have been thinking more of Dom James and Gethsemani than of himself and his Lord. The abbot's mailbox on September 22 yielded a stunning assessment of the increasingly materialistic life of the community. It is too long a letter to include in full here, though it deserves a place. "Perhaps some of [this letter] will test your already heroic humility and patience," Merton began. "But I will try to be simple, unsentimental, and objective, trusting you understand my motives and that you believe the truth: namely that I have no intention of taking a dig at the administration of this house!"[4] He disclosed to Dom James that there were two schools of thought among many of the professed in the community: "The group who think that the place is materialistic and that 'the Abbot is to blame' [and] those who think it is materialistic and no one in particular is to blame (I am in this group)." Merton further subdivides the first group into "those who take Pharisaic scandal at every new machine . . . , simply trouble shooters who are looking for pretexts to be shocked and scandalized. . . . They cause an immense amount of harm by their signs, complaints, etc." The second subgroup was composed of "those who have real ideals and who are really hurt by the tendencies in the community, and who honestly believe that you are at fault. They are, I think, misguided." Both subgroups agree, Merton continued, "in considering you a 'sharp business man.' . . . Without due regard for charity or justice, the following statements about you are common in the community: 'He often refers to Wall Street and the Stock Exchange in chapter talks.' 'His letters from other monasteries are full of nothing but tractors, machines, crops, etc.' 'He will use you as long as you serve his purpose.' . . . Of all this, enough said. But I think you ought to know that this impression of you exists in a large sector of the community."

Where the other group is concerned, those who blame no one in particular, Merton speaks for them in the balance of the letter.

"The very urgent problem of self-support," he writes, ". . . is simply *too big for any one of us* to handle without being to some extent submerged. Hence the sad but undeniable fact that Gethsemani is like an enormous place of business. It does not look like a monastery, it does not sound like a monastery, and the people do not behave like monks. A lot of them do not even try. . . . When you approach the place from any direction all you hear is the noise of a multitude of machines. When you get into it you see business men hustling around in a great lather to get something done. . . . Perhaps this is a caricature, and no doubt I exaggerate—but there is a fundamentum in re. However, I repeat I do not know how to pin the blame on anyone. Our set-up here is simply deficient, we are not strong enough spiritually to cope with the difficulty." Merton ends this amazing *j'accuse* with the thought that the situation needs to be faced rather than ignored and the solution is terribly unobvious. "I say: let us recognize that there is a *real problem* in reconciling modern machine methods with the contemplative life. Both are necessary, but we are not on the way to making them work in harmony. . . . We do have to strive to keep Gethsemani a real monastery. . . . I have no idea what the . . . solution is, but I strongly feel that we ought to stop all expansion and try to get ourselves together. . . . May God have mercy on us. Amen. I hope you do not think I am a complete rebel." He signed, "Yr devoted son –fr M Louis."[5]

Gethsemani then and surely now has its ways of absorbing shocks, both a simple human way by sorting out differences, forgiving, and muddling through, and a religious way by looking upward, inward, and back into the long tradition of prayer, which can settle conflicts by a change of atmosphere. *De profundis clamavi ad te Domine*—Psalm 129 in the Latin psalter: Out of the depths I have cried to Thee, O Lord. Merton had cried out with great power and analytic precision. Though not a "complete rebel," he was undeniably something of a rebel, serving the abbot's and monastery's good and his own conscientious need to speak truth to power. As far as the documents show, nothing much happened in the aftermath of this bolt of lightning. Dom James continued to rework the abbey's buildings and fields, and, fatefully, young Br. Frederic—the future business manager and treasurer—became a novice in that very year, 1954. On his side, Thomas Merton/Father Louis returned to his inner path, his hope for greater solitude, his excellent person. In his November day-of-recollection report to the abbot he wrote, "I am no wiser than before. . . . I am really beginning to have some interior solitude, in which I am alone before God in making decisions that come from the depths of my being and are genuinely mine, made, I think, in Him. . . . I get into a lot of things—a lot of reading—that might seem strange for monks. It is. But for me it still contains the graces I need. I know more and more that I have my own peculiar job to do, and I am glad to be trying to do it, even though in confusion. Pray for me, and bless me."[6]

[9]
Vincolata la Sua Libertà

AFTER A FOUR-DAY RETREAT at the end of November, Merton sent a peaceful and peacemaking report to Dom James to express his new conviction "that I should stay and do what God wants me to do *here,* even though it may seem like being a square peg in a round hole." He added an apology "for perhaps not being always humble about things here, speaking my mind too brutally and without sufficient restraint. I want to be as loyal and as useful an officer as I possibly can be."[1] This was the sweet calm after the storm—and before the storm. In mid-April 1955, Dom Gabriel wrote to James, "I fear that we find ourselves yet again in front of a difficult situation. . . . I ask myself if Father Louis's attitude is always that of a religious, humbly submitted to the control of his Superiors."[2] The immediate issue in Dom Gabriel's mind had to do with Merton's publications, but a larger issue had reemerged a month earlier. The group of now veteran sufferers—Merton himself, Dom James, Dom Louis, and Dom Gabriel—were about to enter one of the most turbulent periods of their association. Merton's brief surrender to life at Gethsemani was already over.

James felt constrained in mid-March 1955 to write to Dom Gabriel about good Father Louis. "He is not as cheerful and spontaneous as he used to be, at least since the beginning of this year," he began.

> He claims that he feels this great urge to be more a hermit. Although this sounds very high and idealistic, I doubt very much the purity of his intentions. I am almost convinced that what is

moving him in this direction is not to have silence and solitude in which to pray to God and be more united to Him, but really to have silence and solitude to write books and to read books with greater freedom. I believe his dominating passion is the writing of books. . . . I do not think he realizes his dominant passion.[3]

After these broad observations, in which James seems to be consolidating a view of Merton, he signaled to his superior that Merton had been corresponding with the prior general of an eremitical order, the Camaldolese, who were working toward the establishment of a foundation in the United States. "I think that what Father Louis has in mind," James continued, "in trying to get the Camaldolese hermits to come to this country is that it might facilitate a transfer to them for him." The consolidation of view continues from that essentially accurate surmise:

I am convinced that it was Our Lord who brought Father Louis to Gethsemani, and He brought him here to stay here. He has a definite purpose to fulfill. He is the master of the scholastics. There are about twenty-five. . . . He does very well with the scholastics, and I believe his work with them helps himself. . . .

I believe the various trials, contradictions, etc., that he meets here at Gethsemani are all part of God's plan for purifying his soul from all self-seeking. The fact that he finds certain kinds of trials very painful may prove that these are the very points that Jesus is detaching him from. . . . It seems that his urge for a change, which he tries to see as coming from God, comes rather from his own self, seeking to find a means of escaping from the very arrangements God wishes him to comply with and accept. . . .

The fact that sometimes he shows even bitterness and resentment in some of these trials reveals to me the very human element in his urging to greater silence and solitude, rather than the divine. In other words, it is self-seeking and not, as he thinks or tries to persuade himself, God-seeking, that is behind his urges. . . .

> I am convinced that . . . God wants him to stay here in the Trappist life at Gethsemani, for his greater purification and, therefore, greater sanctification.

Dom James noted in conclusion that he was sending a copy of his letter to Dom Louis, who would soon be making a formal visitation. Its reception would complete the circle of participants.

Less than two weeks later, James again wrote to report the results of a letter Merton had received from Dom Gabriel. It had brought Merton "much peace of soul," he said, "especially to have been told by his higher superiors that he was in the right place, and just to keep on going." James took the opportunity in his note to share a judgment of Merton that had a long monastic history. "Way deep down," he wrote, "his innate restlessness and gyrovaguing spirit still lives on."[4] Gyrovaguing? The reference is to disreputable wandering monks in the early centuries of monasticism and at least sparingly ever since—Mussorgsky gave some latter-day gyrovagues a fabulous drinking song in his opera *Boris Godunov*. The sixth-century Rule of Saint Benedict is stern in its chapter on the types of monks: "Gyrovagues . . . are ever on the move and never stable. Slaves to their own will and the delights of the palate. . . . It is better to be silent than to speak of the wretched life style of these monks."[5] In Dom James's opinion, Merton ran the serious risk of becoming one—were he permitted to leave Gethsemani. This too became part of his consolidated view now taking shape under the renewed pressure of Merton's most concerted effort to date to transfer elsewhere.

That letter was dated March 28. Five days on there was another, again to Dom Gabriel. The immediate issue, dispatched in the opening paragraphs, was a bothersome letter Merton had written to some of the order's literary censors—a topic peripheral to us here though typical of many exchanges between Dom James and his superiors as they debated Merton's literary projects. After which

James turned to the topic of Merton himself and further advanced his consolidated view. Exculpating Gethsemani, and by extension himself, from any fraction of responsibility for Merton's recurrent difficulties, he declared that Merton was "neurotic."

> Father Louis knows that his troubles do not come from his Trappist surroundings in general, and Gethsemani in particular. He knows, because he practically admitted it to me, that his problems are all inside himself.
>
> But as neurotics usually do, they blame everybody and everything else for their interior suffering. His problem is that he would like to be without any restraint or discipline over him, so that he could always do what he wished. But if he were in such a position, where would his spiritual life be? Where would his sanctification be? And he knows that very well.[6]

Dom James was struggling to make sense of things. If Merton had all but admitted to him that his problems were strictly internal, why did James go on to imply that Merton blamed external factors for his misery? He must have thought of Merton as both self-aware and partially out of control; on that analysis, the driven part of his divided mind blamed Gethsemani. And did he really believe that Merton craved to live without monastic restraint—at a time when he was striving, hope against hope, to transfer to a hermit order? There was and always has been a time-tested means of living without monastic restraint: leave one's robes and effects behind and walk out the gate. This solution occurred to Merton only once in his twenty-seven years as a monk of Gethsemani, and he rejected it. Of that, more in later pages.

It must reflect the pressures on Dom James—Merton's aspirations were not the only difficulty at the time—that he sent a thoughtful letter to Dom Louis at the end of March, not long before Dom Louis was expected at Gethsemani for a formal visitation. For once James spoke of himself. He felt that he was "becoming nothing but a mere administrator of a monastery. Certainly that is not what Jesus created me for and brought me to the monastery for, at least primarily. My physical, mental, but especially spiritual needs, demanded some change."[7] Without mentioning Merton's influence, which was surely dominant though left unstated, he explained that he had adopted a dual remedy: *lectio divina* (the tradition under the Rule of Saint Benedict of regular spiritual reading) and sojourns in the nearby wilderness.

> I concluded, with the advice of my spiritual director, that I should take Wednesday as a day of recollection and more immediate union with God. Father Prior takes charge of the monastery every Wednesday, and I do not have conferences with anybody or speak to anyone. The intervals in the morning I spend in reading and prayer. In the afternoons I usually go out and just walk across our fields, visit the lakes and walk through our intensive woods. . . . I have been going out every week for over a year now. . . . I usually take some Scripture along, and find a nice sunny spot in the winter and read. It cannot be expressed in words what a great benefit these periods of utter silence and solitude with God Alone have been for my spiritual life, whether in giving conferences to others or in chanting the Divine Office. . . . I do not believe this is in any way contrary to our life. . . .
>
> Father Louis sometimes walks out there in the woods, and it does him very much good. . . . There are a few who may object to this, as not being Cistercian—but as Saint Benedict writes, discretion is necessary in handling individual souls. As long as no abuses creep in.

We have reached one of the rare moments in the long encounter between Thomas Merton and Dom James when a wheel that we justly thought fixed, even rusted in place, rotates. In years past James had cautiously offered Merton solitary hours in the woods as medicine for his nerves, as a concession. Now he has adopted

Merton's approach to living with something like serenity in a monastery of 240 souls—surely at Merton's urging, whether he was or was not the unnamed spiritual director. Characteristically, Merton had opened James to a new possibility, while James characteristically set boundaries for Merton and then tinkered to create a measure of latitude within them. "We live quite packed together," James explained to Dom Louis, "whether in refectory, choir or chapter room, or just walking through the cloisters. It is easily understood that such close packing together wears on people's nerves." So it was not only Merton's sorry nerves that were succumbing. Dom James had written to protect preemptively his own privilege of days apart in the woods—you'll recall that Dom Louis had already once revoked the privilege—and he was shrewdly careful to relate his days of solitude to the enrichment of his life of prayer and service in the monastery. Still, he was mindful of how much access to the woods mattered also to good Father Louis. On occasional Wednesday afternoon rambles, did they bump into each other?

The fixed wheel secretly rotated on. In an appreciation of Merton that Dom James circulated at Gethsemani and elsewhere after Merton's death in 1968, he disclosed what many in the local community had known for a very long time: Merton had served for fifteen years as his confessor. A revision of his appreciation, published as an essay in 1974, made this local fact known to the public.[8] Remembering that we are under obedience to respect nuance in this narrative of intertwined lives, I assess this as an avalanche-sized nuance. Merton's and Dom James's relations in what monastics call "the external forum"—the institutional space between people—could be tense and miserable at length, and in the year we're exploring, James was noticeably building a case against Merton that would endure and even intensify as time went on. But he was doing so only in the external forum, where abbots conferred with their superiors and peers, shaped decisions, and communicated those decisions to their "subjects." Where the internal forum was concerned, at about this time James demonstrated enough spiritual regard to ask Merton to confess him, and that intimate relation lasted nearly to the end of Merton's life. Had he some other reason for this gesture? A friend has suggested that James may have wished to give Merton the opportunity to exercise his objective, priestly function despite the tension that easily developed between them. Fr. John Eudes thought this a most sensible insight. Be that as it may, inside the walls Dom James offered Merton influential posts as his confessor, as master of scholastics, and from late 1955 as the long-serving master of novices. So doing, he entrusted Merton with some large part of the spirit of the house and its future. It goes without saying that he was confident the trust was well placed, and he never had reason to withdraw these key appointments. Yet we are beginning to see that outside the walls it was otherwise. How is it possible that the man he described in the external forum as neurotic, restless, self-serving, blind to God's will—a potential gyrovague—merited posts of influence and spiritual weight in, broadly speaking, the internal forum? What does this contradiction tell us? It is too soon to respond.

Dom Louis's visitation, ending April 24 and something of a disaster for Merton, set in motion a wave of correspondence about the possibility of a transfer—a transitus, in monastic language—from Gethsemani to one of the Camaldolese houses in Italy. Dom Louis had again revoked woods walking privileges for all but one. By James's own report, "Dom Louis made an exception in my case; as Abbot, I should know the farm and fields and woods, as a responsibility on my conscience, since I am responsible for the temporalities of the house."[9] What a wordy way of describing a spectacular injustice—but James was aware of the injustice and developing an idea, at least where good Father Louis was concerned.

In a letter to his trusted friend Jean Leclercq written a few days after the simultaneous departures of Dom Louis to Europe and Dom James to California, Merton said that "the Visiting Abbot concentrated his attention on what he called 'a hermit mentality' in the monastery."

> He strongly disapproved of it, although recognizing in a private conversation that on my side I had a particular spirit . . . and [he] did not really expect to see much change in me. But altogether we reached a point at which I think that I cannot, or even should, remain at Gethsemani, or in the Cistercian Order. There is truly no place for me here. . . . They are willing to receive me at Camaldoli d'Arezzo. I have a friend who is willing to pay my steamer fare. . . . Well, there remains an enormous obstacle: my own Superiors. I believe that my Father Abbot will try to hold me back at all costs.[10]

Merton asked the knowledgeable Leclercq a practical question: "Is there a way of submitting an application for transfer in such a way that it would be accepted even if the Superior of the house is against it?"[11] He knew what he was up against.

During that wave of activity while Dom James was away for three weeks, Merton wrote with disguised desperation to a senior cleric with whom he had sporadically corresponded, Giovanni Battista Montini, archbishop of Milan, later Pope Paul VI. Explaining to him the need for a transitus, he asked whether it would be wise on his part "to take some initiative in Rome," though he didn't know what that might be, and then came to the point: "I am sure that if our Father Abbot here did not have to take the whole responsibility for the decision on himself, and if there were chances of someone in a high position viewing my case with positive favor, he would much more easily assent to my leaving for Camaldoli. I believe the only reason why he really refuses is that he does not want to be criticized and blamed. My Superiors all seem to recognize that I am more of a hermit than a cenobite. . . . Begging your blessing, I kiss your hand and remain, in Christ."[12] Merton was politicking; how could he not? He couldn't help but see that the forces of tradition and judgment arrayed against him likely exceeded his ability to persuade.

Nor could he know that his letter to the archbishop would elicit in August the one authentically kind communication he was to receive in the course of his campaign to find a new monastic home.

When he returned to the abbey in mid-May, Dom James did his best to convince Merton that he should surrender to a "real and utter immolation" of his aspiration to become a hermit elsewhere. Merton replied, in James's account, "that his immolation is trying to follow these inspirations and inclinations and to fight for them in every possible way and manner, come what may. He calls this real immolation of self."[13] It is touching to witness these two men using the monastic concepts by which they lived to urge the other to yield. In the course of May, Dom James with Merton's honest help clarified the overall situation, which had been developing for some time. He understood that Merton had consulted privately with five individuals at the abbey and elsewhere whom he regarded at least informally as spiritual directors, all of whom approved his wish for a transitus. James also understood that Merton had gone over his head during his absence by asking the prior general of the Camaldolese Congregation to arrange for the needed transitus. "I told Father," James reported to Dom Gabriel, "that at least he could have waited until my return to the monastery before he would do that. . . . He excused himself by saying that I would not approve his writing, but I said he could have waited for me to say 'no' and then go ahead."[14] Even in this quite grave conflict, there were moments of petulance.

On his side, Dom Gabriel wrote to Merton in early May that he preferred to form an opinion about the developing situation after receiving Dom Louis's visitation report—but meanwhile he did have something to say.

> What could I think of you, dear Son, and even of your loyalty to God, if, going off to live in complete solitude, you then took up your pen to tell us at length the reasons for your departure and

to share with the public the attractions that drew you to a more hidden life than ours?

If you leave us, be logical and promise to God that, for love of Him, you definitively renounce remaining in constant contact with many publishers and an entire world of readers whose presence in your mind is hardly to be reconciled with the full solitude in which intimacy with the divine takes shape and develops without noise.

Illusion lies in wait for us all. Be vigilant and tell yourself that we are in general bad judges of our own cause.

I confide you to Mary in this month of May.[15]

For those who believe that the restrictions imposed on Merton now and for years to come had really to do with the income his writings generated for the abbey, a letter such as this—and there were others, as we'll see—should persuade us that it wasn't so. The stakes—clearly there *were* stakes—were of another kind. What were they? It is too soon to respond. Like the question about the difference between Dom James's treatment of Merton inside the walls and outside, this question also will linger.

May continued to be a month of letters back and forth. Dom James gathered and communicated to Dom Gabriel his clarified understanding of the situation and persisted in his increasingly consolidated view of Merton's inner state and failings. "The great emotional disturbance of good Father Louis, and various other little factors, all reveal to me the workings, not of the Divine Spirit, but of the merely human spirit in Father Louis himself. . . . I think his great success as a writer has increased his pride, subconsciously no doubt, but yet really, so that he thinks he can have anything he asks for, just because he asks for it. Even that God must conform His Will to Father Louis's will. Of course, this is not deliberate."[16] But he went on in the letter to puzzle out what could nonetheless be done for Father Louis. He must stay at Gethsemani—that was clear. But under what conditions? He recalled that during the visitation, Dom Louis had said that work in the fields and woods was acceptable "because the motive then is work." Now it happened that the state of Kentucky was building a fire tower on the monastery's lands, one of several in the region, to spot forest fires with a minimum of delay. There would be a simple cabin at the base of the tower and communications equipment up above in the watchman's space. James asked: "Why could we not let Father Louis spend some time each day on duty in this little fire tower, say from dinner to supper time or something like that"—and other members of the community could be on duty at other times during the fire danger season. "Father Louis would be completely satisfied with this arrangement and would take it as the expression of God's decision as regards his vocational and emotional crises. We had a very calm and cordial conversation together about all this, and he seems perfectly at peace now, with this hope. I advised him to slow down with his writing for the rest of the year, dropping all new books, and he thought that was a good idea."[17]

A Merton letter of early August to Jean Leclercq confirms Dom James's report; he found the fire tower assignment appealing, and he was already overseeing the work of the state forestry personnel who were raising the tower.[18] He also confided to his friend that he had given up writing. "I intend to renounce it for good if I can live in solitude. . . . Writing is deep in my nature, and I cannot deceive myself that it will be very easy for me to do without it. At least I can get along without the public and without my reputation! Those are not essentially connected with the writing instinct. But the whole business tends to corrupt the purity of spirit of one's faith. It obscures the clarity of one's view of God and of divine things. . . . We must be poor, and live by God alone."[19] Dom Gabriel's message in early May, and those received from others in the course of the summer, had made its way. One might like to think of Merton as separate, invulnerable or nearly so, knowing himself and his way without errors of vision and grave uncertainties. It wasn't so. He had accepted long ago the need to be responsive to his superiors, to listen well. As time went on he would free himself from their judgments, and they in turn would come to better tolerate Merton's integrated vocation as monk and author. But in these middle years all concerned were finding their way. What was "always" in his monastic life early, middle, and late was working things out, searching for what would be truest and best in a given situation. He understood and embraced his integrated vocation through trial and error, and among other things through experiencing what it was to write and not to write.

There were various communications back and forth as spring turned to summer. Dom James checked with Dom Gabriel as to whether, in the order, the word of a confessor took priority over the abbot's word—he was worried by the support Merton had received.[20] A week later he recounted to his superior an unpleasant conversation with Merton: "Father accuses me of deciding on purely natural grounds. He does not seem to credit me with being a man of conscience, and to realize that there is a Last Judgment for me too. . . . I work [many] themes into the explanation of the Rule each day, but . . . the Abbot of Gethsemani is inferior to [Father Louis's] giant intellect and mystical experiences."[21] He was referring here to the Cistercian custom of frequent chapter talks on the Rule of Saint Benedict.[22] He was also momentarily expressing a resentment that may well have had a fixed place in his feelings. Some years later he mentioned that it was a little tiresome when he traveled to be asked so many questions about Merton, the great writer and spiritual teacher resident in his abbey.

The concrete issue facing the Cistercian superiors was Dom James's proposal, welcome to Father Louis, to name him the part-time fire warden, coming and going from an aerie above the vast monastic acreage and the cabin at the foot of the tower. In a letter of May 28 dealing with that issue, Dom Gabriel first responded to

Dom James's inquiry as to who should prevail, confessor or abbot: "In the internal forum, the subject must not disregard the thought of his abbot, but the latter cannot in conscience impose his view, because there may be elements of the problem known only to the confessor. Indeed, it mustn't be forgotten that in the internal forum the religious is not required to say everything to his superior."[23] On the other hand, Dom Gabriel wrote, the abbot retains many powers. But what of the fire tower proposal?

Dom Gabriel didn't think it made sense. He was convinced that, were Merton authorized to live there part-time, he would simply wait it out in the heights until he received the transitus to another order and would be on his way. Further, Dom Gabriel didn't think that part-time status would put to the test Merton's aptitude for the solitary life. It would be a "half-measure similar to those you have already taken on his behalf and which haven't satisfied him." He took Dom James to task for the first time in this correspondence. "You will doubtless tell me," he wrote,

> that you are not departing from the Cistercian spirit by placing Father Louis in this isolated post, because that will be his 'work.' Seriously, dear Reverend Father, don't you think that would be a sort of ruse, a play on words? Were you to describe as 'manual labor' Father's occupation in the tower, you surely know that you would deceive no one: neither the Community, which would quickly know what's what, nor Father, who will carry his typewriter to the tower just as he carried it to the shed, and will completely stop being Cistercian. . . . And if Father Louis completely lost his vocation while in an employment [unsuited to a choir religious], wouldn't certain people be ready to believe that you keep him at Gethsemani for reasons other than the good of his soul?[24]

Dom Gabriel concluded that the best for Father Louis would be a five-year halt in writing, and if that were too onerous, then a five-year halt in publication. In that way, Dom Gabriel hoped, he would find his way to the "calm and collectedness that will permit him to find God even in his work as a writer." The unstated judgment that valid religious feeling and insight were absent from Merton's writings comes as a surprise—but in a time of conflict, not everything said is fair or true. If Dom James thought it advisable, Dom Gabriel added, he could send Father Louis to Gethsemani's daughter foundation at Mepkin, South Carolina, which had struck him as "small, calm, and remote."

Dom Gabriel's letter, dry and interesting, pointed toward various possible resolutions short of what Merton actually wished, the transitus. A few days later, Dom Louis echoed much that the abbot general had written—and added that he would be willing to take Father Louis into his abbey in France, "though I don't know if that would advance something."[25] Two offers to transfer him to quieter places in the Cistercian world, two offers not taken up. Dom James must have been determined to resolve the issue on home ground. Dom Louis had two contrasting solutions to offer, short of transfer to his abbey: either Father Louis recommit himself to a loyal life in the Gethsemani community for a set period of years, after which his vocation to solitude could be seriously reconsidered, or he be authorized to live at the fire tower full time with minimal recourse to the community. "It would no longer be a comedy" under those conditions, he wrote—but he doubted that Father Louis would see it through for long. Dom Gabriel weighed in to ratify the offer: "the hermitage life one hundred percent right away," as Dom James roughly scanned their joint view.[26]

By mid-August, Merton had his own doubts about the entire project, which he had been struggling to advance since early in the year. The messages he was receiving from overseas created seemingly endless complexity; the fire tower as principal residence was terribly remote. "It seems to me more and more clear," he wrote to Dom James,

> that somewhere, somehow Our Lord wants me in solitude—a real life with Him alone, and the question to be answered is *where? How?* . . . While I believe it would be simple and beautiful to live as a hermit in the woods, here, it seems in fact that this will be so complicated and involve so many headaches for you and for Gethsemani, and so much opposition on the part of the anti-hermits, not to mention higher superiors, that I wonder if it is not altogether hopeless. Dom Louis has permitted this solution in theory, but in fact it would seem that he wants to surround it with impossible conditions. . . . May God guide us all. But let's get a real answer.[27]

Every one of the participants in this controversy had been telling Merton over these long months that he shouldn't disregard the multiple unfortunate impacts his departure would have—on the community at Gethsemani, on the order, above all on his readers who justly counted on him to express and live the values to which his books introduced them. One correspondent spoke of him as "riveted" to Gethsemani—for that reason. Another spoke of him as "wedded until death" to Gethsemani—for that reason. His fame as a writer, as one of the most widely read and respected voices of Catholic spirituality, pinned him in place—so they said, and he could not altogether disregard their well-intended judgment. While his superiors were urging him, rather successfully in these years, to minimize his writing activities and especially publishing activities, they were also arguing that the tremendous result of those activities in the past now required him to remain at Gethsemani. As Merton observed, there were complexities, more than enough.

No one delivered the message of stability more wisely and gently than G. B. Montini, the archbishop of Milan. His letter to Merton radiates light and warmth, as if he were the only one with no axe to grind, no pride to protect, no feeling of superiority or expectation of docile obedience. It is true that he hadn't a direct stake in the drama; nonetheless, his warmth and humanity reveal the harshness of much that we have been reading. Montini wrote in lovely Italian: "Il Signore, io penso, ha vincolato la Sua libertà dando alla Sua presente vita religiosa una fecondità, che non appartiene più a Lei solo, appartiene alle anime, appartiene alla Chiesa."[28]—"The Lord, I think, has set chains around your freedom by giving to your present religious life a fertility that no longer belongs to you alone, it belongs to souls, it belongs to the Church." Montini also sent a brief separate note to Dom James to inform him that he had written to Father Louis and to suggest that it would be "necessary to favor his desire for silence and solitude, not to ask of him overly absorbing relations with the community," and to let him set his own schedule as a writer.[29]

Both Merton and Dom James replied. Writing at length about the whole matter, Merton said among other things, "I am glad for this trial, and I thank God for it, although I regret having been a source of trouble for Superiors. I would have been less than God wanted me to be if I had not at least made this attempt to verify the attraction He has given me."[30] On his side, Dom James observed that "you certainly wrote him a most powerful and moving epistle, because he has been a changed man ever since he received it."[31]

The "changed man" did in fact find a path of reconciliation with Dom James and his superiors. In mid-October, at some point between the two replies to the archbishop, Dom James had to part with the master of novices, just elected abbot of Gethsemani's daughter house, the Abbey of the Genesee, in the Finger Lakes region of New York State. Merton's internal assessments may forever escape us, but the fact was that he freely offered Dom James to serve as Gethsemani's new master of novices. James could not have been more surprised. Gone the fire tower, gone for the moment the imperative longing for solitude, the long-sought transitus—he would instead, if James wished, become the teacher and guide of the youngest members of the community. Sedately, James told him that he would need a day or two to think it over and sent Merton away. But it is fully and solemnly documented that, after Merton left, James "danced a jig" around his office.[32] He knew at once that his long trial was over. Of course Father Louis would be perfect for the task. A few days later James required two promises of him: that he would serve for at least three years, and that he would teach Cistercian spirituality and community life exclusively. Were he to slip up in this regard—notably by praising the hermit orders—he would at once report it to Dom James. Merton had no difficulty accepting these conditions, and as things turned out he served for ten years.

His heart relaxed. Merton's own communications in the aftermath of this stunning change were measured, sweet tempered. To Jean Leclercq he wrote in early December:

> I am now master of novices! In fact, I am somewhat more of a cenobite than I expected to be. Strange things can happen in the mystery of one's vocation. . . . I shall cease to be a writer at least as long as I am in charge of the novices. The prospect does not trouble me. I care very little what I do now, so long as it is the will of God. Will He someday bring me . . . to perfect solitude? I do not know. One thing is sure, I have made as much effort in that direction as one can make without going beyond the limits of obedience. . . . I have found a surprising amount of interior solitude among my novices, and even a certain exterior solitude which I had not expected. This is, after all, the quietest and most secluded corner of the monastery. I am grateful to God for fulfilling many of my desires when seeming to deny them. I know that I am closer to Him, and that all my struggles this year formed part of His plan.[33]

On his side, Dom James wrote several letters to his superiors about the surprising outcome. He couldn't resist mocking Merton's decision: "He could appear before us all as making a heroic self-sacrifice for the good of the community," when in fact he had gotten "cold feet" about the fire tower hermitage.[34] And he continued with no trace of restraint: "[Father Louis said] that he never had greater peace than at the moment when this was settled. He really feels now that he is doing God's Will. Anything I say goes." James remained mindful that some questioned his motives. "Some may accuse me," he continued, "of opposing Father Louis's change for interested reasons. Whereas I am conscious of the great harm his change would have on souls, yet I know also what tremendous harm it would do to his own spiritual life." In a later communication that fall to Dom Gabriel, James was still thinking about the outcome. "And so, without pressure on my part," he wrote, "but just letting God's grace take its course, we see how much was self-will and how little was really divine."[35]

Merton closed out the year with Dom James through a handwritten note. "As for the novices, I will try to really teach them, instead of displaying my 'learning' (if any), and I will try to guide them instead of trying to make them like me. . . . Pray that I may have courage." And he signed as so often, "Your son in Jesus, fr m Louis."[36]

Essentially everyone involved in this long ordeal—with the exception of the archbishop—asserted that he knew God's will. Remembering this rather grand story from the distance of years, I find myself thinking that God's will was evident neither to Merton nor to his holy adversaries. Perhaps it was God's encompassing will that this conflict occur. It began to loosen unnecessary artifice. It began to open the order to new ways of living the Rule, revered by all participants in the ordeal.

[10]
The Shadow Abbot

AT THE BEGINNING OF 1956, Dom James uneasily noted to the abbot general that Merton seemed steady enough. "Thus far he is quiet and cooperative, but the fire can break out again at any time. However, I do not think it will assume the proportions it did before."[1] On his side, Merton sent a day-of-recollection report to James in February that reflected with his customary, devastating candor that he wasn't all that sure of himself. "I need plenty of grace now," he wrote. "I am coming to a crucial point in my life in which I may make a complete mess of everything—or let Jesus make a complete success of everything. On the whole, my nerves are not too good. . . . I have plenty of peace and trust though everything is *really* dark. But I hope it is the darkness before dawn."[2] He didn't neglect from time to time to remind James of his wish to be authorized, after three years' service in the novitiate, to live as a hermit in Gethsemani's outback. "But it is so easy," James commented to the abbot general, "to talk about something which is three years away."[3]

Merton innocently backed into the world of psychiatry in early 1956 and within a year's time would need to struggle away at great cost from its engulfing influence. As novice master he was faced again and again with evaluating postulants—young men applying for a place in the novitiate—and understanding the psychological difficulties of novices, some of whom encountered problems. Throughout his years as novice master, the most relaxed zone of communication between Merton and Dom James concerned the novices—the ones coming along well, those who found that after all they weren't called to monastic life, and sadly the few who cracked psychologically and had to be sent away either to their families or into psychiatric care. Merton and Dom James were eventually joined in this perennial concern by Fr. John Eudes Bamberger, already an MD when he entered the Gethsemani community. Dom James arranged a leave so that he could undertake a psychiatric residency under the auspices of Georgetown University—a residency interrupted by Dom Gabriel, who doubted its value, and resumed to completion when the forward-looking Dom James persuaded him of its value to the community.

Merton began experimenting with the Rorschach inkblot test as a compact, seemingly intuitive method of psychological assessment, and his first test subject, justly enough, was himself. Working with a Louisville psychiatrist, he had himself tested and, according to James, immediately got into a fuss over the results. Merton had good-humoredly described his experience to Dom James, who would need to approve use of the test in the novitiate. The psychiatrist told Merton, "You are not meant to be a hermit, you are a very social being, and that's that—voilà!"[4] You can imagine Dom James's delight. Rorschach tests found their way into the novitiate for a time.

Meanwhile, James and his superiors settled into a routine of denial where invitations to Merton were concerned. They came from all over, the flow never stopped for long, and they varied in character. That spring Merton had received an attractive invitation to participate in a conference in Paris organized by the Catholic Center for French Intellectuals. "Your presence and your word would be a normal complement," he read, to the Center's efforts to infuse the best of Christian thought into French intellectual milieus.[5] Merton was nearly French: born in France, he was thoroughly fluent in the language and linked by friendship to some of the key minds of French Catholicism, notably Jean Leclercq and Jacques Maritain. In a letter later in the year to Dom Angelico Surchamp, abbot of the Benedictine Abbey of La Pierre-Qui-Vire (justly famed for its books on French medieval art and architecture), Merton had written, of course in French, that he had "such need for voices from France, from *my native land*. . . . It is a continual sacrifice for me to be far from France, and to know that I shall doubtless never see it again. No one here can understand how hard that is."[6]

To put an end to the whole matter, Dom Gabriel wrote both to Dom James and to the somewhat hapless Parisian cleric who had extended the conference invitation. Dom Gabriel praised the "quality and intensity of the effort" undertaken by the center and acknowledged that Merton's books unquestionably made a contribution. But Father Merton, as he called him in this letter, should not depart from "the solitude whose benefits he has so proclaimed" and, were he to do so, one would be "well justified in thinking that he hadn't been altogether serious in what he had written about solitude." Were he to attend the conference, he would be "denying his own affirmations," and for that reason, Dom Gabriel explained, his participation would be "harmful."[7]

He wrote much the same to Dom James with what seems calculated naïveté: he was quite certain, he said, that Merton himself wouldn't even think of attending the conference because it would break into his solitude.[8] Of course, there is a problem here. As Dom Gabriel knew but seems to have conveniently overlooked, Merton had ended his campaign to transfer to a hermit order or to live a partially eremitic life at Gethsemani. He was now dedicated to a central role in the community as novice master. He slept in the novitiate, he was constantly concerned with the monastic education and well-being of some twenty novices, he had little though precious time on his own. Dom Gabriel's prevarication—let's use a vast Latinate word for what has occurred here—demonstrates that, in cooperation with Dom James, he viewed restricting Merton's movements for the sake of his soul as a more important value than honesty. Merton's campaign in the prior year shaped the attitudes of his superiors for a long time to come, and their "consolidated view"—the case against Merton in the external forum—continued to ramify.

It was inconceivable to his superiors that an integrated vocation as a contemplative monk and author was healthy, deserving of support, and not least deserving of the cross-fertilization that naturally occurs when like-minded people meet and exchange. That a monk and author would have two parallel needs, for solitude and for company, was too hybrid, too distant from what they perceived as the standard Cistercian pattern. And yet . . . The first Cistercian generations included remarkable authors, not least Saint Bernard, who had also taken an active role in the politics and international life of his era. So too would Merton in years not far ahead. Armand de Rancé, originator of the Trappist reform of Cistercian life, was a prolific author and correspondent. I search wonderingly in Cistercian origins and culture for the impediment that made it holy and sensible to thwart Merton's integrated vocation in these years. In the 1960s it was no longer so; when Merton resumed writing, the torrent of books, articles, and correspondence broke through the impediment. But Dom James never permitted him, with one exception, to accept invitations that would let him roam independently some little part of the world. As James permitted a number of other monks to travel for scholarly research, duties in other monasteries, and seminary education, the impediment may not after all have been in Cistercian culture but in his mistrust of Merton.

"Father Louis is going along," James wrote that June to his father immediate, Dom Louis. "But you never know what is going on in his head. He does very well as Master of Novices." And he added that "[Father Louis] is quite interested in the study of neuroses and psychoses. But having a very keen mind, he does not become unbalanced by it. These studies really are necessary today in the handling and screening of vocations."[9] James was almost certainly defending America against Old World thinking. He wanted to ensure that Dom Louis would tolerate the introduction of psychological testing. An opportunity to build greater sophistication into Gethsemani's screening practices and care of souls came up that summer, starting in late July: a two-week workshop on psychiatry and its applications to the religious life at Saint John's University in Collegeville, Minnesota. For some details that follow, I rely on Michael Mott's superb biography of Merton, *The Seven Mountains of Thomas Merton;*[10] Mott found his way to this topic and to eyewitnesses at a moment when the story could be richly gathered in and narrated. New here will be the correspondence that followed for some months after the workshop. Adding to the attractiveness of the workshop, its keynote speaker was to be Dr. Gregory Zilboorg, a renowned New York psychiatrist and author who is said to have counted among his patients George Gershwin, Gershwin's girlfriend Kay Swift, Ernest Hemingway, and captains of industry and finance. Of Russian Jewish origins, with a richly complex history ranging from early service in the ill-fated Kerensky government in Russia to the hard struggle to reestablish himself in America as a physician and psychiatrist, Zilboorg had converted not many years earlier to Catholicism. He was certainly an ideal choice as the presiding spirit of the workshop. Dom James dispatched Merton and the monk-physician Fr. John Eudes to the workshop, which he himself joined in the second week. He had heard from Merton's literary agent and friend, Naomi Burton Stone, that Zilboorg was excellent and had in mind to ask him to cast a professional eye on Merton. Zilboorg had already been shown a draft Merton article, published posthumously decades later as "The Neurotic Personality in the Monastic Life."[11]

Merton enjoyed and valued the first week; his journal, resumed days earlier perhaps in anticipation, records points he found stimulating.[12] Zilboorg had told him in the firmest possible terms that he should not write about psychiatric issues without thorough knowledge, but that seems not to have upset Merton—he could agree with the doctor's point, though apparently roughly delivered. In the second week, with Dom James now participating in the workshop, Merton had a private meeting with Zilboorg and a second at which James was present. In the private meeting, lasting an hour and a half, Zilboorg had obviously decided on the basis of scant direct acquaintance with Merton—they had spoken very little—to be extremely provocative. He must have been coached in advance by Dom James; as we know, James viewed Merton as neurotic, and it is clear from what follows that he had shared his view with the formidable doctor. Much of what Zilboorg said in the initial meeting was taken from Dom James's playbook. Zilboorg surely had personal reasons to align with James, the abbot of America's largest monastery and a respected figure in the Church, to which Zilboorg now belonged. Psychologically informed essayists in later years have looked at the sequence of events and attitudes we are about to witness and attributed motives to the psychiatrist—for example, competitiveness and projection—that he himself failed to recognize.[13] In this book that is not our terrain; what we have is an abundance of little-known correspondence written in the aftermath of the Collegeville workshop, correspondence that asks to be read with lay but concerned eyes.

By his own report soon after in his journal, Merton heard in the first private meeting that he was "in somewhat bad shape and . . . neurotic" and that addressing his treatment needs would be difficult. He learned that he was "a gadfly to his superiors" and "very stubborn," "afraid to be an ordinary monk in the community." Presumably because they used psychological tests such as the Rorschach, Zilboorg lumped Merton together with Fr. John Eudes: "You and Father Eudes can very easily become a pair of semi-psychotic quacks." "You like to be famous, you want to be a big shot. . . . Megalomania and narcissism are your big trends." Merton regarded all of this, he recorded in a midday journal entry, as things he did and did not know. While Zilboorg was speaking, Merton

FIG. 5. Thomas Merton and Dr. Gregory Zilboorg, August 1956.

found himself thinking how much he resembled Stalin—he had something like Stalin's moustache and facial breadth, a Russian accent, and for the moment at least Stalin's aggressiveness. A photograph taken during the workshop (fig. 5) should not be overinterpreted, but it seems to show the two men uncomfortable with each other. Who knows? But the photo gives pause, as if one were seeing emotions.

Zilboorg wasn't quite done. "Your hermit trend is pathological," he said, again from Dom James's playbook. "You are a promoter. . . . It is not intelligence you lack, but affectivity. . . . It will do you no good to be forbidden to write. . . . It needs to be prohibited in your heart—if it is merely prohibited, it will not seem prohibited to you."[14]

As Mott points out, Merton was willing to record all of this in his journal; it didn't bowl him over, it made a kind of sense he could hear and perhaps learn from. Mott also writes that Merton did not record the second meeting; it was more than he could bear. Mott's account of it is from other sources. Zilboorg laid into Merton as he had in the first meeting, but "Merton was not ready to be exposed in front of Dom James," Mott continues. "He flew into a fury and cried tears of rage. . . . Zilboorg went on repeating in a level voice what he had said before about the hermitage idea being pathological: 'You want a hermitage in Times Square with a large sign over it saying 'HERMIT.' . . . Merton . . . sat with tears streaming down his face muttering 'Stalin! Stalin!' The worst thing that could have happened had happened: Zilboorg . . . had staged a situation in which the most exaggerated misgivings of Dom James were dramatically confirmed."[15] That the situation was staged is beyond doubt, but psychiatrist and abbot were cooperating all along—why not also now?

Merton's next journal entry is four days on, well after that session. It is striking in that context. He was looking out over the lake on campus and considering the pair of loons that made it their home. They became figures of due solitude, of untrammeled wildness. "The loon, I think, is a very serious bird and I take him seriously. To me it is not crazy but even, in a way, beautiful. It means: distances, wind, water, forests, the loneliness of the North."[16] He had heard a few days earlier from a renowned psychiatrist that he was mentally and emotionally unbalanced, cracked in places. The loons, with their seemingly crazy call and paired solitude, delivered a different message that only a writer and poet could perceive. A message of comfort.

The combatants went home. Fr. John Eudes, traveling by air with Merton, recalls how deeply discouraged he was.[17] Through that summer, until the journal breaks off again in mid-September, Merton makes no mention of his encounter with Zilboorg; he is, as always, self-searching. "Let us walk along here . . . and compose a number of sentences each one of which begins with the words 'You think you are a monk but . . .'"[18] We know this voice in Merton; he owed it to no one, it was his own. That summer he gives the impression of returning wholeheartedly to his roles as master of novices and as a writer freely exploring literature—returning to the company of early Christian fathers and contemporary religious thinkers, to his caring observations of the steps forward, hesitations, and occasional falls of the novices and young priests. All of this was his world; his spirited sense of belonging to it restored him in some measure. Nonetheless, a bolus of grave self-doubt had been injected into him. It would have its effect. Behind the scenes Dom James launched an exchange of letters with Dr. Zilboorg about how best to build on what had been accomplished. He kept Dom Gabriel informed.

James's first letter to Zilboorg, August 13, assumed that Merton would be spending several months in New York to receive psychiatric treatment. Perhaps Merton could take academic courses to fill out the day?

> As I said to you when saying goodbye—and it really came from my heart—you were the soul of that workshop. . . .
>
> No doubt Father Louis has written you already. He mentions something about taking courses.
>
> You did say you were going to be the boss, dear Greg, but if you will allow me to express my opinion on this course affair—it does not strike me favorably for Father Louis.
>
> If he took a course, he would have to attend the lectures, mixing with a lot of other people. He would have to register under some name or other. A priest hardly could use a false name. He is bound to be known—and you know his volatile dynamic spirit. He just would not keep quiet.
>
> Also, I think it would affect his therapy with you.
>
> The less Father Louis runs around in New York for any reason . . . , the better off he will be.
>
> It can be said, however, that he is looking forward to his encounter with you, and he really wants to be straightened out; and so do we want him to be straightened out. . . .

> We want a one hundred and ten percent job done on poor Father Louis, and you are the only one who can do it. You know that.
>
> So, let us know . . . and we will make the arrangements. . . .
>
> All for Jesus—thru Mary—with a smile[19]

They continued to correspond, working out the conditions under which Merton might live in New York for some months. "He is going to be a hard man to manage, dear Greg. You will have to put him under absolute obedience," James wrote a few weeks later.[20] This is in part the language of the cloister. Zilboorg had become a shadow abbot.

Dom James turned to the troubling fact that Merton had resumed his journal. "Wherever he goes he carries a ledger under his arm and is writing his journal, his diary of all the things that happen. Actions and reactions. He had it under his arm when he came back from Collegeville in the plane. This is a mania with him. If he writes a journal of your sessions with him . . . , it will surely make wonderful reading. But how will it affect the psychology of the cure? . . . I hope you will have him so cured that he will not be writing anything at all. . . ." Did Dom James feel threatened by the ledger all too evident under Merton's arm? If so, he had reason: as the years passed, and increasingly from this point on, Merton recorded there his difficulties with his abbot and his criticisms, sometimes extreme, of James's attitudes and acts. Merton should have tucked it away somewhere. Dom James must have felt that he had an investigative reporter in the monastic community; how unwelcome.

Dr. Zilboorg didn't like it either. "The ledger business of which you speak is a dangerous thing—analysis or no analysis," he replied on September 10.[21] "It betrays an overestimation of the external, and I need not tell you how very bad this is in anyone, particularly a monk belonging to such an important contemplative order. . . . It is definitely a serious impediment to the treatment which is being contemplated." But this wasn't the main business of Zilboorg's letter; he had had second thoughts about treating Merton in New York. "May I prayerfully ask you to be patient with me and read this letter with all the patience and tolerance which is in your heart as a priest. The letter is apt . . . to be a little hard." There was no question in his mind that Merton was a disturbed individual. "Father is a gifted and also a restless person," he wrote. "His talent is from God; his restlessness, I am afraid, springs not from his ecclesiastic state, or from his spiritual calling, but rather from his human, all too human, worldly, and even revengeful personality. This is his neurosis. . . . His trouble is that he almost always plans to write a book on a subject before he has even started studying the subject." Clearly, Dr. Zilboorg hadn't managed to forgive Merton his awkwardly trespassing article on neurosis in the monastery. He went on to say that he could not in conscience impose a monastic style of obedience on Merton in New York; the patient must be free to make his own choices, that is a condition of proper treatment. However, "Father is not stable enough to be trusted in ambulatory therapy. He is not stable enough to be trusted outside his abbey without direct and authoritative spiritual supervision. . . . To undertake treatment outside his religious house is to risk a great deal: his own reputation, my reputation, possibly a scandalous moment. The Father, in short, is in my opinion a sick man—and the more normal he appears, the more reasonable to outsiders, the sicker he really is." With this remark, Merton is as undefended—at least before these two men—as he could possibly be. His normality itself is evidence of mental illness. "My heart really aches to undertake this job," Dr. Zilboorg continued.

> It is a great, God-given opportunity to save a man so that he could save his soul fully, but I know, you will be the last to assume that I am equal to the job, unless the Father matures a little more spiritu-

> ally and stops (yes, stops!) writing. . . . You sense the problem correctly when you ask me to put him under absolute obedience, but what can I do to achieve compliance with that obedience? Absolutely nothing—unless the man is ready to sacrifice something in order to be treated. What kind of sacrifice could it be? Well, his neurosis must be treated like an addiction. He must stop indulging himself: as to writing, as to keeping a journal. . . . Let him learn what Charity really is as an experience, not just a concept. In other words, let him spend a couple of years in his monastery with only one perspective—his inner spiritual one, the one he has chosen. Let him milk cows and mix their feed, let him work until he is spiritually stabilized. His neurosis could then be taken care of medically. . . . He could write books, and better books, later.

In short, Dr. Zilboorg had decided not to undertake Merton's analysis in New York and could not commit time for an analysis conducted over some months at Gethsemani. Dom James naturally questioned his decision. The opportunity was unique, the analyst unique. "I have no confidence," he replied to Zilboorg, "in any other analyst apart from you, for him."[22] And at that point, surely unknowingly, he returned to the perspective of his Trappist predecessor, Abbot de Rancé. "Isn't there some monastery around New York where Father could be imprisoned?" As far as Dom James knew, there was not. Where milking and feeding cows was concerned, he sensibly wrote that it "would do more harm than good. It would be too sudden. If one is driving a car ninety miles an hour and throws on the brakes in one sweep, the car will be shattered." For the rest, he reported that Father Louis seemed in better shape and said so himself. As well, "he has cut out writing all books as such. . . . Personally, I know he is, as you say, a sick man, and I wish something could be done now. He himself certainly wants to be cured, although naturally he dreads the purifying fires through which he would have to pass. But that is understandable. I feel he would be most faithful in obeying anything you would say." And he closed the letter as so often, with his motto.

As noted earlier, Dom James hadn't neglected to keep Dom Gabriel informed. In a letter of September 4, he explained the occasion (the Collegeville workshop), the cast of characters (Dr. Zilboorg), the direction of events (psychiatric sessions in New York), and their necessity. "Of course, Father Louis definitely has some very serious neurosis," he wrote with more emphasis than in the past. "In fact, that is the explanation for all his occasional upsets and crises he has been going through the last several years, and pulling the rest of us along with him. . . . Dr. Zilboorg is very sharp and intuitive in his insights into souls. He saw that truly, as he told me, Father Louis is a very sick man psychologically. He said he could go on as he is now, but he never could give his full energies and talent to producing the best for God in the souls of others or in his writings with his present crippled psychiatric apparatus. . . . He believed he could correct Father's neurotic problems and make a new man out of him. He said it would either make or break him. . . . It is really almost a question of life and death spiritually for Father and also for his future work for the Order and for Gethsemani." And Dom James recalled for Dom Gabriel's benefit the drama he had witnessed: "Some of the things the Doctor told Father in my presence at Collegeville were something terrific. He had Father crying from the tremendous punch behind his penetrating remarks. . . . Yes, . . . he is the only man who can straighten out Father Louis, if he is to be straightened out at all."[23]

It is time, and past time, for my own day-of-recollection report to the reader. You'll recall those monthly reports by monastic officers to their superior—not required, not necessarily written, but Merton wrote many. I find this concerted attack on Thomas Merton for being Thomas Merton nearly unbearable. It grieves me to write this part of the long narrative. I do so because it is more preferable to know than not to know. I do so with love for Merton—

the brother of us all—and love of another kind for the abbot his tormenter, who by the inscrutable design of Providence was placed to challenge Merton and unknowingly contribute to the formidable independence of mind and heart of his maturity. A while ago I was speaking of Merton with James George, the Canadian high commissioner in New Delhi in 1968, who helped him find his way to the Tibetan community and in other respects. After listening for a time to what I could then tell him about Merton's trials with Dom James, my friend said something that periodically haunts me: "They should have gotten someone else for him." This concludes the day-of-recollection report.

You must have noticed in Dom James's accounts of Merton's state that he had come to view himself as neurotically unstable and in need of therapy. That was James's view, but three letters in September and October from Merton to Dr. Zilboorg confirm that Merton shared it. On September 14, the very day when Dom James was writing to Zilboorg about Merton's "dread of the purifying fires," Merton also wrote a letter measured in tone to say that he was aware of the doctor's decision not to offer treatment in New York: "I bow to your better judgment. All that remains is for me to prove my good will by following your suggestions. And waiting patiently for treatment in the future."[24] He committed himself "to concentrate on leading my monastic life, on being a monk and nothing else. It is all I want to be, all I mean to be. . . . In what I say now, I am not just expressing my own velleities, but the resolutions and decisions arrived at with my Abbot and my confessor. If I am to live as a monk exclusively and attend first of all to my own soul, I give up all writing activities and contacts of that kind . . . including the writing of a journal, of occasional poems, etc. Until further notice, I cease to be a writer." Zilboorg had accused him of having read too little in the Church fathers, in the Angelic Doctor Thomas Aquinas. It was this reading he would now pursue, he wrote, "just for the sake of my own soul and for union with God." All of this was capitulation; it was as Zilboorg wished. However, Merton mounted a strong defense of his role as master of novices: it would unsettle the novices to shift the assignment to another monk, but beyond that the role was perfectly suited to his need to focus on the pure Cistercian life. "Believe me, Gregory, I am not trying to put anything over on you when I say that in actual fact the closest I can get to being a real monk and fulfilling what you want . . . is precisely the novitiate. . . . I am not really asking anything special, except perhaps that you consider letting me try to be a monk in the novitiate for another year at least, before we change anything there. . . . I . . . beg God to enlighten you, and to give me the grace to carry out His will."

The shadow abbot: even Merton for the moment has accepted Dr. Zilboorg in that role. It was not by any stretch of imagination Zilboorg's role to make or unmake monastic assignments, nonetheless Merton was reading the situation correctly and appealed to Zilboorg as if he wielded the abbot's authority.

Less than a week later, Merton wrote again to defend his role in the novitiate. He reported that he had been praying and meditating deeply, doing everything possible "to put aside my own will and my neurosis and use my reason and my freedom to do God's will for me."[25] He hoped to write "without injecting too much that is neurotic into my answer." The word *neurotic* had become a dark pivot in his view of himself; he was subjugated. "It is not for me to say whether I should continue to be novice master or not. I leave that for Rev. Father and you to decide between you." But he made clear that to be removed from the novitiate would break his heart—so he put it—and would be a "real blow for them also," for the novices. "Again, Gregory, I appreciate your suggestions and your wisdom, and I shall do everything I can to do what you desire. . . . It would be so nice if we could see you and talk it over here. Can't it be arranged?"

On October 9, he wrote again to welcome the news that Zilboorg might soon find his way to Gethsemani for a short visit. "You will be able to get a closer look at the community, you and I will be able to have a little talk, and I am sure I will profit immensely from any revelations you may care to offer me."[26] For the moment Merton is submissively ready to receive Zilboorg as a thaumaturge, a bringer of revelations. (From his vantage point, Dom James seems to have had an even more elevated vision of the man. In a late communication summarizing much that had occurred since the Collegeville workshop, James wrote, "It took you, dear Greg, to bring the light of the Holy Ghost. Meeting you was a real Pentecost."[27]) Merton's October letter had one purpose only, as before: to safeguard his duty as novice master. "In dealing with the novices, I am working hard to avoid exhibitionism if I can. Of course, you understand that I have not been conscious of much before. . . . I will do my best to really teach them, and to guide them, and help them. . . . I want them to be happy and proficient monks. I know of course to some extent what great limitations I have, and I will do my best to keep this in mind."

During these weeks of fall, Merton felt moved to take leave of one of his closest friends by correspondence, Sr. Thérèse Lentfoehr. He didn't expect to be free in future to correspond with her often; "the ultimate in iron curtains has descended on me," he explained.[28] "Although I have always put on a show of being very ascetic," he continued,

> I do not hesitate to confess that letters from my friends have always and will always mean a great deal to me. You see I am not so ascetic after all, and I am glad of the fact, if it means that I can get some of the graces Our Lord reserves for those who are not ashamed to be human. . . . With me writing is less a talent than an addiction. Father Abbot hopes I can be cured of it now, and so do I. Nothing has been said about *never* writing again, but at least everyone wants to see how I get along without writing over a period of several years and I think it is certainly a necessary step to take.

"Those who are not ashamed to be human." In these few words hope makes itself known. The storm could pass, and will pass. The refusal to accept the other as he is, to accept oneself as a thing well made and promising, though of course imperfect—these distortions can and will pass. The massed authority and harsh judgment that Merton had faced, and to which he nearly yielded, would in time lose its power. Dwelling with oneself in prayer and silence, reading the wisdom of the world, hearing the voices of the world, teaching the novices to be the humble and grand thing to which they felt called—to be Cistercian—all of this and more remained possible at Gethsemani. It was Merton's way; it had merit.

Dom James continued to exert pressure against Merton's integrated vocation as monk and author. To Merton's literary agent and friend, Naomi Burton Stone, he wrote in late November, "[Father Louis] cannot think of writing as comprising a major part of his vocation, regardless of how much good his works accomplish. When he writes again, he must think of it as an obedience of monastic and religious life imposed by God through his Superiors, rather than something he has obtained permission for himself."[29]

Dr. Zilboorg did pay a visit to Gethsemani at Christmastide. Dom James hoped that he would give a few talks in chapter. "You can think over what might be the best subjects," he wrote in advance, "that will help most in our spiritual life, or some other subjects that would be interesting, like your work among the criminals of New York. Something that will put the fear of God in us and make us appreciate our cloistered vocation, and how we should persevere in it and live up to its high standards."[30] The doctor's visit was more like a coda than a new beginning; relations afterward became looser, correspondence rarer—and in point of fact, Dr. Zilboorg became ill in 1958 and died the following year. One gain for all concerned was that doctor and monk had private time together, and Zilboorg soon after wrote to Dom James that he had quite liked Merton as he came to know him better.[31] The

Collegeville episode had been so heated, rushed, and controlled by Dom James that starting over with a simple "Hello, who are you?" made best sense. In a note to Zilboorg after his visit, Dom James released the entire conception to which he had held so strongly. "I am glad you were able to come closer to good Fr Louis. Certainly you can write to him at any time, but I know you are a busy man. He sort of surmises or suspicions that you are never going to analyze him. But that is all right. What of it."[32]

Merton's farewell to the episode occurred much later, in the late winter of 1963. "I thought today at adoration what a blessing it was that I did not go in 1956 to be analyzed by Zilboorg. . . . What a tragedy and mess that would have been—and I must give Z. the credit for having sensed it himself. . . . I am afraid that I was willing, at the time, to go, which shows what a fool I was."[33]

[11]

Out of a Chrysalis

"Good Father Louis goes along quietly," Dom James reported to the abbot general in early February.[1] To go along quietly was of the essence. Merton and Dom James needed rest from the stresses of their relationship. Merton was serving as well as ever in the novitiate and concerned, as we know, to remain there. He resumed his journal in April, no doubt invisibly. He was reading widely with intense interest. Now and always, he *lived* in literature with a sense of belonging. He thought with authors; the centuries of writing collected in him. Whatever communications there were between abbot and subject in 1957 have left little trace, and what has survived is not alarming. If the encounter with Dr. Zilboorg left a wound on Merton, there is scarcely a sign that it was so. This is surprising, but as a physician once said to me concerning one of her patients, "he knew what he was about." Merton knew what he was about. His fundamental health and confidence reappeared, accompanied by a new and still shaky attitude of noncombative detachment. Of course he wasn't entirely free. It was a test of his patience when Dom James insisted on speculating with him about suitable names in religion for newly arrived novices: "As soon as anyone comes in who is a little fat," Merton recorded in his journal without love, "Rev. Father insists on calling him Aquinas, because Tho. Aquinas was reputedly fat. This I find extremely silly—but it is one more thing I am finally getting used to."[2] Similarly, when a complex quadrille of sorts was introduced in church for the schola—the monks assigned to lead the chant—his patience blew. "The revival and creation of ridiculous rules has gone up 100% since

Fr C. was appointed choirmaster. He and the abbot abet one another in their madness."[3] Post-Zilboorg, Merton was both more detached and more willing to criticize Dom James. This was not the anticipated result.

On his side, Dom James was surely content to address matters other than Merton. It was clear, however, that his view of Merton had been confirmed and enhanced by the encounter with Dr. Zilboorg. In response to especially significant invitations to conferences or requests for articles that stopped at his office on their way to Merton, their intended recipient, he would unhesitatingly convey some or all of the Fox/Zilboorg vision of good Father Louis in order to quell further interest. In the course of 1957, Dom James and his abbatial office paid the price for coming so resolutely between Merton and the publishing world. "We have had to answer almost 50 persons . . . imploring articles," he complained to Jean Leclercq.[4] At the time Merton was scarcely writing, although topics in the novitiate were beginning to point toward some of his best work of the 1960s.

But Merton was reawakening. "What on earth am I doing here?" He asked himself in a mid-November journal entry.

> I have answered it a million times. "I belong here" and that is no answer. In the end, there is no answer like that. Any vocation is a mystery and juggling with words does not make it any clearer.
> It is a contradiction and must remain a contradiction.
>
> I think the only hope for me is to pile contradiction upon contradiction and push myself into the middle of all contradictions.
>
> Thus it will always remain morally impossible for me simply to "conform" and to settle down and accept the official rationalization of what is going on here. On the other hand it in no way helps matters for me to replace the official statements with slightly better rationalizations of my own. . . . If you want to find satisfactory formulas you had better deal with things that can be fitted

> into a formula. The vocation to seek God is not one of them. Nor is existence. Nor is the spirit of man.[5]

The nested sequence here—vocation, existence, the spirit of man—points toward the widening and deepening awareness of his maturity. I don't know exactly when the ascetic stripling in early photographs of Merton at Gethsemani became the full-bodied man encountered in photographs of the 1960s (fig. 6). At some point he began to look something like a longshoreman and something like the writers Henry Miller and Jean Genet. Miller thought he looked like Picasso, and Merton thought of himself that he looked like Picasso, Genet, or "a Barcelona hotel keeper." Where the writers and artist are concerned, if not the hotelier, he had in common with them qualities evident in their faces of vitality, complexity, and recognition of the human tragicomedy in which they knew themselves to be implicated. Merton did indeed "push himself into the middle of all contradictions" and make his home there; it was a better fire tower by far. That transformation occurred in these years. In the spring of 1958, he noted in his journal: "Thinking of the new and necessary struggle in my interior life. I am finally coming out of a chrysalis. The years behind me seem strangely inert and negative, but I suppose that passivity was necessary. Now the pain and struggle of fighting my way out into something new and much bigger."[6]

In later 1957 a theme emerged in Merton's thoughts that would dominate a drama lying some months ahead: the need and promise of a South American monastic foundation, later expanded to include Central America. He came to the theme by two avenues. Publication of some of his works in Spanish exposed him to the language and soon to contemporary poets in Spanish; their work delighted him. And then, he valued conversations with an outstanding novice, Ernesto Cardenal, a Nicaraguan poet and revolutionary ten years his junior, destined to leave Gethsemani in 1959 to take a direct role in revolutionary scenes both in his

FIG. 6. Thomas Merton, 1960s, in a woodshed where novices gathered on rainy days.

native country and elsewhere in South America.[7] Merton had few friends in the community over the years, though he had cordial relations with many. Cardenal, then known as Br. Lawrence, was one of those few. Merton knew that Dom James also was thinking about a possible foundation in South America, not right away, but sometime. Merton made of this a topic for exchange between them. A letter of mid-July 1957 summarizes his conclusions from reading he had been doing that summer about the conditions in various countries—Colombia, Ecuador, Chile, and others. "Any foundation we may make there in the future will probably be harder than anything so far, but it may also be more fruitful," he wrote.[8] The possibility took root in him. On Christmas Eve, as the year was ending, he recorded in his journal words very close to a prayer for God's help to discover, through a foundation in Ecuador or elsewhere, "how best and most genuinely the monastic life could be lived in our time."[9] The revolutionary content of this sweet wish is hard to miss.

Early in 1958, Merton was inwardly in motion. "I am obscurely convinced," he noted in his journal, "that there is a need in the world for something I can provide, and that there is a need for me to provide it. True, someone else can do it, God does not need me. But I feel He is asking me to provide it."[10] This is both a declaration of independence and an acknowledgment of interdependence—of a world to which he is bound, though by a still somewhat unclear duty. He was speaking with Dom James from time to time about a South American foundation and longing to be part of any such venture. James put him off—the moment hadn't come to think seriously about the project, though an offer of land had been received from a wealthy Colombian. We could "grow corn and frijoles," Merton speculated.[11] There was ever a child in him.

We are now on famous ground. Everyone who cares for Merton's life and writings is likely to remember something of his dream about a young Jewish girl who gave her name as Proverb, and likely to remember in detail his spontaneous visionary experience at "4th and Walnut" in Louisville. Proverb appeared to him one night at the end of February. "I am embraced with determined and virginal passion by a young Jewish girl," he recorded in his journal. "She clings to me and will not let go, and I get to like the idea. . . . I reflect 'She belongs to the same race as St. Anne.' I ask her name and she says her name is Proverb. . . . No need to explain. It was a charming dream."[12] A charming dream, easily dismissed—but almost at once Merton felt drawn to write a letter and within a few days drafted it into his journal. "Dear Proverb," he demurely began what must be his first love letter since entering the monastery in 1941,

> How grateful I am to you for loving in me something which I thought I had entirely lost, and someone who, I thought, I had long ago ceased to be. And in you, dear, though some might be tempted to say you do not even exist, there is a reality as real and as wonderful and as precious as life itself. I must be careful what I say, for words cannot explain my love for you. . . . I think what I most want to say is that I treasure, in you, the revelation of your virginal solitude . . . yet you have given your love to me, why I cannot imagine.[13]

An excerpt from the letter may make it seem syrupy; it is anything but. It is an acute recognition of emotional and sexual energies within Merton which, in the uncanny play of character and Providence, now declared themselves and hereafter might move aside but never disappear. Instinctively making her as real as possible, Merton wrote in the here and now to a girl irretrievably there and elsewhere. We can better understand his choice of the name Saint Anne for the little shed where he used to pray and watch and write (it had long since been overtaken by the noise of farm machines and all but abandoned): Saint Anne, the mother of Mary, to whom all Cistercian monasteries are dedicated and whose initial used to appear first in all Cistercian names—Fr. M Louis, Dom M James. Not a random choice, the name placed Merton under the caring eyes of a lineage of women now joined by Proverb, who prefigures others to come—Sophia, or Wisdom, of whom he wrote a remarkable prose poem, a dreamed Chinese princess much like Proverb, and in time the student nurse with whom he fell in love.

Merton's encounter with Proverb in late February–early March was renewed in the incident at 4th and Walnut two weeks later. Here again, famous ground—and in our context we need only acknowledge the event rather than explore it at length. "Yesterday, in Louisville, at the corner of 4th and Walnut, suddenly realized that I love all the people and that none of them were, or, could be totally alien to me. As if waking from a dream—the dream of my separateness, of the 'special' vocation to be different. . . . Thank God! Thank God! I am only another member of the human race, like all the rest of them. I have the immense joy of being a man!"[14] And he concluded the entry with a second letter to Proverb, as if they had met at 4th and Walnut. "Only with you are these things found, dear child sent to me by God!" In a letter to the novelist Boris Pasternak later in the year he was clearer still: "I was walking alone in the crowded street and suddenly saw that everybody was Proverb and that in all of them shone her extraordinary beauty and purity and shyness, even though they did not know who they were."[15]

Toward the end of the year Merton was able to articulate his new insights and feelings at a moment when he was looking back over his published poetry in a measured but critical frame of mind. He could see the good in what he had written, yet he had become a different person, as fervent as ever but in a wholly new way. "The new fervor will be rooted not in asceticism but in humanism," he wrote in his journal.

> What has begun now must grow but must never seek to become spectacular or to attract attention to itself—which is what I unconsciously did in those days, proclaiming that I was a poet and a mystic. Both are probably true, but not deep enough, because then it was too conscious. I have to write and speak not as the individual who has cut himself off from the world and wants the world to know it, but as the person who has lost himself in the service of the vast wisdom of God's plan to reveal Himself in the world and in man. How much greater, deeper, nobler, truer and more hidden. A mysticism that no longer appears, transcendent and ordinary.[16]

From Proverb by night and the streets of Louisville by day to his new sense of purpose there is little distance; those encounters gave rise to it.

As this is Merton, there was an intellectual element at work in his passage out of the chrysalis and into the middle of all contradictions. He was reading widely—perhaps for the first time in nearly two decades about social and ideological forces—when he found his way in April to Martin Buber's compact masterpiece, *I and Thou*.[17] Like so many of us, he discovered in its pages Buber's classic insight: I-Thou, the living relation of dialogue between human beings and between ourselves and God; and I-it, the lifeless relation in which we objectify one another and think about God in a way that reduces Him to an object of thought among others. But beyond that, Merton wrote into his journal paragraphs from Buber that he described as "among the wisest religious truths written in our century." Buber was drawing out an implication of his fundamental insight:

> "Meeting with God does not come to man in order that he may concern himself with God, but in order that he may confirm that there is meaning in the world.
>
> "All revelation is summons and sending. . . . God remains present to you when you have been sent forth; he who goes on a mission has always God before him: the truer the fulfillment the stronger and more constant his nearness. He cannot concern himself directly with God but he can converse with Him."[18]

Responding to this passage, Merton continued, "Ten years ago I would have been perplexed and scandalized by [these thoughts], but in the depths of my heart I realize how true they are. And I realize how monumentally we fail, in this monastery, to understand this!"

This is breathtaking in a quiet way. It is the subtext or chant accompanying much to come in Merton's life and work. As Merton acknowledged, he was never a theologian, never one to write effectively *about*. But he lived and moved and had his being—the words of Saint Paul are fully applicable—in a world where God also lives and moves. He had no difficulty now sharing Buber's dynamic vision that "all revelation is summons and sending," and that dialogue with God is a necessity for some if not all who are summoned and sent.

Three linked epiphanies: Proverb, 4th and Walnut, and Merton's reception of Martin Buber's religious humanism. There is a fourth element in the new configuration: Merton's greater willingness to look critically at Dom James and at community life as James shaped it. From 1958 forward, these themes recur in his journal and correspondence far more than in the past, sometimes with penetrating lucidity, sometimes with righteousness he would later regret. Gethsemani and its abbot became central objects of meditation; he felt compelled to understand them better. That understanding would have a place in his valediction when, as he again began to hope, he would leave for elsewhere.

[12]

The Moon, Venus, or Mars!

THERE WAS A LITTLE FUN TO BE HAD, all the same. Merton was not to write, not to keep a journal, not to correspond except in small doses. So it was for a time. But in mid-March 1958, Dom Gabriel faced a peculiar problem: the abbess of a Cistercian sisters' abbey in Wrentham (Massachusetts) had asked him to evaluate poems written by one of the sisters; they were to be published soon. This was not Dom Gabriel's field. After the fact he explained to Dom James an initiative he had felt constrained to take: "Given the nature of these writings and their small number, I thought to ask Fr Louis, *most exceptionally,* to give me his evaluation. No one is more qualified than he to judge these poems. I thought it wouldn't take him long to read them and form an opinion. For me this opinion was more interesting . . . than that of any ordinary censor."[1] It was a minor departure from the literary fast imposed—and for a time willingly accepted—by good Father Louis. He was there for you when you needed him.

That spring Merton received a letter and books from a justly famed Italian Jesuit, Riccardo Lombardi. A strong and sensible liberal voice in the Church, familiar to the public as "God's microphone," he was a gifted public speaker in several languages, a radio commentator and author. Fr. Lombardi was destined to influence the substance and course of the Second Vatican Council, convened by Pope John XXIII (now Saint John XXIII) in the fall of 1962. With the support of Pope John's predecessor, Pius XII, he had founded in the postwar period the Pius XII International Center for a Better World, which exists to this day as the broadly international Community for a Better World (www.communitybetterworld.org). By letter Fr. Lombardi invited Merton to contribute in some way to the movement. At that time and always, people outside the monastery—writers, religious, scholars, and others—had their own evaluations of how Merton could help; their logic derived from what they appreciated in his writings. They had no knowledge, at least initially, of the quite different evaluation prevailing inside the walls.

Merton was sincerely touched to hear from Lombardi. "It was to me a pleasant surprise and a very great honor to receive your kind letter," he wrote in reply, "and I will not conceal from you the deep impression that it made on me. I feel, in fact, that this letter of yours has a definite providential meaning for me."[2] He took the occasion of responding to Fr. Lombardi's communication to give what he called a "first tentative formulation" to thoughts he had been mulling for some months. He wrote that he had "written enough about the contemplative life for the time being," although it scarcely needed saying that he would continue to live that life "as God gives it to me to be lived." Second, he had discovered in himself a gift from the Lord: "the desire and the ability to engage in a dialogue with intellectuals outside the Church, particularly literary people, artists, etc." And to this list he added "intellectuals of many different races and nations . . . [whose] forms of thought, religious beliefs and way of life . . . are most strange to occidentals." These reflections led on to the crucial one:

> For many months now I had been thinking that it would be a wonderful thing to *found a small contemplative monastery* which would serve as a spiritual and intellectual center in some South American nation, for instance Ecuador, where there is a small but important intellectual and artistic movement, a certain cultural vitality. . . . When I read of your Center and its program . . . , I saw that this was almost exactly the kind of work I would have hoped to do in this

> monastic foundation.... Intellectual leaders, and other important persons, would be invited to come, together with clergymen, etc., to participate in what would be partly a retreat and partly a symposium on spiritual and cultural matters, especially with a view to the formation of a better world, a more just society, a more true philosophy of life, etc.
>
> For the rest, the community would live an enclosed contemplative life, in silence and solitude.
>
> I am convinced that such a monastery is badly needed, could easily be founded and kept up, and would be an immense success....
>
> However, I have not mentioned a plan for this kind of monastic community to my Superiors because it falls outside the norm of the Cistercian Order... and I do not feel that it would meet with their sympathies because of the emphasis on contacts with people from outside and the element of study and intellectual life which it also implies....
>
> It is a pleasure for me to be able to mention this idea to you, knowing that you cannot fail to be interested... since it is so very close to what you yourself are doing.

It has surely not been lost on you that Dom James and his office had and exercised the right to read all mail addressed to or written by members of the community, excepting only mail identified on the envelope as "conscience matter" or "sub sigillo conscientiae," under seal of conscience. Generally, such mail passed through unopened, although where Merton was concerned in this period James sought the abbot general's agreement that letters even so marked from individuals likely to have a harmful influence could be opened at his discretion or returned unopened to the sender. Where James lost control was during his frequent absences; at those times the mails moved without oversight, and it was at just such a period that Merton had received Fr. Lombardi's letter and responded. Upon his return to Gethsemani, James did see the correspondence, incoming and outgoing, in some form and put his own letter in the mail to Fr. Lombardi on August 4.

He began with extravagant praise for Fr. Lombardi's future plans for the Center for a Better World. "Grandiose, bold, and courageous. . . . It is indeed a gigantic undertaking, when one thinks of the vast fields to be harvested and the almost insuperable obstacles to be overcome."[3] James expressed the most fervent sympathy and solidarity. And then alluded to the Gospel distinction between Martha and Mary—between practical work in the world and the work of "cloistered-contemplative souls." He noted that the Sacred Congregation for Religious, a powerful Vatican department, had recently called upon the Cistercian Order to emphasize still more the values of poverty and separation from the world. "Therefore, dear Father Lombardi, you can appreciate how jealously we must guard ourselves against the all-too-attractive tendency towards the field of Martha."

All of this was preamble to the actual theme: good Father Louis. Dom James was about to deliver his deadliest judgment yet—a newly expanded, more extreme, more psychological version.

> In regard to good Father Louis in particular, dear Reverend Father, I can understand easily your point of view and desires. But I, on the other hand, have lived with him for some 17 years and have been his superior for 10 years. So I know him most intimately. You have no idea what a very complex and complicated person he is.
>
> As you know, he is a convert to the Faith and did not have that wonderful opportunity of being brought up in the Faith from the cradle.
>
> What I write to you here now, dear Father Lombardi, is in the *strictest confidence,* and is the closest to the "sub sigillo" as I can make it.
>
> He is a very neurotic person due to his family background when he was a very young boy. The Providence of God has brought him to a cloistered monastery. If he were allowed to travel around

> outside his monastery, he would be one of the biggest dangers that the Church could ever have in the present day.
>
> As you know, his pen is terrifically powerful. He could gain tremendous followers. But his temperament is one which utterly lacks stability. First, one idea hits him, and he is all for that. And a second idea hits, and he is all off for that. Then a third, etc. . . .
>
> Dear Father, if there is one request that I have to make to you—please, please do not disturb good Father Louis. He means well. He is very sincere, but outside of a strict monastery, he is most dangerous.

At this point in his letter, Dom James harked back to Merton's encounter with an unnamed but "very good psychoanalyst" who had told him that he obviously wanted to be a hermit in the middle of Times Square "with electric signs on the outside," as James put it, signs reading "Come and see the hermit!"

> My dear Father Lombardi, I could tell you much, much more than this. . . . At the basis of all this is the terrible neurosis. It makes him do and say things—and especially dream things—in spite of himself, and against his better judgment. . . . And what is this neurosis? Well, as this good Doctor said, *and this you must keep strictly in your own heart forever,* dear Father Lombardi: "That under the guise of good, is the drive for fame." . . .
>
> In regard to good Father Louis, please leave him in peace in his cloistered monastery. There is where he can do most for Holy Mother Church and for the salvation of his own soul. In good Father Louis you have not an atomic bomb—you have a hydrogen bomb!
>
> Count on us, dear Father Lombardi, as one of your main supports.

In a postscript the following day, Dom James added that the abbot general had just suggested that he meet Fr. Lombardi at his headquarters near Rome—and James would soon be in Europe for other purposes. Both abbot and abbot general were worried. The meeting did in fact occur; James subsequently alluded to it.

What did Dom James fear? What dreadful explosion? As Merton had been outside the monastery walls so very little—the two-week workshop at Collegeville, closely supervised, was by far the longest divagation—it was surely fear at work. There was no basis for knowledge, apart from the fact that periodically Merton wanted desperately to leave and Dom James used his abbatial authority to keep him in place. James's repeated request for discretion on Fr. Lombardi's part—"this you must keep strictly in your own heart forever"—conveys some sense of his uneasiness about what he was writing to a perfect stranger though a brother in the Church. This ferocious letter set the pattern of others to come on other occasions.

In the course of the summer, Merton drafted into his journal the plan for "a small monastery." It would be without a "program," as he put, "without a special job to do. Monks to *live,* not to be 'monks' as distinct from every other kind of being, but to be *men*—sons of God," and on from there.[4] Its Rule would return to Saint Benedict "or an application of St. B"—he obviously felt that Gethsemani's observance of the Rule left something to be desired. During the days when he was working this out, he also noted in his journal that he hadn't received a reply from Fr. Lombardi ("Dreamt that Rev. F. was angry about my letter") and recorded without love that Dom James had written a letter to the community, from the daughter house in Utah, in which he expressed contempt for "the arty people of Aspen Colo . . . and some hot-air phrase about them which made me indignant—especially in the context of all his talk about bulls and chickens."[5]

Merton's reference to bulls and chickens calls for a commentarial note. It was James's attractive custom when traveling, particularly to the daughter houses or related monasteries, to write a general letter to the community intended to be read during meals in the refectory and no doubt posted on the community bulletin board. In later years he also wrote from Gethsemani, or wherever he happened to be in his travels, to what he called the diaspora—community members temporarily elsewhere, quite often in Rome for several years of seminary training. These letters home and letters to the diaspora, of which many examples are preserved in the Abbey Archive, became a particular target of Merton's revulsion. It's true that they convey James's exuberant interest in the physical and quantitative life of the monasteries he visited—in their construction projects, their herds, their products, their earning capacity, the number of choir religious and novices, and all such. Another focus was the details of liturgical practice, for which he had a nearly photographic memory. He was always upbeat and spirited in what he wrote and never forgot for long that he was a man of God, but his preferred focus was objects, activities, and anecdotes. For example, in a letter home from Atlanta after visiting the nearby daughter house in April 1956, he gave half the letter to considerations along these lines: "Cinnamon rolls are really rolling—about 700 of the half-dozen rolls per aluminum tray, per day, selling at 21 cents wholesale. Br Moses conceived the astute idea to put the same amount of ingredients not into six buns but into one big bun and call it 'cinnamon cake,' or coffee cake, and because of the new name, charge 35 cents, up 14 cents from the rolls. He claims it works. There are about 1600 chickens and hens."[6] This is the monastic entrepreneur James speaking. Who can doubt that Merton writhed.

Dom James had written to Fr. Lombardi on August 4. The following day he wrote at length to Dom Gabriel, and again a few days later, and had Dom Gabriel's reply within a few days more. Merton's contact with an innovative thinker and institution builder close to the pope alarmed them. That kind and quality of support for Merton had the potential to break through the boundaries they had imposed. Dom James reported that within the last year Merton's "dynamic and roving spirit has been getting restless. . . . Good Father Louis would be ready to make a foundation tomorrow. But he dreams of something more than a mere Trappist foundation—sort of a center for intellectuals, writers and artists. Of course, he would be the head of the monastery."[7] James speculated—or had he read a letter I've not seen?—that Merton was hoping for Fr. Lombardi's endorsement, that Fr. Lombardi would discuss the project with the pope, and that pressure from the top would be brought to bear to authorize the project. Dom James noted that the community had recently been reading in refectory an account of the Jesuit Matteo Ricci's missionary activities in sixteenth-century China. He wore Chinese dress, he spoke the language and understood Chinese culture, he offered far more of Western culture than standard missionary fare. "Good Father Louis," he concluded, not unwisely, "hopes to duplicate Father Ricci in South America." Merton's project and its contradictions, the proposed mix between cloistered solitude and cultural dialogue, struck Dom James as the latest edition of folly. "To me," he wrote, "it is all so ludicrous. I have to hold my sides from laughter." On the contrary, he continued, the Trappist life properly lived, a life of "utter immolation to His loving good pleasure, . . . calls for the highest form of courage, grit, stability, and self-assertedness [*sic*]. . . . That is my conviction, and that is what I am personally aiming at."

Dom James was fed up. His next letter was as slashing as anything Merton ever wrote about him. About Merton's journal: "He couldn't get along without writing everything down in a journal—I mean the inspirations that were going to come to him for the benefit of the human race."[8] About Merton's search for solitude: "I often wondered [during Merton's service to date as novice master] what happened to his so-called Divine Vocation of inaugurating the hermit vocation in these latter days." About Merton's volatility: "He lacks stability of emotion. He jumps first at this project, and then at that, and then another one." About his hunger for fame: "He thirsts for recognition—not the recognition of ordinary people. That doesn't seem to mean anything to him. But he thirsts for the recognition of those in high places." James must have been thinking of Fr. Lombardi, and perhaps of the embattled Russian novelist Boris Pasternak, with whom Merton had been corresponding. Dom Gabriel was a good deal more composed in his reply. "Let us acknowledge," he wrote, "that it calls for humility out of the ordinary to live a hidden life such as ours with the talents, certainly exceptional, that Father Louis has received. That the Good Lord grant him this grace, that is what I ask with all my heart for this dear Father!"[9]

On into the fall season they continued periodically to correspond. Dom James did Merton a good turn by obtaining the abbot general's permission to simplify the order's censorship process for what he described as "little literary articles" and "short poems." He also reported that "the pendulum of [Fr. Louis's] emotions has seemingly swung back to normal—for the present." One never knew what "dream or illusion" would hit him next: "Maybe he will want to take a shot at the moon!—or better yet, Venus or Mars!"[10]

On his side that fall, Merton wasn't contemplating interplanetary travel—but he was pushing further into the middle of contradictions. He had heard, for example, of a letter from a monsignor in Bogotá, intended for him but intercepted, which discussed a foundation project of some kind. Knowing something and nearly nothing of the letter, Merton was "bitter and depressed for a while," he recorded in his journal, "and even woke up in the night thinking about it, and about the frustration of all my ideas and hopes for something sane in monasticism. But no! To be always a prisoner of *vanitas monastica* and its crudities, incomprehensions, and falsities! Brought back face to face with my vow of obedience—and the paradox that this is what matters most. And it must matter not only on paper but in life."[11] Here is a stunning contradiction with Merton clipped to the middle. Two months later he returned to the topic in his journal. "I honestly begin to wonder whether my being bound by vows to this situation is not in some way a great mistake. Not that I want to be dispensed from my vows; but I can at least hope for some relief, under the vows themselves. Perhaps this hope is also a vain one."[12]

Meanwhile, he was sharpening his critique of Dom James and of monastic life as he experienced it from day to day. A journal entry too long for inclusion here explores analytically in what respects Gethsemani's way of life and customary attitudes were more Protestant—as he envisioned Protestantism—than Catholic.[13] Whether his analysis was true or not, he wrote, "one would look in vain for any trace of the spirit of Medieval Catholicism in America or in this monastery—its broadness, its universality, its all-embracing compassion, its joy, its understanding of man and nature, its cosmic outlook, its genuine eschatology, its asceticism, its mysticism, its poetry." He was drawing confidence from earlier Christian centuries at the very moment he was developing a critique of the Cistercian reality he lived from day to day. This too was a contradiction, and from it some of his best writings of the 1960s would emerge.

In the last days of 1958, he wrote, "The end of a year—and the beginning of a very grave year of struggle. Christ, may I not go under!"[14]

Meanwhile life went on. A letter somehow made its way into the archives from a French Cistercian who was preparing to publish his doctoral thesis on the twelfth-century Cistercian abbot and author Aelred of Rievaulx. The young scholar had previously asked Dom James whether Merton could be authorized to write a preface—what could be more natural? However, the scholar reported to his superior that autumn in slightly skewed English that Dom James "with smiling" had preferred not to impose the task on good Father Louis, who already had more than enough to do. However, it happened that Gethsemani's father immediate, Dom Louis, had recently passed away; the letter was addressed to his successor, Dom Colomban Bissey, from whom the scholar asked a favor: Could he resubmit the request? "I am sure," he wrote with worldly cunning, "that now it would be a pleasure for Dom James to say 'Yes' to you, with a smile."[15] In the event, Dom James did grant his approval, and Merton quite liked the text; preface provided, after all.[16]

[13]
When Will We Become Christians?

We haven't asked Dom James to serve as a guide to Merton's writings. He was involved administratively in censorship processes and in correspondence with publishers and Merton's literary agent, and he was capable of generosity in this role; he would ease the way on occasion and even protect Merton. He would often enough praise Merton as a writer with sincerity and something like wonder before turning to harsh judgments of what he took to calling Merton's "ex abrupto" nature—brusquely subject to change. But there is little evidence of deep reading. I know of just one book he prized and reread with greatest appreciation, the German theologian Karl Adam's *The Christ of Faith,* which confirmed with rich intellectuality his conviction, as Adam puts it, that "Christianity is Christ."[1] All the more surprising, then, that a letter from James to Dom Gabriel at the end of August 1959 provides invaluable orientation in a year, as Merton foresaw, of grave struggle.

Merton had been working for some time on a selection and translation of passages from a Latin anthology of sayings and instructive anecdotes of the fourth-century desert fathers. The resulting book, *The Wisdom of the Desert,* with Merton's introduction and translations, carries a copyright notice of 1960 with the full panoply of Church approvals, notably the imprimi potest (it can be published) of Frater M. Gabriel Sortais, OCSO, Abbas generalis. A typescript was circulating in the summer of 1959, when Dom James took time to read the introduction. To my mind this book represents the beginning of Merton's new authorship, promised to himself and his readers in the December 1958 journal entry about a new humanism. The desert fathers' legacy is made of conversations, incidents, and strikingly original characters—Abbot Agatho, John the Dwarf, Abbot Pastor, Abbess Syncletica, and many more (note the presence of a female anchorite, many more of whom are now recognized than in Merton's era; he made a start). In their desert setting; in their lives of prayer, askesis, and subsistence through weaving palm fiber mats and bringing them to market; in their unforgettable way of encountering and speaking with each other, they are vivid to this day. To recover knowledge of them by transferring anecdotes from the Latin *Verba seniorum* (Sayings of the Elders) to a new and widely read book was an exercise of the new humanism. If the Gospels can be likened to a series of images captured in mosaic—still, beautiful, and fixed—the desert fathers are a mobile, unpredictable crowd of ancient seekers moving in front of that mosaic. Merton's Christian sensibility was now rooted in them both: in the unique sacred narrative and in the hum of conversation in the desert. Merton had hoped for a cointerpreter in his book of tales: D. T. Suzuki, the venerable Japanese scholar of Zen, periodically teaching at Columbia University, with whom he had recently begun corresponding. It hadn't been lost on Merton that the desert fathers, with their often koan-like wisdom and mercurial intelligence, had much in common with the Chan and Zen masters of Chinese and Japanese tradition. His proposal to coauthor with Dr. Suzuki had been denied by his superiors; their linked essays, already carefully written, appeared some years later in another context.[2] But Merton's recognition of cross-cultural similarity and fruitfulness was another sign of the new humanism, Christian at the core, open to the world.

Dom James read Merton's introduction as a guide not so much to the desert fathers as to the dubious tendencies of its author. He rather sulkily observed that Dom Gabriel had granted his imprimi potest and advised that Dom Gabriel's chief aide "skim through it. He will find very much of Fr. L.'s problems revealed in this

Introduction. He pictures the monks of the desert according to the ideas that he would like to live himself. You can read between the lines . . . how these monks were practically 'their own boss,' as we say in America—that is, they had no superior, they would do practically what they liked all day. He mentions some vague acknowledgment of some distant Bishop, of course, but this Bishop was not supposed to ever interfere or become too inquisitive into their lives. . . . In practice they live as if they were under nobody."[3] James's commentary is unfair; Merton said nothing of the kind. But this much James grasped correctly: this tribe of hermits who came together periodically, men and women of independent mind and tough spirit living with a minimum of hierarchical imposition yet with ascetic rigor, was indeed Merton's paradise idea. This was how it should be, serious and mobile, genuinely contemplative, spontaneously ethical, moved from within by faith and shared values.

He closed his letter to Dom Gabriel with a further invidious comment: "Good Fr Louis says on the last page: 'We must liberate ourselves *in our own way*.' That is very important, 'in our own way.' And finally: 'Defy compulsion and drive out fearlessly into the unknown.'" In the first quoted passage, with his own italics added, James resorts to the method of tendentious reviewers: stopping the citation before the author has fully said what he means. Merton had actually written: "We must liberate ourselves, in our own way, from involvement in a world that is plunging to disaster."[4] Our way, he wrote, could not be the same as the desert fathers' because the conditions of life are so very different. And then, where James perceived a dangerously independent spirit, Merton was actually writing about the rediscovery of "our great and mysterious vocation" in a world that demands courage from religiously minded individuals who wish "to build, on earth, the Kingdom of God." He continued: "We need to learn from these men of the fourth century how to ignore prejudice, defy compulsion, and strike out fearlessly into the unknown."[5] This is good Merton, his mature voice.

Merton's long meditation on the desert hermits' values and conversations as he selected and translated is the silent counterpoint, which we might not have discovered as such without Dom James, to the disillusioned observations in his journal for 1959 about monastery and abbot. Such observations are sometimes, but not often, reversed the next day or soon by remorse that he had assigned blame to others without equally assessing his own shortcomings. But on the whole he meant what he said and let it stand. He was again in the middle of a contradiction: it is unmonastic to criticize at length one's abbot and monastery, it is unchristian to shield one's eyes from reality. John 8:32: The truth shall make you free.

Merton's critique began forcefully in 1959 and continued until Dom James's retirement in 1967, when the atmosphere of the monastery changed. We can't take it all into account in these pages; there wouldn't be pages enough. Nonetheless, we should listen. This cannot help but be a heavy passage in our travels with Merton. "I believe more and more," he wrote in January, "that the rigidity of our spiritual categories and the obtuseness of our monastic minds produces results that are fatal to many monks morally, psychologically, and spiritually."[6] He was thinking particularly of a monk and priest at Mepkin, the daughter house in South Carolina, who had left after twelve years. Dom James must have faulted the man in chapter. "Does anyone stop to consider the possibility," Merton asked privately in his journal, "that it was also the 'fault' of the monastic community, the Order, the Superiors?" Across monastic practice Merton was perceiving superficiality, delusion, and complacency, and bearing witness to it all in his journal—at least there. The practice of silence, for example: "In monasteries, we agree that it is 'more perfect' to keep silent than to speak. So if someone speaks we think him imperfect. . . . If we ask to see this famous perfection—why, it is a spiritual reality, an object of faith! . . . How great is our reverence for nothing."[7] And then, a distorted understanding of love that he was encountering in persons unnamed: "Love =

emotional pressure to make others conform to ourselves so that we may not feel insecure. That is the terrible thing: the fundamental treachery of . . . personal values, under the guise of love. In perfectly sincere people. When will we ever become Christians?"[8]

Twice in the journal for 1959 Merton stages an imagined event that he supposed could never occur: a session of telling Dom James the truth as he saw it. Here is the first such session.

> If I had to explain now to Dom James that I wanted to leave to go to Mexico—what on earth would I be able to say? I would be tongue tied. The things I could never say:
>
> I hate pontifical masses. I hate your idea of the liturgy—It seems to me to be a false, dead, repetition of words and gestures without spontaneity, without sincerity. You like to sing hymns because the melodies delight you. I can think of better ways in which to waste my time. The Africans, with their drums, have got it all over us. There is no routine with them. They are saying what they mean.
>
> I think the monastic life as we live it here warps people. Kills their spirit, reduces them to something less than human. The way people verbalize like parrots in sermons and theological conferences seems to me to indicate a perilous falsification of their spirit. Many of them are no longer quite sane.
>
> I would say this and many other things, all adding up to one: our life here is too much of a lie. If that is really the case, then, since I can't do anything about it, I had better leave. But always the question remains: perhaps it is I who am the liar and perhaps leaving would be the greater lie.[9]

There is anger here and a measure of self-doubt, but above all anguished protest against the lack of inner substance at the heart of monastic practice—the liturgy, the conversations about life and the Way. In June, Merton recorded that four monks had left the community within days of each other. He took it as an occasion for self-examination. The "general spirit of rebellion" in the community, he wrote, "is very disturbing. The almost universal unpopularity of Dom James. His unconscious ambiguities, which he himself cannot see, are far too much for most people. Yes—he is a well-meaning man, with all his blind spots, and he is after all a superior. There is not enough supernatural spirit of obedience to superiors and that is why I must be . . . very careful not to simply force my own ideas or my own will on him. May God preserve me from that."[10] But he also took the occasion to set down in terrible, terribly lucid words his anguish over "subjection to a whole false idea created by a man, and a community. What I find intolerable and degrading is having to submit, in practice, to Dom James' idea of himself and Gethsemani and to have to spend my life contributing to the maintenance of this illusion. The illusion of the great, gay, joyous, peppy, optimistic, Jesus-loving, one hundred percent American Trappist monastery. Is it possible to be here and not be plunged into the midst of this falsity? Is it possible to abstract from it? And if that is possible, is it healthy—is it anything better than a defeat?"

Merton was wary of himself, searching for a middle way between asserting the errors of others and asserting solutions of his own that struck him as having no merit. "The great problem in this crisis of mine is to keep from going from one fiction to another: from the communal fiction which we cherish as a group, to the private fiction which I cherish as an individual. The more I let myself dwell with desire upon 'a solution' the more I become involved in a new fiction of my own. I can tell it immediately by the immense weariness that comes from entertaining falsity."[11] Merton spared no one, least of all himself; his sorrow and lucidity admitted no self-serving boundary. Yet his vision through these months was occasionally cruel. While there are some in the community "who believe in mechanical regularity, . . . a series of gestures and external acts without much inner meaning, . . . Dom James's myth is vaguer and in the long run more harmful: that of the jolly, fervent family of girl scouts and little boys. . . . None of us are really monks. The top sergeants of regularity are only sergeants. Rev. Father is a girl scout. The others are frustrated scholars or business men or housemaids. And I—a frustrated intellectual, pseudo-contemplative, pseudo-hermit." Merton ended this cry of misery and denunciation with Hamlet-like doubt: "It is imperative to do something. And I am not yet rightly prepared to act, and hardly know where to begin."[12]

That very day he had a reasonable talk with Dom James about possibilities for change—perhaps living in the Gethsemani out-back as a hermit (James not categorically opposed) or living in solitude elsewhere such as on a small island (James categorically opposed). They listened to each other; Merton deliberately sacrificed any impulse to argue, and James must also have taken himself in hand. "The point is not 'who is right,'" Merton recorded later in his journal. And he recorded the essential question: what conditions would foster inner growth? "Rev. Father . . . takes the status quo as the will of God that 'cannot' be changed. But I think that to submit passively to this false situation is a kind of practical despair—it means really despairing of a truly monastic life. No, not that either: this is a monastic life of its kind. It means despairing of a real growth and development. If our founders had believed this they would have stayed at Molesme, and Cîteaux would never have been founded."[13] He was thinking back to the courage of the first Cistercians—the monks of the new monastery in the wilderness, which gave the order its name. As they went forth, Merton needed to go forth.

And yet . . . Even in this year of disaffection there were links of affection of some kind between the two men. I don't know whose tears Merton mentions in the following brief journal entry in late July—but it seems they are his.

> Rev. Fr. preached sadly, sadly, on kindness in chapter. In a voice almost extinct. Afterwards, it turned out that on his feast day the

> Brother novices had sent him an *enormous* . . . spiritual bouquet—The Choir novices—nothing. That is sad. I suggested they write him personal notes—only two did. . . . Yet they could all have sincerely written him little notes. . . . Tears, tears, tears![14]

You'll recall that Merton was responsible for the choir novices at a time when the brother novices still received separate novitiate training. His team had let him down. Common decency mattered.[15]

Dom James had preached on kindness. If he used a written text, it hasn't come to light, but there is a later text for the same time of year, late July, and the same topic. As he repeated much the same homilies year after year, it is more than likely that the excerpt below from the extant version duplicates what he had said years earlier. We should hear him if only because his words cannot help but remind us of the intellectual and spiritual distance between Merton and his abbot. Merton at this time was acknowledging the need to "strike out fearlessly into the unknown." He would not have Dom James's company. The homily is a verbal prayer card: syrupy sweet in the nineteenth-century Catholic style of imagery known as saint-sulpicien, which survives to this day as an unassuming folk art.

> Suppose that you were asked to write a book, which would give the best *pen picture* of JESUS.
>
> Suppose that you were allowed only *one page,* and on that one page, *one line,* and on that *one line*—only *one word*—of only *one syllable.*
>
> Of all the some 500,000 words in the big Dictionary, what one word—what one adjective, would you select, that would bring most graphically before your mind, the picture of JESUS???
>
> Would it not be, that little word K-I-N-D???
>
> JESUS is KIND!!! . . .
>
> Once—and I'm sure that it happened more than once, JESUS

> was seated under the cool shade of some waving palm trees (Mk 10:13–16). Some mothers brought their little tots to HIM, for HIS Blessing.
>
> You know that with kiddoes, their faculty of reasoning is not yet developed. However, with unfailing instinct and accuracy they can *sense* a kind heart. With keen intuition, this day, they *zeroed in* on JESUS, as one with whom they could have *a grand good time.*
>
> You can easily imagine, that the youngsters were soon climbing all over JESUS—
>
> Jumping on HIS knees—pulling HIS beard—tugging at HIS long locks of hair—and in their charming—unabashed innocence—, throwing their little arms around HIS neck, pressing their little faces against HIS face—and all glowing with smiles,—looking right into HIS Divine eyes!!![16]

The day before Dom James gave a homily much like this one, Merton had been thinking about his sweetness. That trait too figured in the nearly unrelenting critique. "Rev. Father is a good, sweet, and dangerous man," Merton wrote in his journal,

> because he believes in his own sweetness and does not see the inexorable, self-righteous appetite for domination that underlies it. He is terribly possessive, in a feminine and motherly way, and his reactions to serious opposition are feminine, passive, tearful, moralistic and indomitably stubborn. He cannot and will not see any other view but his own, and this is because of the *fear* that underlies all his outlook and spirituality, without his knowing it. The fear of facing the pitiable falsity of the whole structure to which he has completely committed himself here— It is a great theatrical front with little or nothing behind it—except a lot of pitiable and wasted good will.
>
> And he will not call things by their right names.
>
> He always picks some dramatic, emotional word or phrase to dress up and justify what is essentially stupid and trite.

> Hence—life at Gethsemani is a "perpetual martyrdom." "It costs, it costs." "Utter, utter immolation." It is like being "boiled in oil."
>
> In reality the life is utterly comfortable, stupid, harmless. . . . The pain is the pain of a perpetual bad conscience over our pretenses. . . . I think it is better simply to face the fact that I am not honestly a monk here. . . . The search for truth. . . . Here, as far as I can tell, I am at the end of the line—as far as my own personal search is concerned.
>
> For others, the situation is entirely different.[17]

I may have tested your patience by including in these pages so much of Merton's critique of Dom James, though there is a great deal more both in the journal for 1959 and in years following. From this point forward we'll look at such passages when they advance the narrative or add intriguing color. But there is one, from December 1959, which we shouldn't ignore: it is the second occasion when Merton recorded in his journal what he would have said or written to Dom James, had he felt free to do so. It is a declaration of affection and refusal, a reasoned but passionate cry from the middle of contradiction. "There are so many things you simply cannot say to him," Merton began.

> He is one of those people you have to address only in certain terms he wants from you. They can be flippant, absurd, sentimental, conventionally pious and ascetic, even "mystical." But not just straight, honest statements of what you really feel.
>
> What would I have said to him today?
>
> "You have the misfortune to be one of those people for whom I have, in my own way, a deep affection. Deep affection, of course, disturbs me, and I am very exacting and difficult with those who claim my affection. Hence my resolute refusal to accept you except on certain very definite terms, and especially since you too are a very demanding friend, and very masochistic about it, too . . . Thus

> you see that we are bound to get into difficulties, sensitive, subtly aggressive, you under a cloud of sweetness and I behind a curtain of reserve. Certainly it is difficult for us, between us, to arrive at a clear and frank appraisal of the will of God in anything that concerns us both deeply, in a personal way. Hence though you seem to feel that you are the only person capable of directing me at this juncture, and are very hurt because I barely consult you, I on the other hand have reached the conclusion that you are the last person in the world whose direction I would really trust. Though in most things I can obey you there are very few in which I can agree with you, and this agreement is, to you, all important. . . . You somehow seem to think that I have, by making vows, become your personal property . . . etc. etc."
>
> What I did was write him a short note wishing him a happy birthday and a prosperous trip to California, though I must admit during the Mass I prayed for him to have a little light to see himself as his monks see him. I regret it as usual, but perhaps it was worthwhile. . . .
>
> It is, of course, Providence that has thrown the two of us together.[18]

Surely we have accumulated enough nuances now to satisfy even the hermit teacher of the Genesee, Fr. John Eudes. Troubling, strangely satisfactory nuances: first, Merton's acknowledgment of affection for a superior who had caused him ordeals, was now causing him an ordeal, and in time would doubtless cause other ordeals; and then, his intuitive acknowledgment that Providence had thrown them together to work out, if not their salvation, then their humanity. The affection is pure, cleansed by self-knowledge with no trace of masochism; Merton writes of it from the best of himself with admirable lucidity. The acknowledgment of Providence is equally pure. Whatever the transaction was between them, however much or little ruled from Above, it was not yet complete.

[14]
Fuge, Tace, Quiesce

TOWARD THE END OF 1958, the famed Jesuit Fr. Riccardo Lombardi expressed the wish to visit Gethsemani. While he could offer much food for thought to the entire community through chapter talks, he undoubtedly had in mind to explore with Merton possibilities for collaboration and seems not to have been deterred by Dom James's off-putting letter of August 4 or their meeting in Rome soon after. He was traveling and speaking with audiences worldwide; his book *Towards a New World* had just been published in English translation (its author disarmingly renamed "Richard Lombardi, S.J.").[1] James resumed correspondence with Fr. Lombardi early in the following year to turn him away as graciously as possible. He spoke again of his own enthusiasm for Fr. Lombardi's movement and of the need to safeguard the cloistered vocation from engagement even with the most inspiring active ministries of the Church. He spoke of prayerful hours before the Blessed Sacrament and of consensus-seeking correspondence with his own superior—all to ensure that his decision to forestall a visit from Fr. Lombardi was well judged. "Our Most Reverend General is quite emphatic," he wrote, "in his declaration that a visit from you, dear Reverend Father, . . . would be a grave inconvenience to the Community as a whole, and to good Father Louis in particular."[2] He described the ill effects of prior visits from participants in active ministries—for example, one poor soul at Gethsemani was so touched by a visitor from India that he quit the order, moved to India, and ended up "working in some parish as a diocesan Priest" not even in India, an outcome that struck Dom James as pathetic.

Where good Father Louis was concerned, James reiterated many of the charges in his earlier letter. "He is ever and will be dominated," James wrote, "by his poet's temperament, imagination, and sensibility," all of which could "carry him out of the monastery completely. What then would the Mystical Body have gained if a monk has lost his vocation? The attraction of the world is far too strong in good Father Louis. . . . He is certainly not made for living in the world. He could easily destroy himself, and perhaps others, in his own uncontrollable and neurotic fires of enthusiasm—and all, of course, with the best of intentions, at least in the beginning." James reminded Fr. Lombardi that when they had met in Italy that fall, they had agreed that "it would be amply sufficient if from time to time you would send me literature for an occasional article by good Father Louis."

Dom James must have mentioned this plan to Merton toward the end of the month. Merton's reaction—of revulsion—was immediate. From the journal: "I am to write for Fr. L. without having any direct contact with him, even by letter. It is all to go through Rev. Father. I am—why say it?—sickened by being treated as an article for sale, as a commodity."[3]

But more was in motion than the deflected opportunity to work with one of the boldest leaders of the Church. James wrote to Dom Gabriel in March that "in the back of his head, Fr. Louis dreams, at least, of some kind of a foundation he would like to make somewhere—India or South America or the Rocky Mountains."[4] He was making geography mistakes, but the gist of what he wrote was correct. Merton was thinking through the possibility of joining an experimental foundation in Cuernavaca, Mexico, guided by the Benedictine Dom Gregorio Lemercier, an interesting rebel who for some years tested the limits of the possible in the Church. In the course of that winter and spring he was also in touch with a bishop in San Juan, Puerto Rico; with a sympathetic bishop in Nevada; and with Ernesto Cardenal, his former novice now in Nicaragua, who thought it might be possible to establish a modified hermitage on an offshore island sparsely populated by Indians. Through much of this correspondence, Merton was relying on his right to "conscience matter": letters to and from, so marked, were not to be intercepted and opened. Dom Gregorio, who visited Gethsemani several times in this period and currently enjoyed good relations in Rome, discreetly took it upon himself in late summer to obtain for Merton an indult. This thudding term in the Church lexicon refers to a grant of exclaustration issued by the Sacred Congregation for Religious—permission to leave an order. For some, exclaustration ends a monastic life; the individual takes up work in a parish or returns to the world, already in that era often to marry. In Merton's case, the request was for an exclaustration of three years' duration so that he could experience other monastic possibilities, after which his status would be reviewed.

Merton kept Dom James generally informed of his need and wish to live elsewhere in another way, but he bypassed him entirely as he labored through the official process. He was in touch by mail with key authorities and churchmen of influence—with Dom Gregorio, of course, and Dom Gregorio's bishop in Cuernavaca; with Archbishop Arcadio Larraona, secretary of the Sacred Congregation for Religious; with Valerio Cardinal Valeri, prefect (senior leader) of the Sacred Congregation; with his friend and adviser Dom Jean Leclercq; and with Fr. Jean Daniélou, a French Jesuit and well-known scholar destined to be named some years later both a cardinal and a member of the French Academy. Dom James knew little of all this, though correspondence not identified as conscience matter allowed him to catch glimpses of Merton's initiative. Juridically speaking, Merton was within his rights to navigate around his abbot and the abbot general, Dom Gabriel. He could be certain, of course, that sooner or later there would be hurt feelings and reactions, but he accepted that eventuality. Late in 1959, in a time of explanations, he made chapter and verse clear to

Dom James about his rights. The entire campaign was nonetheless a desperate measure and a new contradiction. "Is there any hope of obtaining an indult from Rome in the first place?" Merton asked in his journal at an early stage of the campaign. "It would be disastrous to stir up a great official fuss and then have nothing come of it."[5]

As the secret campaign gained traction in the summer of 1959, Merton checked his conscience often and did what he could to preserve conversation with Dom James. In late August, for example, he recorded that he had had "a fairly sane and sensible talk with Rev. Fr. yesterday about . . . my problems here and my desire for a more primitive, isolated, and simple life alone and away from the *vanitas monastica* of the community life. Not that we settled anything, but at least it was a matter of a genuine exchange of thoughts and not just two individuals . . . refusing to communicate with one another. . . . I felt . . . that I had sufficiently manifested the state of my mind to him, and that he now knows my desires in a general way."[6] Later he found himself thinking about how one might best write a book entitled *The Years with James*. He was reading James Thurber's classic memoir, *The Years with Ross,* about Harold Ross, founder and editor in chief of the *New Yorker*.[7] "Very edifying in its subtle way," was Merton's assessment, "and yet there is also something weird about it."[8] That mix would do, were one to write a life of Dom James Fox. He didn't.

Apart from his agon with Dom James and its attendant anxieties, Merton was capable that summer of being the Merton we know and admire, the writer and man of spirit. In an August letter to a Nicaraguan poet, he distanced himself from his difficulties enough to see them in a remarkable light. "Our lives go on," he wrote,

> at times it seems they are fruitless. We must always pray to be attuned to the mysterious language of events, and shape our actions accordingly. It requires prayer and humility and vigilance and love. Although it says in Ecclesiastes that there is nothing new under the sun, yet there is always the creative newness of our deci-

> sions, in the service of God. May they be filled with His Spirit and His "new life."[9]

It was this spirit, gentle and inquiring, humane and contemplative, that he was striving to protect. Where did he belong?

Merton was still checking his conscience and soon confronting intimate demons. "Put two people like Dom James and myself together," he wrote in his journal in late August, "and we react on one another with sincerities that cover deceit. . . . And if I say he is worse than I am, it is probably in order to justify my own duplicity. I only hope the whole project is not shot through with duplicity and I have to be careful to see that it is not." He was fearful of being "hated and rejected for what I feel I ought to do," and steeled himself for the very things he seems most to have feared: rejection, vilification, "complete loss of face and of reputation." Much the same fears had assailed him when he was campaigning for the fire tower hermitage. He had scant comfort: "Rev. Father is clearly informed anyway, that my life has reached a turning point and that I may turn some unexpected corners. But let me really turn them and keep going and not come back around the corner to see if he approves and to placate him before going further. So far as I am concerned he is the Mother over whose prostrate body one must step in order to follow one's vocation."[10] Merton's disorientation is evident in this difficult language, its doubts and burst of violence. Three weeks later, in mid-September, his inner situation remained much the same: "Probably this week Dom Gregorio will present my petition to the Congregation in Rome. I wish I were in some sense more 'ready.' I feel helpless and confused, not knowing at all what will come next." He could already foresee "the silly and petty battle that will be waged with Rev. Father. His emotionalism, his recriminations. . . . It could be infinitely unpleasant. I will have to bear it in a spirit of truthfulness and calm. . . . It is a question of the difference between pleasing God and pleasing men."[11] A few days further on, he had managed to take himself in hand. "There are no more special difficulties as far as I am concerned interiorly. I have a job to do and I am going ahead with it. The request for the indult has been presented and I have a feeling it will be eventually granted."[12]

In the interval between these two journal entries, Merton had taken an initiative toward Dom James, prompted by a felt need to be as open as possible without revealing the undisclosed campaign. He had placed in his mailbox a letter about the life of the monastery, the poor state of their relations with each other, and the consequences. "I am really a little disquieted," he began,

> by the trend in the Order, or at least in this house, to add up and accumulate novelties that are along the line of more and more public vocal prayer and communal demonstrations of piety in ceremony, etc.—the trend to replace silence and solitary meditation by things in which people "get-together" and "do things." If that is the need of the majority and if it produces, as it must, a conflict with what has always seemed to me to be the contemplative life—or at least the contemplative life to which I personally am called, then this, along with everything else, simply adds to the personal problem of which you know.
>
> You also know that between us the matter has reached a dead end in which there is no solution. I have repeatedly tried sincerely to accept your decisions as final, but they just don't stay final. Everyone else I consult seems to think I have a perfect right to seek a leave of absence in order to make a concrete trial of some other form of life. You alone categorically exclude this from consideration. When I see religious in other orders liberally granted the right to solve problems of conscience, and see how persons with this kind of problem in our own order are treated as lunatics or men possessed by the devil, I find it difficult to have confidence in the decisions handed down. However, since there is no point in discussing the matter—there being little or no common ground on which we can meet—I just leave you with these reflections.

> I see no point in molesting you further with my desires, hopes, and aspirations. And I see, from experience, that attempts to gain some light by means of letters are very much subject to deviation and falsification of the real issue.
>
> Since it does remain a problem of conscience for me, however, I may perhaps feel obliged to ask some help from higher superiors. If I do so, it will not be in a spirit of vindictiveness or aggressiveness, and it will not represent personal antagonism of any kind. Nor will it be an attempt to get out of the Order but only a desire to obtain that leave of absence to which I believe firmly, with my directors, that I am really entitled for a very serious motive.
>
> Dear Rev Father, I know you don't like this kind of thing, but what can I do? I have to let you know the state of my conscience, even if it is a state which you will promptly interpret as hostile to yourself, when it is not so.[13]

Fuge, tace, quiesce—flee, be silent, be still: words quoted by Merton in his introduction to the desert fathers. They were spoken by an inner voice to a fifth-century man of learning, Arsenius, tutor in Rome to the children of a Christian emperor. He heeded the voice and made his way to the Egyptian desert, where John the Dwarf received him. Merton heard that call no less vividly.

Not all of the spring and summer's business was focused on advancing or detecting Merton's secret campaign. He and Dom James campaigned together in full agreement to ensure publication of a quite wonderful book of photographs of Gethsemani created by Shirley Burden, with an introduction by Merton: *God Is My Life: The Story of Our Lady of Gethsemani* (1960). When finally published, the book didn't entirely please Merton: he found the captions sentimental and realistically feared they would be blamed on him, though they weren't his.[14] The book needed special pleading with the abbot general because it was arguably a bit immodest to publish an entire book about the abbey. As well, some photographs showed monks' faces. The tradition had long been to preserve anonymity by showing hooded figures only. "We know that rules are rules," James wrote to Dom Gabriel, "but once in a while an exception can be made, when there is really a compensating reason for it. We all think deeply in this case that there is such a reason, since [the book] will show a monastery without any glamor or tinsel, without any falsifying, but just as it is every day, with all its common ordinary nooks and crannies."[15] Altogether chilling in this letter is Dom James's attitude toward the American public to which the book would be addressed: the "American pagan public," as he put it. "After all," he continued, "this country of America is really a pagan country. There is much religion, and there is some Christianity, but at basis, it is really pagan in its outlook on life, and something like this will have tremendous power and influence to meet the common ordinary pagan on his own level of everyday life, and yet lead him to God." My willingness, and perhaps yours, to follow Dom James with interest wherever he may go, whatever his attitudes may be, reaches full stop here. Was *this* his vision of America? Were Gethsemani and the Church isolated preserves of sanctity on a gladiatorial continent? Admittedly he was promoting a project he cared for—Shirley Burden had a poet's eye and he was a wealthy friend of the abbey's—but all the same, his pride and prejudice are unbecoming. Dom James had not been to 4th and Walnut. He traveled the world but had somehow missed 4th and Walnut.

In the event, Dom Gabriel gave his imprimi potest and life went on—sometimes in unpredictable directions. In early September Merton received unexpected visitors: Natasha Spender, wife of the English poet Stephen Spender, and her friend Margot Dennis. They were driving coast to coast and naturally found their way to the poet Thomas Merton. The afternoon idyll that ensued was pure Merton: despite the high tension of that period in his life, he was able to accept—and gladly set in motion—a good time for all. He must have had abbot's permission for the initial conversation with his visitors. It's inconceivable that he had permission for the rest.

> We were very decorous and intelligent walking up and down the front avenue talking about Zen, Freud, music, St. John of the Cross, and the Dark Night of the Soul. Then it went down a notch, became more familiar, and amusing, as we went out to St. Bernard's lake and ate sandwiches and fruit cake and talked about monasteries and abbots, bishops and popes, Corn Island, Mexico, God knows what. This was very charming and maybe I began to look a little less scared. Finally we went to Dom Frederic's lake and went swimming which was the most enjoyable of all. I forget what we talked about. . . . Margot, once dipped into the water, became completely transformed into a Naiad-like creature, smiling a primitive smile through hanging wet hair. We sunbathed a bit, then finally they trundled off to Cincinnati.[16]

Should we add this naiad with her wild smile to the lineage of women, holy, dreamed, and real, who touched Merton? What pleases is that Merton had enough sense to drop out of the drama of that time to play. Early the next morning at the day's first office he was quite dazed, though he had slept well: "perhaps did not really wake up, just stayed asleep, watching and singing in my sleep."[17] The hangover of joy—from misconduct that would have sent any novice home, had it become known.

In late September Dom Gabriel informed James that he could not object if James opened and read letters to and from Merton marked conscience matter.[18] A letter not so marked to the bishop of Nevada, which both had read, made them suspect that Merton was abusing the privilege. This was not a small issue; the privacy of conscience-matter letters was fundamental to Merton's constricted, defended freedom. At the end of the year he would confront Dom James about it. Later, at the end of the year, mails became something of a combat zone. In July, after reading Merton's exchange of letters with Fr. Daniélou in which the older man conveyed richest sympathy for Merton, James sent Daniélou one of his classic denunciations. "I am not supposed to know," he began, "that he has been writing to you these last few weeks . . . but Divine Providence, in most loving ways, has brought the entire matter to my attention."

> I cannot but write you this letter to give you another side of the question, and to warn you to go very, very slow in encouraging Father Louis in something which may lead to a great catastrophe in his own soul, and perhaps greater harm to the souls of others, if not to the Church. . . . Unfortunately, I must say this at the beginning, dear Reverend Father, [Fr. Louis] is a person who has a very deep and serious neurosis—in the strict and scientific sense of the word.
>
> That is to say, he has a twist in his deep, subconscious emotional life which makes him a most unpredictable person. . . .
>
> We must remember, dear Father, that good Father Louis was not born into the Catholic Faith. . . . Thus the spirit of private judgment, independence from authority, and the spirit of subjectivism, assert themselves very strongly at times of trial and crisis. . . .
>
> The loving Providence of God it is which brought him to this monastery. His electric spirit needs four walls and some superior over him. . . . He knows deep in his heart that he needs a monastery to protect him from himself.[19]

It is a seven-page letter, typed, single-spaced, concluding of course with the motto "All for Jesus. . . ." James sent it off on the very day Merton was contemplating how to write *The Years with James*. The correspondence from others elsewhere in response to Merton's inquiries, event sharing, and indult request was warmly thoughtful—the word *civilized* comes to mind. Fr. Daniélou must have searched his mind and heart before sending James a tidy, handwritten note in mid-July. He had small, precise handwriting, as if the words themselves kneel. He understood now from Dom James that Father Louis should not be long absent from his monastery.

"But I think," he wrote, "that Father Louis has received from God a precious gift for understanding today's world and bringing it the message of prayer which it needs. This is, it seems to me, a genuine mission in the spirit of St. Bernard. . . . I am persuaded that, to accomplish this mission in a fertile and truly spiritual way, Father Louis needs to be sustained by monastic life. . . . This I have written him. . . . Yet I ask myself if, given the tension . . . I sense at the moment in Father Louis, it might be good to leave the monastery for some time. I am thinking for example of a journey in Europe. . . . I submit this suggestion to your wisdom."[20]

Dom James's response I've not seen, but Fr. Daniélou drew on it in a follow-up letter of mid-August. He acknowledged James's conviction, no doubt strongly restated, that Merton must not leave Gethsemani but offered his own restatement that a "temporary mission outside the monastery could have been an element of the solution" to Merton's unrest. "I fear," he continued, "that if nothing is done the question will become graver still, which would be truly regrettable. Of course, it is above all a grace of light and peace which would resolve all things. . . . That is my prayer for Father Louis."[21]

Dom James replied that Father Louis's attitude had changed since he had received a letter from Daniélou that echoed James's views about the need for stability at Gethsemani and thereby keeping faith with his readers. "He is his own true self again," James wrote, "happy, relieved, spontaneous and seeming to have come out of a deep, deep fog. I feel very sure that he was quite relieved to receive the opinion which you gave him. He was looking simply for some authority to support what he knew is his true vocation. . . . He told me . . . in your letter to him that certainly it was in God's plan that he should continue writing—that he should remain in a monastery—and that his influence with other souls is largely due to the fact that he is in a monastery."[22] James noted that he would be in France in mid-September for the general chapter meeting at

Cîteaux and proposed to meet Fr. Daniélou in Paris in the course of things. "With all my heart I thank you," he concluded. "You have tremendous influence in keeping good Father Louis on the supernatural path." Dom James in turn had exercised tremendous influence on the learned French Jesuit.

I have invited us to dwell for a moment on this exchange of letters because it vividly illustrates the unlike forces at work as Merton, yet again, strove to find the exit from Dom James's world and, just as important, a new entrance into monastic life differently felt and ordered. As we know, Merton was periodically anxious, concerned by the somewhat duplicitous path he had been obliged to take. Nonetheless, he was hoping that all would work out for the best. He was searching for the internal texture of the time: "We must always pray," he had written to the poet, "to be attuned to the mysterious language of events, and shape our actions accordingly." For his part, Dom James was doing his all to restrain Merton and undermine his reputation with those who could help or advise him. He did so also with Jean Leclercq, the distinguished Benedictine scholar who recognized Merton's call to solitude. In early November, intercepting a letter from Leclercq to Merton, he returned it with stern advice: "What I want to ask of you is that in the future when you write to Father Louis, you simply omit anything in regard to his vocation, whether it is legitimate or not legitimate—whether it is an illusion or whether it is really from God. . . . So, therefore, dear Father, if you would rewrite your letter and leave out that last part."[23]

In early October Merton heard from Dom Gregorio in Rome that the congregation was likely to grant the indult but final approval would of necessity rest with Merton's own superiors. "This may be quite an obstacle," Merton knew all too well, "but it seems as if in the long run the move will be completely successful."[24] Later he heard a little more, again from Dom Gregorio: "[Archbishop] Larraona said that he would almost certainly grant the indult even though there might be opposition. . . . He felt that it was well founded."[25]

On November 15, the hopeful atmosphere changed abruptly. Dom James announced without explanation that he would be leaving for Rome the following day for an important conference. "A complete bombshell," Merton wrote in his journal that evening, "and I have no doubt that one of the main reasons for the trip is my petition to the Congregation. . . . It is not going to be easy just sitting here powerless to do anything while he has full power to completely wreck everything by fair means or foul."[26] He was right: it wasn't easy, and it wouldn't be easy for more weeks of suspense than he anticipated. Dom James returned a week later but kept his counsel. "It reminded me of a game of cards," James recalled a few weeks later, "that two men are playing together—one is not going to show his hand, because then he might lose the game."[27] He told Merton that he had indeed seen the archbishop—but said no more and left in doubt the reason for the sudden trip. Merton read his attitude in a positive light: "I gather that he is now happy with the unconcern of one who has shifted an unpleasant problem on to the shoulders of higher superiors. This is a great relief to me also because we can now go ahead more objectively, without animosity and resentment. I think my relations with him have never been better and I am very glad of that fact."[28] James's unconcern had another cause. In cooperation with Dom Gabriel, he had gained a great though still unstated victory.

In a letter dated November 8, received at Gethsemani shortly before Dom James's departure for Rome, Dom Gabriel informed him that a signed indult on Merton's behalf had been delivered to him by the Sacred Congregation for Religious.[29] To ensure that James realized the gravity of the situation, he cited the specifics of the indult in the Latin in which, as a matter of course, it was written: "P. Thomas Merton . . . implorat Indultum exclaustrationis," ending with "concedat petitam facultatem exclaustrationis non ultra triennium"—in paraphrase, Fr. Thomas Merton pleads for an exclaustration permit; the petition is granted for a period of not more than three years. The signature on the document was Archbishop Larraona's. "I have no need to tell you," Dom Gabriel wrote,

> the feeling of stupor with which I scanned this document. Dom Déodat [his second in command] was no less dumbfounded than I because we knew NOTHING about this request of Father Merton's. . . . There is no question for me, not even for an instant, of signing this Indult and thereby validating it, since the Sacred Congregation leaves the decision to me.
>
> Yet I cannot withhold an Indult without conveying to the Sacred Congregation the motives behind my attitude. And here I need your help.
>
> We don't know what channel Fr Merton used to obtain this document. He may possibly have secured the consent of a bishop who has responsibilities in Rome. . . . We have no idea.
>
> It seems to me that we must exercise extreme care in preparing our response so that, today or tomorrow, through one channel or another, Fr Louis does not come into possession of this document without our knowledge or despite us.
>
> For this we must explain to the Holy See the very grave reasons why we think that Fr Louis is suited neither to the active ministry, to life in the world, nor to the eremitical life. I know your thinking well enough to know that you are completely agreed with me on this point, namely, that *for the soul of Father Louis,* his departure from Gethsemani would be a catastrophe.
>
> Further, we must ourselves remember and tell the Holy See that, if it is to be feared that Fr Merton may lose himself by leaving the monastery, it is no less to be feared that he will lose not only himself. Multitudes of souls will suffer grave harm through his departure, beginning with the novices he has formed, the religious who have known and loved him, and the innumerable readers who have been touched by the witness to the hidden life brought to them by Father.

All these things must be made clear to our Most Reverend Father Larraona. But I think they will have much more weight in his mind, and eventually in the minds of the Cardinal Prefect [leader of the congregation] and other personalities whom we may encounter in the course of this affair, if you come personally and expressly to Rome for this reason.

Given the importance I attach to this initiative of Father Louis's, I urgently appeal to you, dear Reverend Father, to come to Rome. I should add that your arrival must not be delayed; you understand that I cannot hold this Indult for very long without explaining why to the Sacred Congregation. . . . During your absence [from Gethsemani] no letter from Fr Louis should be posted until your return, even those marked "conscience matter."

Dom Gabriel concluded by asking James to bring with him extracts from letters written by Merton that demonstrated his "lack of submission, not only to religious Superiors but to the Church hierarchy itself." Dom James did so and assembled in Rome a thirteen-page typewritten report which was instantly translated into French and delivered on November 19 to the senior leaders of the Sacred Congregation for Religious.[30] Dom Gabriel and Dom James also explained their views in direct conversation. The best surviving account of that moment is in a letter written by James quite a few months later, in October 1960, to a highly placed official, likely the newly appointed secretary of the Sacred Congregation, Paul-Pierre Philippe. James wanted him to be aware of the course of events at the end of the previous year. He knew that Merton had been writing to him to reopen, in principle and without urgency, the possibility of leaving Gethsemani for another monastic home, and an invitation to Merton to travel somewhere had also come up. The letter opened with an account of Dom Gregorio's visits to Gethsemani and contacts with Merton. "I had no inkling," he wrote, "of what was going on between them, except once in a while Father Louis would write to some of his friends mentioning something about 'a bomb which when it explodes is going to surprise everybody.' I had no idea of what this 'bomb' was."[31] James went on to explain his urgent trip to Rome and Dom Gabriel's difficult situation: "Our Most Reverend General did not know how he could execute an indult according to his conscience when he knew nothing about it. . . . I did not know anything about it either, and was utterly and speechlessly surprised. . . . When good Cardinal Larraona heard the real situation, that Father Louis was trying to make a detour around the ordinary channels through which a good monk would pass, he simply took the indult and tore it up as invalid."

At that point in his letter, Dom James turned to his standard judgments of Merton, though with a notable addition.

> I want to, however, insist, good Monsignor, that Father Louis and I are the best of friends—in fact, he is my Confessor, so you can see how intimate we are.
>
> Since he is really sick emotionally, neurotically, he cannot see his very deep and serious faults. However the pride of his intellect does not allow him to put too much confidence in my advice. . . . Good Father Louis is safe for Eternity only within the four walls of a monastery under a superior.

It is not clear to me how Dom James could feel comfortable confessing to a "really sick" member of the community; he too found himself at times "in the middle of all contradictions" but seems not to have noticed. It is not clear to me how James could claim Merton as a very good friend. They were friendly at times, friendly for certain purposes such as care of the novices, friendly in some liberated way that occasionally allowed them to laugh at themselves and the lives they led—Br. Patrick Hart can recall their peals of laughter at times in the other room. But they were not friends if friendship means mutual trust and the fruitful meeting of minds over long stretches of time. They were not friends if friendship means encouraging the other's authenticity and freedom.

Dom James's report to the Sacred Congregation is far too long to include here in full. Its style is a blend of mainstream James with a novel French flavor. Using extracts from Merton's correspondence against him, it seeks to demonstrate that he had "much attachment to his own judgment, a strong spirit of independence in relation to authority, a large dose of subjectivism in his notions of moral rectitude, and scarcely veiled contempt for the ecclesiastical hierarchy."[32] Concerning his warm, thoroughly creative relations with the Zen author, D. T. Suzuki: "[Fr. Louis] manifests profound contempt for his Order and admits that he prefers Zen, which he finds much more congenial, more *sympathique*." But the most serious feature "in the case of good Father Louis," as James put it, is his lack of emotional stability. "He is a neurotic in the strictly scientific meaning of the word." Casting a long shadow forward, here enters Dr. Zilboorg. "As one of the most famous Catholic psychiatrists in America told him in my presence," James wrote,

> in his subconscious there is a formidable force that impels him to acquire renown, celebrity, grandeur.
>
> I am speaking of Dr. Gregory Zilboorg of New York City, who passed away in September 1959.
>
> Father Louis cultivates in the sanctuary of his imagination a grandiose portrait of his own person. He is not unaware of the extraordinary impact he has had as the author of works on the spiritual life. It has gone to his head. . . .
>
> The origin of his neurosis is to be found in his early childhood, due to the treatment he received from an unnatural mother who lacked maternal instincts. He has never recovered from the first years of his life.

This too can only be Zilboorg's view; we haven't encountered it before. There is more of Zilboorg—the bright sign in Times

Square, "Come see the hermit!," and much else. Dom James wound up his letter by speculating about the outcome, were Merton to be granted the indult.

> Let us suppose that he can obtain permission to live outside his monastery, far from all superiors, if only for a short time. How long would he remain in the place he had chosen? And, given the instability of his character, who would wish to assume responsibility for directing such a soul?
>
> In all this he imagines he is seeking God, but it seems rather that he is seeking the satisfaction of his Ego disguised by the good he has in mind to accomplish, that he allows himself to be guided by his subjectivism, by his desire to free himself from all external control, by his large and unhealthy need to add to his fame and assure himself of people's increasing esteem.

At the very end of the letter Dom James again referred to himself as an "*ami intime,*" an intimate friend of Father Louis's. These views and many more were addressed to a major department in the Holy See and to men close to the pope. They became part of the written, perpetual record. And there was just a little more, apparently unwritten but communicated. Fr. John Eudes, who stood between Merton and Dom James as the trusted friend of both, had heard Dr. Zilboorg say—presumably at the Collegeville workshop more than three years earlier—that, left to himself, Merton "might well leave the Church, go off and marry a woman, etc., etc." Concerning which Merton said, when told of this, "Obviously we are all human. But the Abbot will have a great deal of ammunition.... So long as Rome considers me a Don Juan in prison, there is nothing to hope for. It is very heartrending."[33]

A Don Juan in prison. . . Here the natures of abbot and monk intersect with a crash. Like the claim about Merton's mother, this claim also is new—but for some of those who knew both men, it wouldn't come as a surprise. Fr. James Conner, Merton's undermaster in the novitiate and long since a respected elder and teacher at Gethsemani, had this issue in mind when we spoke in January 2014. "I think James was influenced by Merton's early history," he said, "and particularly by the fact that, whether true or not, there was talk that he had fathered a child. James had a real hang-up about sex, a tremendous fear of it, tremendous repression and denial of anything pertaining to that whole area within himself. In Merton's case especially, I believe his restrictions were based principally on the tremendous fear that if 'I give him an inch, he's going to take a mile'—and it would end up a real scandal."[34] Dom James's vehemence over years and years now makes better, even sadder sense; many monastic leaders of his generation are said to have been much like him in this respect. The power of sexual desire was almost certainly the "hydrogen bomb" he feared. It can't really have been rebellious ideas, though Merton had plenty about a new monastic spirit and order of life, and soon about the indecency of war. It can't have been anything else I can think of, apart from a few stiff drinks—in later years Merton liked a drink when he could have one. It must have been sex. Within the monastic enclosure, the possibility of scandal was extinguished. (It is worth mentioning that Merton wasn't naive about the possibility of homoerotic relations in the monastery. There is very little on this topic in his journal and correspondence, but a note to Fr. John Eudes about the admission of novices reflects with good humor his recognition of the issue. "I notice that in picking people," he wrote, "we all have certain demands. Some seem to need people who will be pretty and girlish. You need people who are 'interesting,' and I will settle for people who do not develop a hostile transference for the Fr Master"—namely, himself as novice master.[35])

There is something more we can now better understand in light of Dom James's letter to the congregation. Within the monastic enclosure, James tasked Merton with the key educational positions from 1951 through 1965: initially as master of scholastics (the priests in training), later and at length as master of novices. As noted in an earlier page, this entailed responsibility for shaping the spirit, practice, and conduct of an entire generation of monks—many of whom to this day are grateful for the opportunity they had to know and learn from him. Dom James *trusted* Merton as an educator, as a monk who understood what it is to be a monk, as a scholar of the teachings of the order and the Fathers of the Church. And then, he chose Merton as his confessor. Even if, in the secrecy of confession, there were issues he could not or would not broach with Merton as his confessor—we shall never know—his choice of Merton reflects trust. Yet Dom James *blackened* Merton's name and reputation among his superiors and peers. How else to characterize the succession of letters we have read? Merton was mentally unstable, emotionally buffeted, uncured of childhood traumas, wobbling between docility and rebellion, lurching after one project and then another without considering consequences. . . . Not someone you want at your side. And then, were he to leave the monastery, even for a more contemplative, quieter institution, he would betray what he had written and his readers. We can be quite sure that Dom James believed what he wrote to others. We can also be sure that he fully trusted Merton as the central educator of the abbey, and this for years on end. Here again, and no less than Merton, he was in the middle of all contradictions, trapped by his attitude toward Merton and treatment of him. His authority and institutional reach as abbot gave him means that Merton lacked, but they did not confer self-knowledge. "The unchangeable holiness of power," Merton wrote in his journal during these months.[36]

While awaiting word from Rome about the indult, Merton continued to correspond with friends and advisers. To Fr. Daniélou, whom he obviously still trusted, he sent a lengthy *vue d'ensemble,* including a hot critique of Dom James, who had, in Merton's judgment, stepped past any reasonable boundary by opening and delaying the delivery to him of conscience-matter letters. "You see what kind of man he is," Merton wrote.

> Extremely convinced of his own rightness in everything, *absolutely incapable* of understanding that there can be a more perfect form of contemplative life than this, unless perhaps the Carthusians. But utterly incapable of seeing anything outside the conventional cadres. . . . He is utterly committed to the prosperous, established, bourgeois type of big monastery with all its comforts, façade, etc. At present we are becoming a prosperous cheese factory, and our advertising is utterly sickening. . . .
>
> I have an acute problem as regards liberty of conscience. . . . Father Abbot acts in practice as if it were a sin to consult anybody but him. He arrogates to himself sole rights to decide . . . in both forums, internal and external. . . .
>
> It is a question of choice between a bourgeois, inert, decadent façade of monasticism, and a genuine living attempt to renew the inner spirit of the monastic life.[37]

On December 16, after what felt to him to be a very long wait, Merton received from the Sacred Congregation for Religious the letter denying his application for an indult. We need his journal to understand how he felt. "It was a long, personal, detailed letter," he wrote,

> in fact a very fine letter, signed . . . by two cardinals. What could be more definitive and more official—what could be more final?
>
> They were very sorry. They wanted the right words to pour balm in certain wounds. But my departure would certainly upset too many people in the Order, as well as outside it. And they agreed with my superiors that I did not have an eremitical vocation. That therefore what they asked of me was to stay in the monastery where God has put me, and I would find interior solitude. . . .
>
> I felt no anger or resistance. . . . It could only be accepted. And the first reaction was one of relief that at last the problem had been

> settled . . . , settled in some wider and deeper way than just by negation. . . .
>
> Went out alone, in light rain, to get Christmas trees for the nuns. . . .
>
> The letter is obviously an indication of God's Will and I accept it fully. So then what? Nothing. Trees, hills, rain. And prayer much lighter, much freer, more unconcerned. . . .
>
> Actually, what it comes down to is that I shall certainly have solitude but only by miracle and not at all by my own contriving. Where? Here or there makes no difference. Somewhere, nowhere, beyond all "where." Solitude outside geography or in it. No matter. Coming back, walked around a corner of the woods and the monastery swung in view. I was free from it.[38]

"An absolutely final negative decision," as he put it that day to his friend Ernesto Cardenal.[39] He was thinking further, quite sure that Dr. Zilboorg's judgments, conveyed by Dom James, were responsible for the refusal. In this he was partially mistaken. He had never seen the full suite of judgments against him that Dom James now wrote almost routinely, and they were the substance of the document submitted to the congregation. Merton continued in his morning-after letter to Cardenal: "I think the reason the Congregation swung in favor of Dom James is that he told them a lot of irresponsible remarks about me by Gregory Zilboorg [who] said of my desire of solitude that I just wanted to get out from under obedience and that if I were allowed a little liberty I would probably run away with a woman. I don't pretend to be an angel, but these remarks of Gregory Zilboorg. . . . Well, anyway, I think that is why Rome rejected my case, for certainly Dom James will have made everything possible out of these statements by Zilboorg. He has probably made enough out of them to queer my reputation in Rome forever."

Merton's quiet acceptance of the congregation's verdict is

remarkable. He was a vowed man, a religious—this cannot be forgotten. He lived within an icon in which the Hand of God is held out over the mean affairs of men. He wrote further to Cardenal, "So many people prayed hard for me; their prayers will not be lost. I received the decision of Rome without emotion and without the slightest anger. I accept it completely in faith, and feel a great interior liberty and emptiness in doing so. This acceptance has completely liberated me from Gethsemani, which is to me no longer an obstacle or a prison, and to which I am indifferent, though I will do all in my power to love and help those whom God entrusts to me here." This, then, was the result: a great interior liberty and emptiness, indifference to the monastery as an institution, continued love of those in the community whose lives touched his.

Merton and Dom James needed to cleanse their relation insofar as possible if there was to be a future between them. On the day when he was, in effect, writing his life, writing to save his life (the long journal entry, the letter to Cardenal, another to Dom Gregorio), he also wrote and placed in his mailbox a letter to Dom James, who was expected to return from a trip the following day.

> Dear Rev. Father:
> I want you to receive this news when you come home, and before I see you. The whole question of my vocation has been finally settled once for all by Rome. There is no question in my mind that this is God's Will, and that I am to accept it without hesitation, and this I do. . . .
>
> The Lord has given me the grace to see this without difficulty and to accept it gladly and with deep peace of heart. I only took the steps I did in order to find out what the Congregation thought, and hence what was the will of God. I know of course that the Congregation was considerably influenced by you and Dom Gabriel and I know that human feelings must have entered in, but still I have sufficient faith in my Superiors and in the Church to see that this does not matter.[40]

To this humble preamble Merton added a series of what he called "resolutions." He resolved to take no further steps to leave the order. "I will make no move to do so, and will apply no pressure to do so. At most, I will content myself with manifesting my thoughts to Superiors or those competent." He wished to remain as novice master. Further, he looked forward to working with James "to solve some of the difficult problems of formation that arise with the new generation coming in (college, etc.)." However, were Dom James to remove him from the novitiate, he "would like to put in a request to try out living as a hermit in the woods." He regretted any inconvenience he may have caused; "this will not be renewed." And he concluded: "I really love Gethsemani in spite of the reaction against certain aspects of the set-up. I am grateful to God for the graces He has given me here and know that He has many more in store. The decisions made have left me very free and empty, and I can say that they have enabled me to taste an utterly new kind of joy."

On the following day, Merton noted in his journal that he "had a good talk with Rev. Father, who is tired after coming in late last night from California."[41] What a human expression of concern. But there was one further written communication that Merton felt compelled to place before Dom James. It concerned the rights of conscience. It was in part an exculpation of his conduct: "The reason why I did not directly consult you about my application for an indult was that there was in fact no necessity to do so. I was fully aware of your views on the subject. I had every right to appeal to a higher Superior."[42] This being said, he went on to lodge serious charges against James in the form of unyielding questions.

> I fully recognize your right to refuse permission for a leave of absence. In this you were following your conscience and within your rights. But I wonder about the way in which you have done everything possible to prevent me obtaining permission from anyone and in any way whatsoever. I do not deny you this right, but

> in point of fact it seems to me to represent an arbitrary and tyrannical spirit. Are you not so intent on your own views, in this matter, that you are willing to stifle the Holy Ghost in a soul? . . . Do you not have an inordinate tendency to interfere in the workings of conscience and to suppress by violence those desires and ideals which run counter to your policies?
>
> Do you not tend to assume that your own policies represent the last word in the spiritual perfection of every one of your subjects? . . .
>
> I have always striven to be perfectly obedient to legitimate commands in the external forum, but I beg the right to form my conscience according to the guidance of my directors, in the internal forum, without demands that I follow your directions and no other. I hope you understand this rightly as a humble and filial petition.

Though Merton accepted the congregation's decision and acknowledged his continuing obedience to his abbot, he drew a line here that James surely could not dismiss. It is not a declaration of independence; it is a declaration of integrity capable of withstanding tyranny. Humble and filial, yes—and afire.

Dom James wasn't able or inclined to jump out of his skin, to become other than he was. In a letter to Dom Gabriel the following week, he described Merton when they met after his return from California as "a completely changed person. It seemed as if a great load had been taken off his shoulders. He acts like a young boy 15 years old ever since—jumping around, smiling—his own spontaneous self has come back to him. I am convinced more and more it was just a tremendous temptation that had him in its iron-bound vice [*sic*]."[43] Merton's declaration of integrity went unmentioned; the depth of Merton's reception of the congregation's decision was apparently invisible or not worth mention. What James saw was an adolescent jumping around.

At the end of the year Merton recorded without love a few

observations in his journal. "Two days I have inwardly said no to all the Abbot's preening exhortations after Chapter sermons—not because they are wrong in themselves but because they are all implicitly summations to conform with the party-line, which is that this life is a life of great suffering and heroism and therefore most noble and exalted. . . . You do not agree that this is a life of suffering? At least I can hold you here and bore you, because I have the power."[44] And Merton added a surmise that would prove to be fateful: "The attitude of the abbot seems to be that as long as I am in this monastery he doesn't care much what I do." On January 4, he sent a letter to a Nicaraguan friend with a further sign of things to come: "Father Abbot has hired a contractor to build me a very fine little hermitage house back in the woods."[45]

Fuge, tace, quiesce. . . . Flee, be silent, be still.

[15]
Solidity and Ashes

DOM JAMES HAD THE ART OF miniaturizing what Merton wished. And the art, if it was one, of knowing what would make life at Gethsemani tolerable for him. Merton had evoked in his first letter to Fr. Lombardi the vision of "a small contemplative monastery [where] intellectual leaders and other important persons would be invited to come, together with clergymen, etc., to participate in what would be partly a retreat and partly a symposium on spiritual and cultural matters." It was to be in Ecuador—or somewhere else far from Gethsemani. But what if there already existed a monastery where such a program could be organized—namely, Gethsemani itself? Under the circumstances now enforced, Merton found this possibility worthwhile, as did Dom James. Merton sketched out the idea effectively in a letter to Pope John XXIII in the winter of 1960. Although he was not on close terms with the pope—they would never meet—like virtually everyone in the Catholic world, Pope John was aware of Merton's writings. Upon the pope's election in 1958, Merton had written him a heartfelt greeting and had dared to air his ideas for a South American foundation. Now he wrote again to describe the novel ecumenical program he was about to set in motion. "I have just received permission," he wrote,

> to start, very discreetly, a small retreat project here . . . , five or six retreats for what may be called specialized groups and even in some sense elite groups. For example, there will be a meeting of several theologians and heads of *Protestant* seminaries, another meeting of professors of a Catholic university (priests and

> lay people together), another of psychiatrists and writers, and possibly another of artists, poets, etc.
>
> Our goal is to bring together . . . people highly qualified in their own field who are interested in the spiritual life . . . and who will be able to profit from an informal contact, from a spiritual and cultural dialogue, with Catholic contemplatives such as we are, or should be.[1]

It was one of Merton's contradictions that his reputation and sheer intelligence as a writer gave him deserved access to men and women of accomplishment in many walks of life, although he scarcely ever left Gethsemani. He would draw on that ease of access for the retreats he was envisioning, as he also drew on it here to write directly to the pope without the pipeline. Pope John responded ever so kindly by sending Merton in April a beautifully embroidered liturgical stole that he had worn and blessed. Merton was very moved by the gift and sent him in return a version of his translations from the desert fathers, hand printed by his friend the artist and printer Victor Hammer, who owned an artisanal printing house in Lexington, Kentucky, that had captured Merton's imagination. He loved to prepare small works for Victor Hammer's small editions. Merton did not neglect in his cover letter to the pope to cite the words of the desert saint Arsenius: *fuge, tace, quiesce*.[2] In a monastery with an excess of slogans, these few words seem to have become Merton's secret counterslogan.

There was growling in the wings over Merton's exchanges with the pope and the marvelous gift he had received. Dom Gabriel was not happy about an earlier letter: "I don't know," he wrote to Dom James, "whether there are many Father-Masters in the Order who would have thought to send a spiritual bouquet to the Sovereign Pontiff at Christmas. And yet, from the point of view of monastic life and interior solitude, they are as good Father-Masters and as good monks as Fr Louis, committed to forming monks as fervent as his, and who, as a consequence, would have as much title to the attention and affection of the Common Father of the faithful. But in this gesture of Fr Louis's, there is obviously much of Thomas Merton, the celebrated author, and he is the only one who fails to see that."[3] The constraints on Merton sometimes resemble a leash in the hands of a loveless master. Replying soon after to Dom Gabriel, James infantilized Merton's delight over receiving the pope's gift. "You may imagine that good Father Louis was all enthused and excited at this very special and personal gift from the Holy Father."[4]

For once abbot and abbot general had different views, specifically concerning the ecumenical retreat program which James had authorized. In his letter of April 25, Dom Gabriel wrote that he feared, "more for [Fr. Louis] than for anyone else, the 'contacts' and 'dialogues' with non-Catholics. To go down that path, exceptional docility toward the teachings of the magisterium and toward the summons of the Holy Spirit reaching him from the Church and his Superiors would assuredly be needed. The moment does not seem to have come when Fr Louis would enjoy such docility." Dom Gabriel seemed out of sorts. There were quite a few thorny censorship issues in which he was necessarily though somewhat unwillingly involved. In July a publication approval came through, but Dom Gabriel's comment to James was irritable: "One of his censors seems to me nearly as prolix as he is."[5] A few months earlier Merton couldn't help but question why things had become so difficult. He put the question in a letter to Dom James, although they could easily have discussed it directly, because he wanted "[a] quasi-formal and official . . . consultation concerning a spiritual issue, so that I can have your reply as representative of God. . . . It is my impression," he continued, "perhaps . . . unfounded, that actually the Abbot General is unconsciously preserving a kind of rancor for the fact that I went over his head to the Holy See last fall. This may be an unjust supposition: but is it without foundation . . . I wonder! However, I do not mean to raise it. I will willingly bury it in oblivion."[6]

Refining his approach to the ecumenical retreats, Merton dutifully and I think sincerely sought Dom James's advice; the meetings were a shared initiative, in Merton's hands but from James's hands. He hoped that James would see fit to convey to Dom Gabriel that he would be following sensible guidelines: "Would [it] do some good to explain to him—I mean for *you* to explain to him—that I am really not a revolutionary and that I am really not trying to start a fuss or be a rebel, . . . lest he become suspicious of me and have a grudge against me."[7] Suspicion was permanent—no hope there—but, as we'll see, in time the grudge passed off. Merton wrote further to Dom James that he had in mind to treat the visits "above all as conversations among friends . . . and *never* . . . give the impression that I am trying to start a dialogue that will lead to a 'movement.' . . . I must speak to them simply as a humble and ordinary priest who is their friend, no specialist, no expert, . . . just their friend and neighbor who is interested in them."

Merton occasionally recorded his impressions of retreats, never more appreciatively than in June 1960 when he met first with Jesuits and soon after with teachers and students of a Protestant college. "I am convinced of the great value of such encounters," he wrote, "and all that is needed is for *me* to do less talking. For all those who have come so far I feel a very deep respect and affection, and I believe it is mutual. I value their friendship, and this is not just a conventional phrase: it is important for the wholeness of my own life—it enables me to be friends with a hidden part of myself, which I can only find if I give my friendship to *them*. Everywhere, all Christians should be making this same discovery."[8] Merton was conducting, before the fact, an *aggiornamento* of a kind the Second Vatican Council several years later would counsel across the Church. The typical translation of this promising Italian word is crude: "updating." Something more like opening the doors better captures it, at least where Merton was concerned. He was opening the doors of his mind, heart, and faith to groups of others; he was listening as they opened their doors. And he was learning more deeply still to be himself.

As so often, there was rattling at the edges of his life. In October 1960, Merton noted that Dan Walsh, a theologian and close friend through the years, had told him that James was "really very keen" on the ecumenical meetings, but even that provoked misgivings. "I am afraid," Merton continued, "of it becoming some kind of a silly, organized racket to bring publicity to Gethsemani. More glory! I am not in it for my glory or for the glory of the house—but for the good that comes of simple and charitable conversation. . . . If we leave it be what it is, it will give glory to God."[9] And this in fact came to pass; I've seen no sign that Dom James exploited this heartfelt initiative.

Merton wrote to Fr. Daniélou at the beginning of the year that he had sought and received permission to consult periodically with a psychiatrist in Louisville, Dr. James Wygal, who had studied with Zilboorg at some point, knew the monastery well—and, as it happened, would convert to Catholicism at the end of the year.[10] For some time Dr. Wygal had been engaged to provide psychological evaluations of postulants or community members, as needed, and he provided similar service to other Catholic houses in the region. Through Wygal, Merton hoped to fight fire with fire. Thinking of Zilboorg's judgments against him, which he took to be responsible for the denial of his request for an indult, he wished "to know if there is any foundation to those damaging statements, and what I ought to do about it. In any event, it ought to be useful to me and my work." He added that "Father Abbot is really obsessed with the idea that I should not be allowed out of the monastery for more than a day and not further than Louisville—he has many funny ideas about his men." Merton's trust of Fr. Daniélou is evident where he confided to him a concern that would lead far: "It seems to me that it is very necessary to take a political stand in these times and I have been, I regret to say, foolishly apolitical." In a letter of the same day to the head of the Sacred Congregation, Merton made his thinking explicit. Were Dr. Wygal to "assure me that there is no danger for me" in transferring to a more experimental Benedictine monastery, "and that I might even have something to gain by it," he might ask the congregation to reconsider his petition.[11]

Dom James was persuaded—mistakenly, as events unfolded—that Dr. Wygal was his man. In a letter to Arcadio Larraona, now a cardinal and no longer serving in the Sacred Congregation, he wrote with serene conviction that "this psychiatrist . . . has a very fine background of monastic life. . . . He has a tremendous sense of the necessity of authority and right order in religious matters. He always favors the authority of those who are placed in positions of authority and the Church, and always inclines to give a view against one rebelling against authority, even though he thinks this rebellion comes from God. . . . This doctor always emphasizes to the various monks he has interviewed . . . that the main thing . . . is to keep the Rule and follow all the regulations."[12] In reality, Merton and Dr. Wygal became friends, and their conversations about psychological health were genuinely helpful on that basis. In one large incident that lay ahead, Wygal would be a restraining, questioning influence—but as a friend who knew him quite well, not as a servant of abbot and institution.

As the months passed, Merton kept his eye on the small cement-block retreat house and hermitage under construction (fig. 7). It was some fifteen minutes on foot from the monastery, at the forested edge of a field with a view to a distant ridgeline. In its original form it was completed on November 30, the Feast of Saint Andrew; later additions didn't prevent it from remaining austere, as intended. (The Catholic custom of associating nearly each day of the year with a saint is a lovely parallel to cities with named rather than numbered streets—it allows one to travel the year with interest in people and creates street corners in time.) As Merton worried about nearly everything that touched on the abbot, he worried now.

FIG. 7. Merton's hermitage today.

"The hermitage grows," he recorded in October, "but I find that anxiety grows with it because Rev. Father keeps intimating that it is something he does not want me to have or even to use except in a very restricted way. I mean, he is very clear about my not living in it, or sleeping in it, or saying Mass there. It is exceptionally frustrating to have such a beautiful place as this one is getting to be—tucked away among the pines—and to have to stay away from it. . . . I did not really ask for this, for rather I showed a great deal of hesitation and gave him five or six chances to . . . call the whole thing off."[13] But by the time it was fully built, he had realized that Dom James's terms were reasonably generous, and under those terms the hermitage had so much to offer: a quiet place "for . . . dialogue and conversations with Protestant ministers and professors," as he described it to Leclercq in December, and "it also serves for solitude and I have at least limited permission to use it part-time. This is to a great extent a hopeful solution and I find that if I can have at least *some* real solitude and silence it makes a tremendous difference. It can at least help to stave off the kind of crisis that arose in 1959 when I felt it was necessary . . . to go elsewhere. As long as this solution exists, this can be avoided."[14] Still, Dom Gabriel was expected to make a visitation soon, and *that* was a worry: "Let's hope it will not be closed down or dynamited by the Abbot General."[15] In the event, Dom Gabriel spent several weeks at Gethsemani in late February and early March 1961, and proved to be warmly attentive to Merton, who was the first person with whom he wished to speak privately after seeing Dom James. "This was a kindness and even an honor," Merton noted.[16] Surely to Merton's surprise, they tramped around in the woods together and spent some time in the new hermitage, where they talked about hermit affairs: about a female hermit in southern France and how she was doing, about the value to Merton of the new hermitage provided that he made measured use of it, not living there full-time, "for you are the novice master," as Dom Gabriel put it. "But all his logic (and he is after all very logical)," Merton concluded, "was that this was right for me. He was very kind. . . . He was really very kind."[17]

Yet unchanged. After leaving Gethsemani, in a letter of March 1 to Dom James he acknowledged that "dear Fr Louis certainly makes efforts to understand the attitude of his Superiors, and even to submit to them goodheartedly. Nonetheless, it's evident that he will always be Fr Louis Merton, drawn by his very gifts to seek a public."[18] He made clear as well that he had been in touch with the new secretary of the Sacred Congregation for Religious to ensure that he had a realistic view of Merton; Paul-Pierre Philippe assured him that he had already studied the file and understood that "Fr Louis was a neurotic whose good intentions [*bonne foi*] were beyond doubt but with whom one had to act with the greatest prudence."

Throughout the year, from January forward, Merton was pressing more deeply into the realm of immaterial insight and prayer, his inner homeland—but he was also burning with the issues of morality and integrity raised by his failed effort to obtain a passage to elsewhere. The two concerns were not wholly independent of each other because the solution of the moral dilemma, if there was to be one, called for spiritual insight. And there was a third concern, hinted at in his letter to the trusted one, Fr. Daniélou: the newly discovered need to develop and exercise political understanding by the light of Christian values. The failed campaign of 1959 had something like the force of a spring that projected Merton more deeply into himself, yet also more deeply into concern for humanity at large. Much of this was unpredictable; its source was the hidden logic of Merton's identity rather than the logic of external circumstances. But Merton would soon again disregard boundaries; some, though not all, of his superiors would again be stunned by his initiative and its implications for the Church; and—a great and lasting gain—he would make many new friends who, like him, brought moral fervor and personal courage to the peace movement of the 1960s.

"Struggle in my heart all week," he recorded in his journal at the end of November 1960. "My own moral conflict never ceases. Knowing I cannot and must not simply submit to the standards imposed on me, and merely conform as 'they' would like. This I am convinced is wrong—but the pressure never ceases. . . . I will do what they tell me, but I will not and cannot think as they think. If I did so I would be untrue to God, to myself and to all those who for some reason or other have a kind of confidence in me. Yet I do not know where I stand myself. As though I were standing on 'nothing.' And perhaps that is the only position possible. . . . There is nothing here to which I can assent without reserve except the barest essentials. And I do not even assent to my own way of life."[19] The concluding thought here makes the circle spin, and with it Merton. He had three views of the moral dilemma, each fully articulated, two of them contradictory, the third subtle and difficult to sustain by reason of its impersonal objectivity. From one perspective that he often adopted and explored, Merton was certain that he had been treated unjustly by his superiors, who confined him to Gethsemani out of motives few of which seemed reasonable. "It is the presuppositions in which they base themselves that are wrong," he wrote of his superiors, "—the placid assumption that since 'the will of the superior is always the will of God,' it matters little how arbitrary, selfish, prejudiced and interested they are; they are always infallible and sacrosanct."[20] From a second perspective that he also pondered and suffered, he blamed himself for failures of understanding, acceptance, and compassion. "It is clear," he wrote in the early days of 1960, "that I have been severely tempted for a long time and have not avoided sin—the obscure, easily justified sins of self-will, pride, disobedience, infidelity to duty and obligation, lack of faith. Specifically, lack of faith in the protection and providence of God in the ordinary ways of monastic life. . . . My 'rightness' is only a matter of opinion."[21] He was reflecting along these lines not only soon after the shock of the refused indult but much later in the year. In June, for example: "How silly and unreal are my rebellions. . . . There is no need to rebel, only to ask *mercy*. And to trust in mercy. Which is what I have not done. . . . God is my Father and my superiors are his representatives. And if I live quietly in long suffering and humility and patience, and represent my needs to them, they will have mercy. . . . I must be content to accept mercy from them and be humble."[22] And in September: "Walking to Prime in the grey cloister, realized that I have paid too little attention to a great reality—my love for my monastery community, the love of the community for me."[23]

And then a third perspective from which all concerned—he himself, his superiors—are equally wrong, equally standing on nothing, therefore wholly exposed and vulnerable to the divine will that shapes all things, even these things. "'The truth shall make you free,'" he wrote in mid-November. "And doubtless the truth is that all of us are wrong in one way or another. And the ways in which we are 'right' are so illusory as to be non-existent. The truth is somewhere outside and above the spider's web that they have woven—with 'the best of intentions.' Why get caught in it? What I need above all is to be liberated from my own imagination and from theirs. But I do seek liberation, at all costs."[24] This was the most difficult perspective: to abandon one's sense of being in the right, to abandon blame of the other, to let the situation melt toward a solution beyond anticipation from a source beyond all effort. This was the religious perspective.

Through these difficult months Merton's life of prayer and his capacity for focused insight gained richness and depth. He was rewriting one of his earliest books: *Seeds of Contemplation* of 1949 was becoming *New Seeds of Contemplation,* completed by 1961 and published the following year. Authors rarely revise creative works but often revise textbooks—and this book had become something of a textbook or guide to contemplative prayer. Merton needed to amend it, to offer in its pages the fruits of another decade and more of experience. Alongside that effort, there were more than a few occasions when he entered new ground, planted new seeds in the privacy of his journal. "In emptying Himself to come into the world, God has not simply kept in reserve, in a safe place, His reality and manifested a kind of shadow or symbol of Himself. He has emptied Himself and is *all* in Christ. . . . Christ is not simply the tip of the little finger of the Godhead, moving in the world, easily withdrawn, never threatened, never really risking anything. God has acted and given Himself totally, without division, in the Incarnation. He has become not only one of us but even our very selves."[25] I can't imagine that anyone, of any faith or none, can remain unmoved by the clarity and courage of this vision. It is also a call to engagement with the world and others, keenly heard by Merton.

Merton's prayers in his journal sometimes become the prayers of us all and sometimes stay rooted in his life and moment. Which it is probably depends on one's own life and moment. In mid-August he recorded a prayer which, like Dag Hammarskjöld's prayers in his journal *Markings,* written also in these years, exemplifies the act of writing as an act of prayer.[26] The prayer takes shape in the space between heartfelt thought and words that gather of themselves. It is here that we find the stunning phrase "solidity and ashes," his assessment of his life at that time. Kyrie eleison, Lord have mercy, is one of Christianity's ancient prayers, but it loses force unless the living re-create it.

> Lord have mercy.
>
> Have mercy on my darkness, my weakness, my confusion. Have mercy on my infidelity, my cowardice, my turning about in circles, my wandering, my evasions.
>
> I do not ask anything but such mercy, always and in everything, mercy.
>
> My life here—a little solidity and very much ashes.
>
> Almost everything is ashes. What I have prized most is ashes. What I have attended to least is, perhaps, a little solid.
>
> Lord have mercy. Guide me, make me want again to be holy, to be a man of God, even though in desperateness and confusion.
>
> I do not necessarily ask for clarity, a plain way, but only to go according to your love, to follow your mercy, to trust in your mercy.
>
> If I am to be condemned by men, make me strong and quiet under their condemnation and above all show me how not to condemn them in return, but to forget any harm they may have intended.
>
> Or not even to question their intentions.
>
> I do not go anywhere out of ambition—I seek nothing for myself. (That is: I want to seek nothing for myself.)
>
> Or perhaps I want to seek nothing at all if this be possible, but only to be led without looking and without seeking. For thus to seek is to find.[27]

Should we understand this extraordinary expression to be the fruit of Merton's months of struggle to come to terms with everything that had occurred and everyone in the circle of events? That seems right.

We must not turn aside for long from Merton's working environment. In mid-October, Dom James provided Dom Gabriel an update on how Fr. Louis was faring. "Well," he wrote, "he is something like the waves of the sea. His emotions some days carry him up to heaven—and some days they carry him to earth. . . . He is a sick person."[28] Dom James himself became something of a poet when he had in mind to describe Merton. The only poetry to which we can be certain he was regularly exposed was Psalms and other elements of the Latin liturgy; it was enough. Isaiah 57:20: *quasi mare fervens quod quiescere non potest*—like the tossing sea which cannot rest.

On his side, as 1960 drew to a close, Merton had a new insight, touchingly similar to a thought of Nelson Mandela's decades later: "Perhaps I am stronger than I think," he reflected in his journal. "Perhaps I am afraid of my strength and turn it against myself to make myself weak. Perhaps I am most afraid of the strength of God in me."[29]

[16]
A Deeper Kind of Dedication

"I HAVE BEEN SILENCE. I have been nacht und nebel for my war book. I have been put in the calabozo. I have been shut up in a tin can. I have been shrewdly suppressed at the right moment. I have been stood in the corner. I have been made to wear the cap. I have been tried and tested in the holy virtue of humility. I have been found wanting and tested some more. I have been told to shut up about wars, wars is not for Christians except to support."[1] This is Merton in a letter of June 1962 to his lifelong friend Robert Lax, poet, world wanderer, free spirit. It was their joy through the decades to write each other in scrambled language, a sub–*Finnegans Wake* mauling and re-creation of English. The wacky exercise must have helped Merton restore perspective: scarcely anything was so grave that it couldn't be converted into a divine comedy written by fools of God. And so it was in this letter. Merton was reporting on an expected, nonetheless heavy disappointment: a book of essays entitled *Peace in the Post-Christian Era* had been prohibited at the last minute by Dom Gabriel and his team of censors; it would not appear as a book in Merton's lifetime, although its contents would circulate discreetly among peace activists whom Merton reached by mail.[2] Two years of passionate effort, engagement, and writing separate this sadly comic notice from the first stirrings of political concern in Merton.

I cannot point to the precise moment of Merton's political awakening. He had been aware for years of the Catholic Worker movement in New York City among the poor, and he deeply admired one of its guiding spirits, Dorothy Day, a political activist and practitioner of nonviolence. They had stayed in touch from time to time. And then, Gethsemani was quite close to Fort Knox, a base for nuclear-armed Strategic Air Command bombers; as flights departed or returned, they often overflew the abbey. The hardware of nuclear war was not abstract for the community. But the strongest sign in his journal of political awakening occurs less than a week after the death of the Russian poet and novelist Boris Pasternak, author of *Doctor Zhivago,* with whom Merton had intermittently corresponded since 1958. Pasternak's abuse by the Soviet authorities and by many of his Russian literary peers after he was offered the Nobel Prize in Literature that year may have driven home for Merton a lesson about stupidity and injustice on the scale of nations that he had already learned on the minute scale of monasteries. In his first letter to Pasternak he had written, "Whatever may lie ahead for the world, I believe that men like yourself and I hope myself also may have the chance to enter upon a dialogue that will really lead to peace and to a fruitful age for man and his world."[3] In the week after Pasternak's death on May 30, 1960, Merton wrote out an informal vow in his journal.

> To discover all the social implications of the Gospel not by studying them but by living them, and to unite myself explicitly with those who foresee and work for a social order—a transformation of the world—according to these principles: primacy of the person (hence justice, liberty, against slavery, peace, control of technology, etc.). Primacy of wisdom and love (hence against materialism, hedonism, pragmatism, etc.).[4]

Merton had given thought to many of these themes in the past, but now he set out to approach them deliberately—"to the point at least," he wrote, "of reading and studying in full these questions not speculatively but in order to form my conscience and take such practical actions as I can."[5] By late November his exploration had taken him back to the writings of Mohandas Gandhi, in whom he found an axis of values and methods that would stay with him. "Gathering texts from Gandhi on non-violence," he recorded in his journal. "Sense of obscure struggle to find a genuinely true and honest position in this world and its belligerent affairs. I wish I knew where to stand. I think I stand with a Gandhi more than with anyone else. But how to transpose his principles to suit my own situation? . . . A growing obscure conviction that this country, having been weighed in the balance and found wanting, faces a dreadful judgment."[6] In 1965 he would publish an anthology of excerpts on nonviolence from Gandhi's writings and speeches, proof if proof were needed that he had taken Gandhi to heart.[7] The search for a point of view and a mission deriving from it continued into the fall of 1961, alongside much else: Merton was a pioneer of the art of multitasking, it was not only natural but necessary to him to have varied outer and inner themes in parallel motion. It was a way of being, of thinking combustibly, of ordering purposes and zones of experience from the inside out.

In April he was still searching and unsure. "To what extent is it simply a temptation," he asked himself, "for me to want to take some political position, as distinct from an ethical one? Are the two separable, for instance where war is concerned? . . . Opposition on the moral level demands some kind of open expression of one's position."[8] In late May, on the eve of Pentecost, when thoughts naturally turn to what must be communicated and by whom, infused with what spirit, Merton prayed: "Now Father I beg You to teach me to be a man of peace and to help bring peace to the world. To study here truth and non-violence, and patience and the courage to suffer for truth."[9] By the time fall arrived, he had made up his mind: he would take a position publicly. He wasn't slow to make or renew connections among Catholic peace activists, who recognized him as one of their own. But he was aware of his disadvantages. "I am now perfectly convinced," he wrote in October to a friend, "that there is one task for me that takes precedency over everything else:

working with such means as I have at my disposal for the abolition of war." This is large—but he had no illusions about his resources. "This is like going into the prize ring blindfolded and with hands tied, since I am cloistered and subject to the most discouragingly long and frustrating kinds of censorship on top of it. I must do what I can. Prayer of course remains my chief means, but it is also an obligation . . . to speak out."[10] He wrote in a similar vein to Fr. Daniel Berrigan, the young Jesuit destined to be a true friend and to play a major role in the American peace movement. In touch with Merton years earlier, Berrigan had resumed corresponding with him after reading Merton's first published article on peace issues.[11] "We are going to have to keep in touch with one another," Merton told Berrigan. "I don't have eyes and ears down here and others have to do my seeing for me."[12] This observation, true from start to finish of his peace initiative, points to issues we'll need shortly to explore.

Merton felt pressed into the unfamiliar world of political and moral controversy by the absence of prominent Catholic voices on the calamity of nuclear war. "Why this awful silence and apathy on the part of Catholics, clergy, hierarchy, lay people?" he asked Dorothy Day in August 1961.[13] By October his reading of the situation hadn't changed. "It appears that I am one of the few Catholic priests in the country who have come out unequivocally for a completely intransigent fight for the abolition of war."[14] Several years later, in spring 1963, when his freedom to write on war and peace had been curtailed, he didn't see the situation as greatly changed; there was still a succession of silences in America, broken from afar by Pope John XXIII through his famous encyclical, *Pacem in Terris,* released on April 11 of that year. Despite that powerful statement of principles and policy, change was slow in coming. Merton had been admonished that monks were expected to defer to bishops on public issues. But bishops in turn were expected to wait for the moral theologians to step forth. "And the moral theologians?" Merton asked in his journal soon after publication of *Pacem in*

Terris. "Sitting on their cans and preserving their reputations. This is one of the situations that keep the Church half dead."[15]

He did all that he possibly could to change the situation. Merton's first article on war and peace, "The Root of War Is Fear," appeared in the *Catholic Worker* for October 1961. Long priced at one cent, this newspaper had then and now has humble magic. It was the medium in which Dorothy Day and many others could week in and week out tell stories of poverty and hardship, faith and striving—of religion in action among the most needy in a city that cared little for them. Some in the U.S. government regarded it as Communist controlled; Merton regarded it as controlled by servants of the Lord.

A question has been waiting: As this storm gathered and broke, where was Dom James? Now that Merton had been brought to ground at Gethsemani, James was seemingly absent—but not actually so. At the end of 1959, Merton had surmised that "as long as I am in this monastery he doesn't care much what I do," and that proved true for years to come. Dom James recurs in Merton's journal with some regularity in the early 1960s as a topic for amazement, excoriation, contrition, and renewed amazement—the wheel turned with these not-so-festive flags fluttering from it. In September 1961 Merton acknowledged with pain that he was still angry over the treatment he had received two years earlier in Rome largely at Dom James's instigation. "I should love my abbot, my order, my community," he wrote. "But really I doubt if I do, I doubt if I can love them spontaneously. I am too obsessed by the unfairness, the injustice that was done me in Rome by the Abbot, and above all embittered that he was able to do this with a good conscience, subjectively, thinking himself perfectly right. And he does the same to everybody. His deviousness, his ambivalence, his trickery, his business manipulations are to him pure guileless simplicity because, while he does these things, he does them 'with a pure intention.'"[16] Merton understood that James was kind and considerate to him in some respects. "But all the time," he continued, "I cannot help feeling he is so for business reasons. . . . This I have to live with. . . . All I can do with the man is smile and be courteous and obedient and try not to argue . . . and of course I must understand and forgive."

Wouldn't it be possible to speak in some new way with Dom James, to clear new ground between them? "Impossible," Merton answers. "For twelve years I have failed to establish a real rapport, an understanding in which these things can be faced. There is just no meeting of minds; except on a superficial level. Only our 'well-meaning' efforts to communicate, which break down because we speak different languages. The only meeting is in the realm of perfectly acceptable clichés. Not cliché words but cliché ideas. A real idea has to be emptied of its content and turned into a stereotype before one can use it in a conversation with him. And yet he is so earnest about all those stereotypes!"

Perhaps we regret asking after Dom James at this moment when Merton was launching a brave new venture? Clearly, nothing had changed inside. Yet there was a change: Dom James's tolerance of Merton's peace writings and his discreet support in ways large and small *should* have surprised Merton but somehow didn't. Merton theorized the new latitude he was enjoying in different ways at different times. The first theory is familiar: Dom James didn't much mind what he did, provided he did it at the abbey. The second theory: real or feigned indifference. "It is certain I do not speak for the Abbot and it is good of him to let me speak at all when I often say things he disagrees with—or probably disagrees with, for he says nothing."[17] The third theory is broader in kind, from a letter to Dan Berrigan: "My own abbot always manages to show just enough good will and tolerance on the crucial issues to keep me hesitant about the next drastic step."[18] And there was even a fourth theory, again written to Berrigan. This was the most elaborate and interesting, offered as field notes for managing one's superior.

> My guess is that probably your Provincial wants to keep himself off some kind of a hook, and will probably look the other way as much as he can, which is what I would let him do if I were you. All I know is that one can eventually reach *modus agendi* with these people in which, as long as they do not feel that they are too involved, they will put up with a lot that they would not otherwise tolerate and think they are being generous about it. Also when people get thoroughly used to you being a bad boy, they will expect a certain amount and will not complain too much.[19]

These theories range in date from 1959 through 1966, but they all concern the same abbot and strike me as applicable to the first year of Merton's peace writings, which the late Msgr. William Shannon, irreplaceable guide to these materials, has called The Year of the Cold War Letters for reasons that will soon be clear. However, we need a fifth theory based on Dom James's unmistakable aid to Merton in that year, October 1961 to October 1962, and beyond. James may well have felt that Merton, now securely cloistered, needed latitude. Given the controversial content of his writings in this period, James would also have been aware that the order's censors, and ultimately Dom Gabriel, would eventually throw obstacles in Merton's way. Why, then, should Dom James add to Merton's miseries? There would be misery enough without him. All of this argues for a laissez-faire attitude, and there *was* that—but also more. Dom James allowed Merton to capture, so to speak, some of the monastery's communications resources and divert them when necessary to his campaign. Most important were the novices and perhaps others in the community who typed final drafts of Merton's articles and letters. That they were free to do so represents a permission that need not have been offered. And then, the mimeograph machine. Many readers today will have no concept of this one-celled precursor of today's photocopier and scanning devices. You typed onto a sheet of fascinatingly moist blue film, wrapped the film around the ink-filled drum of a tabletop printer, and let 'er rip. The result was any desired number of identical pages, each smelling like a grammar school exam. By this humble means Merton and his ad hoc monastic publishing team were able to operate what became a samizdat printing operation, loosely patterned on Russian underground models. Dom James allowed it.

He also gave Merton every possible break where censorship and membership were concerned. Under the order's rules, articles in small publications of limited influence were permitted without censorship; James applied this definition liberally and also permitted uncensored letters to the editor as an additional platform for Merton's messages. He authorized Merton to add his name, of course thoughtfully, to boards of directors and advisors of American peace organizations. He appears to have let the mails go through unhindered, and correspondence was the most crucial channel for Merton to know, to connect, to contribute as a writer. Merton had heard and rather believed that Dom James made photocopies of every single item of his mail apart from conscience matter, but he had no reason to think that James withheld mail—of which there were masses. As well, James authorized occasional meetings of peace activists in the hermitage, some of which amounted to coast-to-coast summit meetings in which, as we shall see, Merton played a crucial role. Further, James befriended Dan Berrigan, the rebellious and brilliant young Jesuit, and annually paid his way to and from the monastery, where he gave chapter talks quite apart from meeting privately with Merton. Though there might have been tremors of a "clash of civilizations," all was well—for example, Dom James once offered the services of the monastic barber to Merton's young, mostly long-haired friends, an offer patiently accepted. They surely emerged looking like choir monks, though they weren't.

I do not believe that Dom James was a peace activist in hiding. But he must have measured the forces—the imperative need to keep Merton at Gethsemani, Merton's passionate commitment to contributing a Catholic voice to the developing American forum on war and peace, the likelihood that the order's censors would come along in their own good time. Merton needed to breathe, after all; the long combat could not be sustained at the same level of intensity without unpredictable consequence. For all of these reasons he must have concluded that Father Louis could and should have his day. Merton has already told us that James said nothing for or against, but he *allowed;* that in itself was a statement. And the abbot had support for his laissez-faire policy from Dom Gabriel,of all people. When Dom Gabriel at long last wrote Merton in spring 1962 to foreclose publication of Merton's book *Peace in the Post-Christian Era,* ready for publication but unapproved, he put it this way: "You have wished to say what you think of nuclear war. Although in my view that was not exactly your role as a monk, several times I have allowed you to do so [*je vous ai laissé faire*]."[20]

Merton was fiercely productive in The Year of the Cold War Letters. Msgr. Shannon has collected eleven substantial articles on war and peace in his book *Passion for Peace: The Social Essays* and added to them a further sequence of twenty-one articles in the period 1963–68, predominantly on racial injustice in America, the Vietnam War, and aspects of nonviolence.[21] Speaking of some articles in this second sequence, Merton once said, "I can reach out with an article that is *near* but not *on* the forbidden target," that is, the folly of nuclear war.[22] Partially hidden alongside this flow of public communication was a flow of private communication now gathered in a book, *Cold War Letters,* which we owe again to Msgr. Shannon and his colleague Prof. Christine M. Bochen.[23] This is a collection of 111 letters written by Merton on issues of war and peace to recipients ranging from frontline peace activists to whom he was close to theologians, rabbis, psychiatrists, writers, and more.

The Cold War Letters return us to the unequal contest that emerged between the order's censors and the abbey's mimeograph machine—a contest that the censors appeared to win but, if so, only on points: the blindfolded boxer, as Merton described himself, remained standing and surprisingly effective. Already in October 1961, soon after his first article on war and peace appeared in the *Catholic Worker,* Merton wrote to Jim Forest—the best of men, a friend for the duration, later one of Merton's biographers—that he had "begged [the censors] to be cooperative if possible, but this means nothing. I don't think most of them have the slightest idea of the import of what is taking place, or if they do they have perhaps cultivated a kind of holy callousness that does not seem to me to have much to do with the Gospel of Christ or the spirit of the Church. Let's not blame them, however, but pray and hope they will come through."[24] They came through on some things, not on others, and it quickly became evident that a reliable alternative was needed to putting articles through the sticky censorship process. Apart from prayer and hope, it occurred to Merton in December that the abbey's mimeograph and mimeographs elsewhere—for example, in the office of W. H. "Ping" Ferry, another of his close frontline allies—could be pressed into service. So it was: Merton's letters, conveniently grouped, circulated among the peace activists with whom he was regularly in touch, and among their friends, and among *their* friends, for years to come. The process made a special kind of sense to him—equivalent, in its way, to Gandhi's humble spinning wheel. "I do feel," he wrote to Ferry in January, "that there is a lot of point in sending around copies of things in a small circle of interested people . . . , all the more meaningful because it lacks that mass, anonymous, stupefied quality that everything else has." In this letter devoted mainly to practical matters, he also modestly exemplified what he could best offer the peace-activist community: words of quiet wisdom, rooted in Christian vision, rooted in experience. "What is needed," he continued, "is really not shrewdness or craft, but what the politicians don't have: depth, humanity, and a certain totality of self-forgetfulness and compassion, not just for individuals but for man as a whole: a deeper kind of dedication."[25] A deeper kind of dedication—this is Merton speaking to his friends and to us, drawing from the sense and sound of words a call not easily forgotten. By January 1963, he could report to Jim Forest that "we are mimeographing an enlarged edition of CW letters. . . . It is quite a lot bigger and fuller, and we are doing a lot of copies."[26] Unnoticed by censors, protected by Dom James, the spinning wheel was whirring.

I rejoice to discover Merton's strongest, richest voice in letters to his friends in the antiwar movement and in certain Cold War Letters. I rejoice because the published articles of that period, while bold and true, often—not invariably—suffer from the deficiency he recognized from the beginning: he was not in the fray, had no frontline experience. A degree of abstraction in the place of direct observation, a somewhat fixed tone of indignation where the nuanced feelings of direct experience were needed, secondhand information about places he had never been and could not go: imperfect ingredients, although Merton's antiwar essays were influential and provocative at the time, and many readers today continue to value them. To my mind his best writings, be they based on his journal, on sparks from inner experience, on appreciations and translations of monks at work (desert fathers, Zen masters), or on tales of wandering teachers (Chuang Tzu) are very, very close to his experience. They are transcriptions of what has been lived. Early in this book, we spoke of him as a "scrutator," a monastic word whose meaning can be expanded to designate an observer and interpreter of all things directly encountered, including himself. This remained true; he was and is one of the great scrutators of modern literature.

One further point: he *lived* in his correspondence. There would hardly be so many books of his collected correspondence, and surely more to come, if the person-to-person act of composing and posting a letter were merely pragmatic on his part. Merton's correspondence with friends and even strangers in the peace movement contains much that is practical—about publications, needed ideas, and all else—but also passages that could come only from a spiritual director, unappointed, unofficial, yet influential from letter to letter, month to month. We can ask Dan Berrigan to clarify this theme for us. "In the Catholic community," he has said, "the role of Merton was absolutely crucial. Correspondence with Merton, visits to Merton, prayer with Merton, the wisdom of Merton . . . He had a great gift for digging out the essentials of a situation like ours. He wrote a famous letter, I think it was to James Forest, to the effect that 'you will not survive America unless you undertake a discipline of prayer and sacrament. Period.' That was the gist of his famous letter to a young peacemaker. . . . I came deeply to believe that, and to say and quote it because I believed it so deeply myself. We saw so many young people give up, give in, walk away. It was a long, hard road. We needed help along the way, and he gave it. He was very important to all of us."[27]

We needn't dwell overlong on this aspect of Merton's service in the peace movement, but it's essential to recognize what he brought, from what Dom Gabriel called "the hidden life," to his friends and colleagues. In a letter to Dorothy Day in the summer of 1960, when he was first recognizing the need to speak out, he included—out of the blue, from that good nowhere whence such things come—a poetic and religious reflection that no one else in our time could have written. It has to do with courage, with struggling on:

> We should in a way fear for our perseverance because there is a big hole in us, an abyss, and we have to fall through it into emptiness, but the Lord will catch us. Who can fall through the center of himself into that nothingness and not be appalled? But the Lord will catch us. He will catch you without fail and take you to His Heart.[28]

Merton exchanged more than ninety letters with Dan Berrigan, who with his brother Philip risked and incurred arrest and prison in the course of his campaigns for peace and, soon, against the Vietnam

War. Of course, they were far from the only ones. As Merton wrote to Berrigan in March 1962, "A lot of guys from the *Catholic Worker* were here . . . , went home enthused and are now in jail. I feel bad about it."[29] In the same letter he also wrote the following—to a fellow priest and poet whom he could fully expect to understand:

> There is an absolute need for the solitary, bare, dark, beyond-concept, beyond-thought, beyond-feeling type of prayer. Not of course for everybody. But unless that dimension is there in the Church somewhere, the whole caboodle lacks life and light and intelligence. It is a kind of hidden, secret, unknown stabilizer, and a compass too. About this I have no hesitations and no doubts, because it is my vocation; about one's vocation, after it has been tested and continues to be tested, one can say in humility that he knows. Knows what? That it is willed by God, insofar as in it one feels the hand of God pressing down on him. Unmistakably . . .

Merton's spiritual counsel to Berrigan often drew on his own experience of rebellion against Dom James. He was, in effect, some years ahead of Dan Berrigan, knew the road better, and served as a moderating influence. With incomparably more grace and warmth, he could sound like Dom James. "You do have to consider," he wrote Berrigan in 1963,

> the continuity of your work as a living unit. You must be careful not to rupture that continuity in a violent and drastic way without having an exceptionally grave reason and a rather evident sign that this is required precisely of *you*. By this I refer to the fact that a violent break with Superiors would tend to cast discredit on *all* the initiatives you have so far taken and render them all suspect. . . . If you allow this to happen . . . , you must consider that you are turning adrift those who have begun to follow you and profit by your leadership. And you are also at the same time wreaking havoc in the minds of Superiors, who were perhaps timidly beginning to go along with you.[30]

April 1962 and that month again in 1963 brought watershed moments in Merton's efforts to write peace. It was in April 1962 that Merton read a crucial letter from Dom Gabriel. It put an end to the cat-and-mouse game with the order's censors and simply ordered Merton to cease writing on the threat and madness of nuclear war. Dom Gabriel's letter has not come to light—we can see it reflected in Merton's comments to others—but a second letter of May 12 has much the same content. "It was doubtless difficult," Dom Gabriel wrote, "to completely refuse you the right to express your opinion on the question of nuclear war. But one can ask oneself whether, for yourself and for the cause you defend, it is better to permit you to speak once again or to invite you rather to remain silent." He reminded Merton that "your combat is conducted in the presence of the Lord and not amongst men. Your contribution to the common victory is the grace you obtain through your hidden effort in the Lord, in support of those who are responsible for word and action.... You understand that I do not ask you to take no interest in the fate of the world. But I believe you capable of influencing it through your prayer and your withdrawn life in God much more effectively than through your writings. And this is why I do not think I harm the cause you defend by asking you ... to abstain hereafter from writing on the subject of nuclear war, preparations for it, etc."[31] As we have noted already, this was not unexpected. "For a long time I have been expecting trouble with the higher Superiors," he wrote to Jim Forest, "and now I have it.... I have to be careful even with privately circulated stuff, like the mimeographed material.... In substance I am being silenced on the subject of war and peace.... It reflects an astounding incomprehension of the seriousness of the present crisis in its religious aspect. It reflects an insensitivity to Christian and ecclesiastical values, and to the real sense of the monastic vocation."[32]

Merton could be funny about the new restriction—after all, he knew it was coming. In a note to Forest he imagined his superiors asking, "Who do I think I am, and will I permanently shut up about everything except the Rosary."[33] He could also reach for his best thought about "the perhaps impossible task of purifying, humanizing, and somehow illuminating politics."[34] And he moved on. The Cold War Letters became a hidden institution, circulating his support, his ideas, and whatever wisdom he could summon to a discreet readership. As noted earlier, he turned his attention to social issues not proscribed by his superiors, and did so with a relatively easy heart. He had done all he could, and he had done it quickly.

In April 1963, Pope John XXIII issued the major statement *Pacem in Terris,* Peace on Earth. There seems to be little question that Merton influenced its perspective, particularly through a letter he sent to the pope in November 1961, when he was beginning to publish on war and peace. "The most agonizing problem here," he had written, "is the very grave threat of a nuclear war. . . . There are many who hate communist Russia with a hatred that implies the desire to destroy this nation. . . . Sad to say, American Catholics are among the most war-like, intransigent and violent; indeed, they believe that in acting this way they are being loyal to the Church. Just recently a very small peace movement, bringing Protestants and Catholics together, has come into being in the United States. I try to be a part of this movement as much as I can."[35] *Pacem in Terris* is a comprehensive statement of considerable length, but we should know from it these few words: "In this age which boasts of its atomic power, it no longer makes sense to maintain that war is a fit instrument with which to repair the violation of justice. And yet, unhappily, we often find the law of fear reigning supreme among nations and causing them to spend enormous sums on armaments" (paras. 127–28).

Merton read the encyclical with close attention and could not resist—simply couldn't—sending a few words tinged with bitterness to Dom Gabriel. "I . . . wanted to tell you," he wrote, "how interested I was by the encyclical *Pacem in Terris*. Now the Holy Father clearly says that war can no longer be used as an instrument of justice in a world that possesses nuclear arms. Fortunately he does not need to be approved by the censors of the Order in America, for they said very energetically last year that this thesis, when I proposed it myself, was wrong, scandalous, and I don't know what more."[36]

A mystery remains. James received Dom Gabriel's first letter of prohibition at the beginning of the year—but he passed it on to Merton only in April. Msgr. Shannon comments that this too was a kindness: Dom James must have wanted to give Merton as much time as possible to finish and publish the articles he had on his worktable. It is not at all clear how James justified this maneuver to the abbot general, or whether he even bothered to do so. Merton was puzzled by the delay. "Yesterday Rev. Father gave me a bunch of letters and reports, the main item being a letter of the General dated Jan. 20th which Rev. Father for some unaccountable reason had been saving up."[37] The unaccountable reason must have been Dom James's unaccountable willingness to give Merton his chance.

[17]

Who Can Say?

We have been looking at major correspondence filled with crucial attitudes and decisions at the forward edge of Merton's life. But there were other written exchanges at Gethsemani, so ephemeral that they had no reason to survive and find a place in archives—though they did. Such minor survivals possess a peculiar poetry, as if through them we perceive daily life with special clarity. In his journal Merton meant to write: it was a composition. But this typed note is not a composition:

> Dear Fr Eudes
> I don't know if you saw the note on the door opposite yours, but about eleven thirty last night as the corn drier was running all night and I wasn't getting any sleep, I came down to use that room. Fortunately the bed was stripped, so I didn't mess it up.
> Thanks, In Jesu
> brmlouis[1]

The scene is easily imagined: in the midst of the nightly Great Silence, a whirring fan keeps Merton up, he finds refuge elsewhere but has the courtesy to pin a handwritten note on the door to alert his friend and fellow priest John Eudes of his whereabouts. And next morning types this further note to ensure that the first was received. All this in Jesu, remembered in the smallest of things. Another example: a handwritten note from Merton to John Eudes about a scrap of music notation or commentary that had somehow come to hand.[2] Carefully inspecting what he called "the palimpsest"—he was already having a good time—Merton concluded that it was almost certainly an "opus chrysogonicus," referring to a community member, Fr. Chrysogonus Waddell, the musicologist and composer who wrote many of the psalm tone patterns and some of the hymns still in use at Gethsemani. The deliberate fanciness of Merton's word choices, his witty dip into monastic Latin, speaks to his affection for Chrysogonus in a way that larger documents might not. We can sense the emotional texture of life—easy assurance between Merton and John Eudes, warmth toward Chrysogonus.

Merton lived for growth. He never expressed this fundamental of his identity better than in a note written at the hermitage, perhaps soon after he began to live there full-time in 1965. "To say that I am a child of God is to say, before everything else, that I grow. That I begin. A child who does not grow becomes a monster. The idea 'Child of God' is therefore one of living growth, becoming, possibility, risk, and joy in the negotiation of risk. In this God is pleased: that His child grows in wisdom and grace."[3] His impulse to grow inwardly gave him a yardstick by which he could, often with pain, measure the monastic environment. "There is something lacking in this life here," he wrote in summer 1964,

> not essentially perhaps, but the way we are living it in practice. Not that it is not strict, or fervent, but do the strictness and fervor have any meaning—beyond satisfying the religious compulsions of a certain type of person that thrives here? After twenty-three years I can say that I have never seen any serious evidence that the strictness of the life as we interpret it was anything to really deepen the spiritual life of the monks. It keeps them in line, but there is no development. The life is static, if you like it is safe, it gets nowhere.[4]

Anything, anyone, any occasion that repeatedly blocked Merton's impulse toward inner growth was likely to cause turmoil: questioning, rejection, remorse for rejection, search to situate the difficulty in a larger religious attitude of forgiving love or penitential acceptance. "Scripture conference in Chapter today," he recorded in spring 1964. "Impression of the whole group sinking deeper and deeper into boredom and resignation until finally, at the 'discussion' when the same dutiful ones as always stood up to speak, the whole place was enveloped in dense spiritual and intellectual fog. Is this irremediable? Perhaps, all things considered, it really is. A community of men dedicated to the contemplative life without too much sense of spiritual things. Earnestness cannot compensate for such a lack."[5]

Merton had another element of ineradicable identity to deal with in himself: he couldn't stand what he experienced as empty display. To his misfortune, Dom James's sincere love of liturgy, including its more elaborate, festive forms, upset Merton nearly beyond measure. As we know, some of Dom James's letters home to the community when he was traveling included meticulously detailed accounts of worship services, written as if he were a choreographer delighting in movement and its capacity to convey meaning (fig. 8). A later page of this book has a notable example of his choreographic sensibility. But within that innocent interest there must have lurked something else that Merton could not abide. Twice in 1963 there were pontifical masses at Gethsemani, celebrated with every yard of fine fabric, every ceremonial cape and glove and jewel in the monastery's closet. Merton was not happy with Dom James on Easter Sunday 1963.

> The less said about the Easter celebration the better. Pomposity, phoniness, display, ultra-serious, stupid. Interminable pontifical mummering, purple zucchetto, long train, Mexican novice as train bearer (he always manages to get a Mexican or a Filipino or a Negro to carry his tail), all of course for the "glory of God." The Church was morally, spiritually stifling with solemn, unbreathable unrealities. . . .
>
> The spring outside was sacred. At the lake, Easter afternoon,

FIG. 8. Dom James Fox celebrating Mass at Gethsemani, 1950s.

the purity of the green buds, the wind skimming the surface of the water, the utter silence, and a muskrat slowly swimming to the other side![6]

FIG. 9. Dom James Fox vested for a Pontifical Mass, 1960s.

The same offense was committed in mid-August, causing the same reaction with a still closer look at dress code.

> Again—the pompous absurdity of Pontifical Mass. I don't usually even look at the sanctuary. Happened to glance at the throne, and the Abbot standing on his platform a little above the general melée—saw his hands and his white gloves. What for? Along with

FIG. 10. Dom James Fox vested for a Pontifical Mass, detail.

> all the other superfluities, the meaninglessness of white gloves and a ring (outside the glove of course).
>
> There are many like myself in the community. The Abbot claims he loves simplicity, but in fact these masses are contrived largely because he wants them—along with . . . others who like a display, and much singing.[7]

I dwell on this further element of discord between Merton and the abbot because a remarkable surviving photograph of Dom James in pontifical vestments allows us to participate (figs. 9 and 10). The traditions of the Church in that era or today are not at issue, whether one responds warmly to the elaboration of costume or, like Merton, turns away. Most interesting, to my eye, is the attitude of the man inside the gorgeous shell. How to read him? Is this man, obviously ascetic, straining to be as he feels he must be or to project what he feels he must project: an otherworldly, hieratic condition, a living symbol of holiness? It seems so. I confess that the image saddens me. It reminds me of the inhumane pressure we can impose on ourselves in the name of the highest good we know.

In the interest of objectivity, I must report that on suitable occasions Merton would wear the elegant stole he had received from Pope John XXIII, a gesture regarded by some members of the community as immodest.[8] He also thought highly of a beat-up denim jacket supplied to him by Fr. Alan Gilmore when he was wardrobe keeper; he had been offered a new one. Merton wears it in many photos of the 1960s.[9]

A few weeks earlier in a letter to a friend, Merton was saying that "I think it is salutary to accept the absurdity and contradictions of life in good part, this is a very effective penance. Unfortunately I get angry and disgusted a lot of the time, and I suppose that spoils it to some extent."[10] Questioning, rejection, remorse, questioning anew—this was Merton's round in these years, but only in the external forum, in the space between himself and Dom James. In the internal forum, his true workshop, where he was an observer, writer, poet, and soon visual artist, these were overwhelmingly creative years.[11] It is as if he were gathering his team for a new effort of large magnitude, a team composed of respected ancients—the desert fathers, Zen masters of China and Japan, the Taoist sage Chuang Tzu, the medieval Muslim mystic Ibn Abbad—and living contemporaries ranging from Dan Berrigan and his friends to thoughtful priests, rabbis, theologians, artists, and writers such as the formidable Czesław Miłosz, with whom he maintained a gravely questioning correspondence. The ancients he published in translation, his own perspective made clear in introductions. The contemporaries he learned from, taught, and listened to; they were his conversation partners. And among them one stands apart from others as his teacher, a second and wholly authentic abbot: D. T. Suzuki, the Zen scholar and author. From this extremely rich context of ancient and modern companions, and from his privacy as a contemplative seeker—a person drawn, however awkwardly and sufferingly, to look within and see more than himself—Merton's best writings of his last decade emerged. I am thinking particularly of the prose poem *Hagia Sophia* (1962); *The Way of Chuang Tzu* (1965), one of his own favorites; *Raids on the Unspeakable* (1966); *Conjectures of a Guilty Bystander* (1966); the two books on Zen (1967, 1968), *The Climate of Monastic Prayer* (posthumously published, 1969); and among shorter works *Day of a Stranger* (1967) and "A Letter on the Contemplative Life" (1967, published posthumously in *The Monastic Journey* [1977]). The immense correspondence of the 1960s, like the complete journals, would wait longer for publication, but they are now part of the canon of Merton's writings, larger perhaps than he could possibly have anticipated in his lifetime.

Merton didn't feel that he had many more years to live. It's true that his health was, to say the least, imperfect—his rugged appearance concealed chronic problems—but his sense that time was pressing also had some more-internal source. Be that as it may, he understood without self-congratulation that his writings represented a very considerable achievement and in future would be read. For that reason he was willing to cooperate with the editor of *A Thomas Merton Reader* (1962) and with librarians at what was then Bellarmine College (Louisville) to create a Thomas Merton Room furnished with a collection of first editions, manuscripts published and unpublished, and other memorabilia. This was the origin of today's Thomas Merton Center at Bellarmine University. Needless to say, Dom James was of two minds about the project. On one hand he thought it made sense to store Merton archives elsewhere, why not at a nearby Catholic institution of learning? On the other hand, the project was an obvious departure from the hidden life of self-denial.[12] On his side, Merton was wary of Dom James. An uncertain politician when his own affairs were at stake, he proposed a pathetic scheme to his friend and adviser, Dan Walsh, in the fall of 1963: "About the 'Collection,'" he wrote, "anytime that Rev. Fr. gets the sense that there is an exuberant activity going on in connection with it, he is going to feel mad, frustrated, and gloomy. I would suggest that the information sent here be kept to what is really necessary. . . . Rev. Fr. should get of course all that he is entitled to, but I would suggest restraint in accidentals. . . . Do you think Bellarmine could offer *him,* Rev. Father, an honorary degree? That might 'cement the relationships' and calm some of his anxieties. . . . Or am I wrong?"[13]

How much do we need to know of daily joys and irritations at the Abbey of Gethsemani in the reasonably tranquil year 1963? "Dom James wrote one of his letters from Mepkin, mostly about chickens," Merton dourly noted in May.[14] It's true that James often gave first place in his letters to the economic activities of monasteries he visited—we have seen a sample—and the egg business at Mepkin, pitched to an industrial scale, delighted and fascinated him. He returned to the topic of eggs and chickens several years later in another letter from Mepkin. "They have about 23,000 chickens, and they make a beautiful sight. . . . The chickens, being pagans, do not observe the Sabbath, and . . . lay just as many eggs on Sunday and Feast of Sermon as they do on Monday, Tuesday, (etc.). . . . So, the chickens really swing the monastery . . . as regards arranging the daily horarium."[15] It's good to see Dom James happy, even if his happiness is not Merton's. "Letter from Dom James read in refectory today," Merton again noted a few months later. "About his visitations at the Genesee, in Utah, etc. These foundations certainly sound dull. . . . Dom James says what he sees and that is not much."[16] Let us leave monk and abbot to this undeclared combat; we must look elsewhere. A few days after his reaction to James's flat field report, Merton came across an enigmatic practice of the desert fathers in his reading—"vomiting up the interior phantoms, the doubter, the double"—and quoted from a source: "The desert fathers practiced this grandiose operation in place of everything [else] and once and for all."[17] This grandiose operation was integral also to Merton's way: to strive to free himself of resentment and self-defeating doubt, to strive to move freely in life without a burdensome, chattering double. Let there be chickens, even twenty-three thousand of them. And let there be love.

In cooperation with other American abbots of the order, Dom James had laid plans for a meeting of abbots and novice masters in 1964 at Gethsemani. "I was told, by implicit and equivocal hints," Merton noted, "that I would be expected to give them all spiritual conferences."[18] Infinitely irritating! He felt caged—he knew himself to be caged, the event was foreseen for Gethsemani precisely because James wanted Merton's participation but wouldn't permit him to travel. "When the canary is asked to sing," Merton fumed, "well, he is expected to sing merrily and with spontaneity. It is true that I have a nicer cage than any other canary in the order. . . . But this upsets me so that I cannot sleep. . . . My . . . neurosis runs like a sore, and I know it, and see it, and see that I am helpless. . . . And am, of course, guilty." But this was a moment when Merton was genuinely ashamed the next day. "Doubtless there is truth in my intuitions about the abbot. But in all his complexity there is also a good will that has to be recognized, and a sincerity—a quest for truth that is quite genuine. . . . It makes no sense to oscillate . . . from the good points of another to his bad points. . . . There is finally a simpler, more existential way of . . . accepting facts. And it is this, not sterile moral analysis, that is demanded of a Christian. The fact remains that I have to give those conferences, I can give them and I don't have to be so frantic, so suspicious, so resentful. . . . There is after all a common sincerity in a common quest for rational solutions. I should be able to join in this too."

The reconciliation he reached in this night and day tumbled far into him. When he was free the next morning, perhaps after Mass, to look out over Gethsemani's land, he saw and felt much neither seen nor felt before—as if he remembered himself, the one he had lost:

> Marvelous vision of the hills at 7:45 A.M. The same hills as always, as in the afternoon, but now catching the light in a totally new way, at once very earthly and very ethereal, with delicate cups of shadow and dark ripples and crinkles where I had never seen them, and the whole slightly veiled in mist so that it seemed to be a tropical shore, a new discovered continent. And a voice in me seemed to be crying, "Look! Look!" For these are the discoveries, and it is for this that I am high on the mast of my ship (have always been) and I know that we are on the right course, for all around is the sea of paradise.[19]

Merton's capacity for discovery and his ability to convert discovery into startling, truthful words is always new, as we read him. "High on the mast of his ship"—but how low he had been just the night before. This is not bipolar disorder; it is living fully in light of an authentic spirituality that can encompass wide swings, sometimes with grace, always with perseverance.

In mid-November the monastery received news of the death of Dom Gabriel Sortais, the long-serving abbot general, ill in recent months. Merton explored their relations in the privacy of his journal. "He was often angry with me, and I must say I was often angry with him. He had the good grace to listen if I was in earnest. . . . I suppose in a way I was very fond of him . . . and his honest, Trappist spirit. . . . It is due to him and Dom James that my attempt to leave the order . . . was blocked, and perhaps not too justly or rightly. I do not say I am grateful for that. Perhaps it was for the best, however. Who can say?"[20]

[18]

The Tea, the Joy

MERTON AND OTHER senior community members cheerfully tormented Dom James as he was leaving for the general chapter in France, which would elect the new abbot general. Three of them separately, as if conspiring, though they hadn't, told him that *he* might just be elected. It was enough to keep him up all night.[1] Merton's view was that Dom James knew too little French, too little of the French Cistercian houses, and had too narrow a concept of monasticism. Still, there was a chance. In the event, the new abbot general was Dom Ignace Gillet, a man of scholarly temperament and, like Dom Gabriel, an experienced monastic leader who had been a prisoner of war in Nazi Germany. Merton and Dom Ignace would not meet until a visitation at Gethsemani in 1967, during which Merton translated for him one evening and found him kind and well-meaning. Well-meaning as he was, he continued the policies of Dom Gabriel where Merton's scope for travel and publication was concerned.

At the beginning of 1964, struggling yet again to distance his perceptions of injustice suffered at the hands of Dom James, Merton realized that he had no model to follow. He wasn't a good monk by standard definition, but he was *something,* and that something deserved its chance. "I have no need to judge and no capacity," he wrote of Dom James, not for the first time. "What matters is the struggle to make the right adjustment in my own life, and this upsets me because there is no pattern for me to follow, and I don't have either the courage or the insight to follow the Holy Spirit in freedom."[2] Words written in January. By midsummer in the year beginning to unfold, he had very different thoughts: "Some conclusions: literature, contemplation, solitude, Latin America—Asia, Zen, Islam, etc. All these things combine in my life. It would be madness to make a 'monasticism' by simply excluding them. I would be less a monk. Others have their own way, I have mine."[3] It was a year that worked change, not only in Merton.

In a late memoir, Dom James took some pride in the fact that he had asked Merton to write very few things. A request he unhesitatingly made was for the script of a short film to be shown in the Vatican Pavilion at the New York World's Fair, opening in 1964 and continuing into the next year.[4] A prayer written by Merton was distributed as a prayer card. The pavilion proved to be a vastly successful effort to project the spirituality and artistic riches of the Church to a global audience. In a white oval building with a glittering tiara-like dome, the pope had seen fit to display for the first time outside of the Vatican Michelangelo's *Pietà,* the magnificently realized sculpture of Mary cradling the body of Jesus in her lap. The fame of the image made the pavilion the second-most-visited in the world's fair; the numbers were astonishing—in excess of twenty-seven million visitors, some carried past the sculpture on three tiered moving walkways, fewer taking time to view it from a stationary platform. The pavilion was strongly sponsored by the New York diocese and Cardinal Francis Spellman, who dispatched to Gethsemani a member of his office to coach Merton on what sort of script was needed. There must have been much unspoken satisfaction that the Church and New York turned to Gethsemani and Merton for this task. Merton cannot have been listening too closely to the emissary from New York. He drafted a script "mostly about charity, peace, racial justice, etc.," reflecting the concerns he longed to share with all people of goodwill. The draft was returned. What was needed, Merton summarized, was an "apologetic text-book piece on the Church as the one true Church" without "all this ecumenical business." He tried again—obedience truly mattered to him—and wrote a script that he hoped would still have "a few lines that will have meaning for someone outside the Church. . . . Will it even support Catholics in their convictions—or just be another four minutes of familiar jargon?" I have not seen the short film shown at the pavilion, but if the prayer card suggests its tone, it would have been difficult to find those few lines. The prayer begins "Grant all men light to see You, by faith, in Your Holy Church, the Mystical Body of Your divine Son," and on from there in the same vein. At the time he was writing for the pavilion he recorded a new thought in his journal: "Real expression—a spontaneous elucidation of what we do not yet know rather than a final statement of what we have 'acquired.' But we go at it the other way: we pretend to say what we know. Our genuine surplus is what we do not know."[5] The Church hierarchy was terribly unable to hear or draw on his authentic voice.

At some point in 1963, rambling as usual in the woods, Merton came upon a massive boulder that suggested to him the possibility of a dry Zen garden at the abbey. There were strange boulders out there, resembling giant sponges from an ancient sea. The garden would need this boulder and others, and additional elements such as just the right gravel raked into just the right watery pattern and isolated plantings of some kind.[6] A neglected, weedy shelf of land adjoining the novitiate invited the project and, naturally with Dom James's permission, it began to take shape in fall 1963. As noted earlier, Merton had been reading Zen for nearly a decade and corresponding with its foremost scholarly exponent, D. T. Suzuki, since 1959. He had quietly incorporated elements of Zen into his contemplative practice and possessed a growing knowledge of the tradition's concepts and tools, among them the repertory of koans—attractively enigmatic questions that serve as meditation themes. In 1962, he wrote to a Chinese friend, "There are times when one has to cut right through all the knots, and the Zen view of things is a good clean blade."[7] It's surprising that Dom James permitted a reasonable facsimile of a Zen garden in the novitiate, but the project met his first criterion: Merton as Zen gardener was bound to the abbey. As well, there was already a Zen garden at Portsmouth Priory in the care of Dom Aelred Graham, the Benedictine author of *Zen Catholicism* (1963); Merton's would break new ground locally but not in the larger sense. James knew scarcely anything of Zen, but he knew when a project was labor-intensive, as this one was, and without irony that would have made good Trappist sense to him.[8]

There was a further and greater surprise. In early June Merton received a letter from Suzuki's secretary telling him that, were he able to come to New York City a little later in the month, Dr. Suzuki would be extremely happy to meet him. Not long before, Merton had been examining the consequences—yet again—of the absolute travel restriction imposed on him. "As I go on," he wrote in his journal, "the ways of escape are progressively closed, renounced, or otherwise abandoned. I know now that I am really committed to stability here, and that even the thought of temporary travel is useless and vain. I know that my contacts with others of like mind by mail, etc. are relatively meaningless, though they may have some raison d'être. I know that my writing solves nothing for me personally and that it has created some problems which are still unresolved. . . . That my position is definitively ambiguous and my job is to accept this with the smallest possible amount of bad faith."[9] Along this familiar path of thought, he had reached a familiar destination, though cloaked in darker light than usual: the resolve to accept his circumstances in the monastic spirit of obedience, with a minimum of what the Rule of Saint Benedict, a document for the centuries, calls "murmuring."

Some days after this journal entry, the letter arrived. "I thought about it," he wrote, "and since it is probably the only chance I will ever have to speak to [Suzuki], I thought it important enough to ask Dom James' permission. I certainly did not think he would give it, but, somewhat reluctantly, he did, and a flight is booked for me next Monday 15th."[10] What was Dom James thinking? Unknown. It seems very unlikely that he had time to consult with the abbot general; the decision must have been his own. He may have felt that a three-day trip to a reasonably nearby city to visit with a ninety-four-year-old sage, with agreed restrictions on Merton's freedom to contact other people, might serve in the future as a model modest in all respects. What Merton said and what Dom James thought at this watershed moment is curiously undocumented, as if both men dropped out of their harrowing shared narrative, and the furious letter and journal writing that surrounds it, to try something else, something freer.

Instead of the explosive joy we might expect in Merton, the prospect of travel to New York caused him acute anxiety. His resource in the face of that anxiety was to immerse the opportunity in the sea of religion. "It was God's will for me to ask, and for some reason I should go, not only for my own benefit. I am not supposed to understand, but have trust. There is more here than I know." Replying promptly to Dr. Suzuki, Merton expressed his grateful acceptance of the invitation and alluded to the conditions set by his abbot: "I must ask you not to let this be too widely known.... It should not become generally known around New York as this would cause difficulties.... I hope to see you in the best of health and spirits."[11] Merton was to come and go with a sole focus. Living in a dormitory at Columbia University, his alma mater, saying Mass at the nearby church where he converted, eating in local restaurants, many of which hadn't changed since he knew them, he willingly accepted the anonymity James had asked of him.

I have written at some length in the past about Merton's visit with Dr. Suzuki.[12] It goes nearly without saying that as soon as he reached New York—even from the air as he approached—he was altogether happy; no further anxiety. The recognition we need here is that he met in Dr. Suzuki, at last, a living spiritual father—

an abbot in all but name with whom he felt instinctively at home. Merton was once a Columbia graduate student exploring the poetry of William Blake, the nineteenth-century poet, graphic artist, and mystic. "Damn braces: Bless relaxes," Blake had memorably written. The conversations of Merton and Suzuki were in that spirit. There are several homages to Suzuki in Merton's writings, among them this:

> One had to meet this man in order to fully appreciate him. He seemed to me to embody all the indefinable qualities of the "Superior Man" of the ancient Asian, Taoist, Confucian, and Buddhist traditions. Or rather in meeting him one seemed to meet that "True Man of No Title" that Chuang Tzu and the Zen Masters speak of. And of course this is the man one really wants to meet. Who else is there? In meeting Dr. Suzuki and drinking a cup of tea with him I felt I had met this one man. It was like finally arriving at one's own home. A very happy experience, to say the least. . . . I did feel that I was speaking to someone who, in a tradition completely different from my own, had matured, had become complete, and had found his way.[13]

"The tea, the joy," he wrote in his journal after the first of two visits with Suzuki. One joy, "profoundly important to me," was "to experience the fact that there really is a deep understanding between myself and this extraordinary and simple man." Another was to feel so magically at home with him and with his secretary, Mihoko Okamura. "For once in a long time felt as if I had spent a moment in my own family."[14] Both experiences were crucial. In dialogue with Dr. Suzuki he could measure how far he had come through his years and struggles and strivings in the monastery—so much farther than he thought. A confirmation of this order would occur just once more, but few are needed: in conversation with the Dalai Lama in the fall of 1968. As for feeling profoundly at home with the ancient sage and his young companion, this too was a confirmation: that the orphaned child, the monastic misfit, remained undamaged. His heart was intact.

Dr. Suzuki remarked to Merton that he should come to Japan. "He said it with meaning," Merton noted, "not in a polite formula. And I know I should go there."[15] The opportunity wasn't far off. In mid-September Merton received a letter from a well-known Jesuit scholar, Fr. Heinrich Dumoulin, professor at Sophia University (Tokyo) since the 1930s and author of a succession of respected books on the history of Zen Buddhism and Buddhist themes, many of them published after Merton's death. With the support of his superiors in Japan, Fr. Dumoulin invited Merton to spend time at the university, to visit monasteries (Zen and Catholic), to immerse himself for a time in Zen culture, about which he was thus far writing from a distance. The idea had initially occurred to Fr. Dumoulin—it "flashed upon my mind," he wrote—in conversation with a retired Cistercian abbot, ethnically Japanese, whom Merton had met.[16] Merton was both thrilled and alarmed to receive this invitation: thrilled because it made sense, alarmed because permission was so unlikely—Japan at length was a different matter from New York for three days. Responding some days later to Dumoulin's kind letter of invitation, Merton said that he had mentioned it to Dom James, who "seemed a bit shaken by the totally unusual nature of the request. . . . I have asked him to look at it objectively and give it his serious consideration, which I know he will do."[17] Merton was somewhat wishful; he could commit unreservedly to leading "a fully monastic life" in Japan rather than accepting invitations to give talks here and there, but he imagined that "Fr Abbot would regard Zen communities as equivalent to our own monasteries." Terribly unlikely. "Naturally," he concluded, "my superiors must decide and I leave the ultimate solution in their hands, in a spirit of faith and detachment. But thank you most warmly for thinking of me, and please keep the issue in your good prayers." He did suggest that Fr. Dumoulin write to Dom Ignace; that letter was duly written.

The very day he replied to Dumoulin, Merton typed out a formal petition to Dom James in which he did everything possible to position the opportunity not only as of greatest importance for his spiritual development but also of importance "for the community here and indeed for the whole Church, since today relations with non-Christian religions are being given much attention and are regarded as one of the most important tasks of the Church"—he was thinking of pronouncements from the Second Vatican Council, still in session.[18] "I ask this permission," he wrote, "not as an exception and deviation from my contemplative life, but as something that leads directly to a completion of what I have been called to the monastery to seek." He used every argument he could think of, some quite far-fetched: "It will . . . be equivalent to an experiment in depth psychology, as if I were undergoing analysis, and this has eminent value. I am sure both Fr Eudes and Dr. Wygal will support me in this wholeheartedly." Understanding that Dom James would consult the abbot general, he encouraged that consultation and hoped for their joint permission at least "to go to one of our houses in Japan, and there visit from time to time the places where the Zen discipline is studied."

There was, of course, an exchange of letters between Dom James and the abbot general. James was suspicious of Fr. Dumoulin's motives, and even somewhat suspicious of his order, as if old mistrust between Cistercians and Jesuits persisted. "In the first place," he wrote to Dom Ignace, "it is necessary to remember that Father D. is a Jesuit. . . . No matter what he may say, . . . it is easy to see that the main reason Father D. is pushing Father L., and trying to influence you, is to have Father L. over in Japan for Father D.'s own advantages. He would show him around to the various monasteries, have him give talks to the students, etc. . . . You know, as well as I do. . . , that Father L. would not go to Japan to stay in a Trappist monastery. . . . Father D. would have him under his control, and show him all over Japan. . . . It would be publicized all over the world."[19] Dom James was advancing now toward a conclusion: "I believe Father L. can do more to bring union between Catholics and pagans and Buddhists by staying in his Trappist monastery, and offering up the sacrifice of a trip to Japan—offering up his prayers and sacrifices to Almighty God in holocaustic love and a true spirit of self-denial and immolation to God, than by this trip to Japan." This is Dom James unmistakably angry, insisting that his own spirituality of self-immolation and holocaustic love should apply in this instance also. It is not clear what he means here by pagans; there had been no question of pagans, but it was one of his anger words, signaling how thoroughly upset he was.

The issue came up again between Merton and Dom James early in November, as James reported to his superior. "What I think will really pacify him, in regard to this Japanese trip," James wrote, "is to think that you have really taken time to consider it—that you . . . did not listen to what he, or I, may have written to you."[20] But of course Dom Ignace *was* listening to James. He had adopted James's longstanding attitudes toward good Fr. Louis. In mid-November Dom Ignace demonstrated how thoroughly he had done so in a letter to James. "It does seem that there is in [Fr. Louis] an element of impulsiveness: he seems capable of allowing himself to be invaded, carried away by a desire, without taking the time and perhaps even without the strength to control it. Under the influence of such an impulse, it must be very difficult for him to judge serenely and objectively, for himself and 'for the Church' (as he wrote me), the timeliness, usefulness, and providential meaning of a project such as this journey to Japan."[21]

Early in the following year, as if prior and briefer lessons needed reinforcement, Dom James sent the abbot general a ten-page, single-spaced letter of the kind we have seen in the past written to Fr. Riccardo Lombardi and to the Sacred Congregation for Religious. Every topic is covered anew: the terrible, deprived childhood; early years in a Protestant milieu "that places much stress on emotions,

FIG. 11. Ink drawing by Thomas Merton, ca. 1964.

feelings, private judgment . . . and lax ideas about obedience and authority." And then, how close Dom James is to Fr. Louis: "For some 13 years he has been my Confessor." And then his Pied Piper genius: "He is very discerning and penetrating. . . . He is essentially an artist and poet . . . , captivating and attractive to so many people, no matter what he is writing about." And then his emotional problems: "His emotions are definitely out of balance, and in many respects quite immature. . . . a person who is very impetuous—'ex abrupto'—precipitous—dashing off on a tangent at the first 'primo primi.'" And then a new admission, difficult to square with the alleged closeness between them: "I suppose, in his mind, I am his worst 'bête noire.'" And then the long history of Fr. Louis's failed attempts to leave the monastery for some other monastic destination. "I could not see God's Will in this." The fire tower incident. The indult refused. And most recently the petition to study Zen in Japan. On this topic he quoted Merton, who had told him that he wanted "to get to some Zen Buddhist monastery, and live there for a while—living their life, if I can. I know it is very tough, their meditations, etc.—perhaps I would only last a day. But I need . . . a thing like that." And, as in past letters, James didn't neglect to infantilize Merton's response to the invitation from Japan: "He was excited about this dream that came to him so suddenly as a little boy at Christmastime or Birthday, when he gets a new toy or a new drum." And toward the end of the letter, the recurrent doubt as to whether Merton, once released from the abbey, would return. "What strange, fantastic conduct might he become embroiled in? Does he not need the control of the four walls of the monastery? . . . Has not God's kind Providence brought him within these four walls to protect himself against himself?" And the standard request for utter confidentiality: "Of course, it is not necessary to add that all this information be handled with the greatest and absolute confidence." We can obliquely rediscover Dom James's recurrent impression of Merton's energy—"ex abrupto," "dashing off"—in his ink drawings and prints from the hermitage years (fig. 11).

Thank goodness, Merton had friends. He heard at the very end of 1964 from John C. H. Wu, with whom he had been collaborating for several years on the texts that would be published as *The Way of Chuang Tzu* in 1965. Wu was a distinguished lawyer in the Republic of China, a Catholic convert, and the author of books on Zen, Catholic spirituality, and related topics. He and Merton had met at Gethsemani, and they collaborated from afar without difficulty. Wu had heard that Merton was denied permission to visit Japan and experience Zen practice—and made light of it in the most warming, magical way. "Our Lord was a Fire-Eater," he wrote. "So are you, Father! . . . I am tickled by what you tell me about the decision about your going to Japan. Their reasons, I am sure, are wrong, but their decision seems to me to be right. You may be shocked by this statement of mine, but, Father, the truth is that there is more Zen in your hermitage than in any of the Zen halls.... For you, Father, you are already *yourself,* the 'Original Face'; who is everywhere, including Japan, and nowhere, not even in Gethsemani."[22] What a dear and inspiring letter. As Merton closed the books on the year and no doubt noticed that he was again running a deficit, he must have been cheered by his friend.

[19]

A Hermit Now

WITH THE GENIUS FOR DESIGN of Providence, two wholly unrelated topics became entangled in fall 1964: Merton's invitation to Japan and Dom James's changing view of the hermit life. The abbot's attitude, rigidly opposed for many years, had considerably altered in recent years: he had authorized construction of the ecumenical retreat house in the woods with full understanding that it was also a hermitage for Merton; he had permitted Merton to spend days there, and more recently permitted him to sleep there from time to time. His purpose was almost certainly unstated, but this stepwise approach was intelligent. Merton was tasting extended periods of solitude without a formal commitment from either man; it was what had been denied him during the fire tower incident. Few words were said—until September 24, a day in what Merton called "a week of Kairos," of special time.[1] On that day Merton received the invitation to Japan and also, serendipitously, reopened the topic of hermit living with Dom James, who of all things was "remarkably interested and open." The abbey had acquired a new tract of hilly, wild land separate from the main acreage, which had suggested to Merton the possibility of a "desert," as he called it—a sparse settlement of hermit dwellings. James was unexpectedly, inconceivably receptive to the draft idea: "He listened to everything I said, raised good questions, had constructive comments to offer and was thoroughly ready to get 'into' it. This was marvelous. . . . Now I look with astonishment across the valley at those hills. Trees hide the ridge behind which 'the desert' is hidden. But I am aware of those silences with a new awareness."

A week later, on the basis of a planning memorandum Merton had given him a little earlier, they spoke again. Dom James had meanwhile visited the valley, approved the general plan, and expressed the view that it was "from God." Though much encouraged, Merton was as wary as ever. The conditions of life James had in mind for hermits in the valley struck him as draconian, excessively idealistic: "*No* contact with *anyone*. . . . *No* letters. *No* visits. *No* talking. To do any kind of productive work would 'spoil the purity of intention.'"[2] But for the first time they were speaking with each other as colleagues with a common interest in the hermit life. What explains Dom James's changed view? It would have been unlike him to give much weight to his personal wishes, but he had transferred decades earlier from the Passionists to the Cistercian Order in search of greater solitude and silence, and despite his brilliant career, so to speak, as a monastic entrepreneur and globe-trotting superior, he had never lost that longing. This was one of *his* contradictions, and in the context we are exploring, everyone has a right to contradictions—they are badges of honor, signs of uncontained and uncontainable humanity. Looking back a few years later, Merton was quite sure that it was Dom James's personal interest that set the hermit experiment in motion.[3] James was getting older. He was now sixty-eight and, although free to serve for life as abbot, he may well have been thinking of a different future. There is still another point: he was aware through the network of his fellow American abbots that good Cistercian vocations were "going off," as he put it, "to more eremitical congregations, such as the Camaldolese or others, which have sprung up here in America, and of which I do not think very highly up to the present moment. But something on our own property, under the obedience of the Father Abbot, without any necessity of leaving the Order or the Community, could be worked out. It is something we do have to face—that is certain."[4] A conversation was beginning among the senior members of the order about the hermit life in the Cistercian past and the merit of cautiously restoring it—both Merton and his friend Jean Leclercq had contributed scholarship on the topic.

Merton pressed ahead with both projects, the journey to Japan and the plan for a "laura," a term he and James borrowed from Eastern Orthodoxy for a semieremitical monastic settlement. Just there was the entanglement. He made clear to Dom James that "the Japan project is of course a matter of secondary importance, and I know you realize that I am not blindly attached to it,"[5] but he didn't quite act that way—he perceived them as a reasonable sequence, first Japan, then the laura project, which didn't need him to progress. None of his superiors took that view. Dom Ignace wrote in mid-November that he "had difficulty believing that the will of God destined Fr Louis to be at the same time in a hermitage and traveling in the Far East. The fundamental question is this: is the man in Fr Louis who dreams of withdrawing into eremitical silence and solitude the same one who wants to go to Japan, with all the fanfare that will result from that? And if they are two different men, which is inspired by God?"[6] Dom James responded promptly: "I have no hesitation as to knowing what I think is God's Will in the matter. Providentially, the question of good Fr. L. and his hermitage is running along parallel with this Japan project. It seems that God has arranged it so, so that one could fight the other. I do not think it would be so easy to have convinced Fr. L. of God's Will, if such a situation had not existed."[7] He concluded that the "Japanese Project," as he put it, was "finished, and for the archives." And he confided a further thought about Merton's drive toward the hermit life: "I think if he keeps on, he will have me out there in the solitude, too. We will see what God wants . . ." (*ellipsis his*). This is touching; we see so little of Dom James's heart, his unspoken search. The hermitage project had become his own. He included with the letter a position paper on hermits in the order, a document looking toward a more complete account he would soon prepare for the 1965 general chapter meeting, chaired by Dom Ignace, which approved the hermit experiment in the order—an approval consequential for Gethsemani, where others in addition to Merton sought hermitages.[8] Merton had influenced Dom James, opened his mind to a possibility that might serve him well in his older years. Merton could hardly have expected this; nor could we.

"Day unto day uttereth speech, And night unto night showeth knowledge"—Psalm 19, incomparable, enigmatic, evoking the round of time and the difference between what day and night know, the difference between worthy projects and remote insistence. Merton sometimes dreamed of a certain kind of woman—most recently of a Chinese princess whom he likened to Proverb. He willingly called her an archetype entering his dreams in various disguises. "She was with her 'brothers,'" he recorded in his journal, "and I felt overwhelmingly the freshness, the youth, the wonder, the truth of her—her complete reality, more real than any other, yet unattainable."[9] She belonged to the night, but related thoughts and feelings found their way into the day. At the end of January 1965, writing in the hermitage, where thought in depth was more possible, Merton weighed his relations with women during his university years and found them grievously wanting. "I suppose I regret most my lack of love," he wrote,

> my selfishness and glibness (covering a deep shyness and need of love) with girls who, after all, did love me I think, for a time. My great fault was my inability really to believe it. . . . So one thing on my mind is sex, as something I did not use maturely and well, something I gave up without having come to terms with it. That is hardly worth thinking about now— twenty-five years nearly since my last adultery, in the blinding, demoralizing summer heat of Virginia. . . .
>
> What I find most in my whole life is illusion. Wanting to be something of which I had formed a concept. I hope I will get free of that now. . . .
>
> Snow, silence, the talking fire, the watch on the table. Sorrow.[10]

The theme persisted from month to month, unnoticed at length, no doubt, then suddenly insisting. In late June he thought again of the past—of an English friend's twelve- or thirteen-year-old sister who had somehow impressed him. "She was the quietest thing . . . , a dark and secret child. . . . If I had taken another turn in the road I might have ended up married to Ann. Actually, I think she is a symbol of the true (quiet) woman I never really came to terms with in the world, and because of this there remains an incompleteness that cannot be remedied."[11] Should we add to this, "Silence . . . Sorrow"? At the hermitage he found solace in the earthly forest: "It is necessary for me to live here alone without a woman, for the silence of the forest is my bride"—a most beautiful journal passage that would find its way into *Day of a Stranger,* written that spring.[12] But the incompleteness remained.

In August Merton received a letter from his literary agent and friend, Naomi Burton Stone. Here we must quote him in full if we are to understand what he means by the risk of tragic chastity.

> I got a very fine letter from Naomi in answer to one of mine admitting my own confusion and self-contradiction. Full of mature realistic understanding, and feminine comfort—the warmth that cannot come from a man, and that is so essential. Psychologically, my doubt is based in this giant, stupid rift in my life, the refusal of woman which is a fault in my chastity (and in the chastity of so many religious!). But I am learning to accept this love (of Naomi, for instance) even if it means admitting a certain loss. (Chastity is in fact my most radical poverty, and my un-poverty in accumulating things is a desperate and useless expedient to cover this irreparable loss which I have not fully accepted.—I can learn to accept it in the Spirit and in love, and it will no longer be "irreparable."—The Cross repairs it and transforms it.)
>
> The tragic chastity which suddenly realizes itself to be mere loss and fears that death has won—that one is sterile, useless, hateful. I do not say this is my lot, but in my vow I can see this as an ever

> present possibility. To make a vow is to be exposed to this possibility. It is the risk one must run in seeking the other possibility, the revelation of the Paraclete to the pure heart![13]

One's mind stops here—with his. He has dared to look directly at the most radical poverty he shared with his fellow religious, vowed long ago, now asking to be understood anew. What has the vow made of him? Toward what does it point at this time in his life—toward drought or toward inner purity capable of receiving and belonging to the Holy Spirit? The question is posed with devastating honesty. The answer, if there was to be one, had nothing to do with words, everything to do with life lived. The hermitage was proving its value: he could face himself there in the most vivid, searching way.

Merton had been working for years on a book, never published, called *Art and Worship*. It was to have been a richly illustrated exploration of sacred art. In pursuit of the needed illustrations and of understanding, he read far and wide and looked at innumerable illustrations. While in New York he had visited two museums, but in general he had no opportunity to see and experience works of art directly. Just as his published writings on peace often seem schematic and a little remote, his worked and reworked text on the history of sacred art was unavoidably superficial. Nonetheless, as he explored, there were moments of lasting insight: the project served him well, even if it never yielded a text of the quality he expected of himself. In October 1965 he came upon an illustration of a justly famous work, a fifth-century Byzantine medallion said to show the regent of the Western Roman Empire, Galla Placidia, with her children (fig. 12)—the young man a future emperor. Merton became absorbed in the image. "A most lovely and fascinating picture. The children are beautiful but dull. She is full of life and character. A fascinating face. How is it that this face is so contemporary to me, so ready to speak to me? As if she were someone I had always

FIG. 12. Medallion of Galla Placidia and her children, fifth century C.E.

known. I can imagine it is mother, perhaps, I see in her; there is some resemblance, the same kind of features. Anyway I am moved by the picture."[14] His mother, or Naomi, or the princess, or Proverb now grown with a family . . . This genuinely haunting image, with its Late Antique or early Byzantine stillness and inwardness, became another link in the knowledge that night shows to night.

There was a further link, less explicit but of compelling energy. A few days after his encounter with the image of Galla Placidia, something more insisted on recognition. "There has been much self-searching," he wrote in his journal, "some futile, some disquieting. It may be excessive, but there is something in the core of my being that needs to be revealed. I wonder if I can face it. Is it futile even to try? 'Let sleeping dogs lie, leave things as they are, etc. . . .' I will try to do whatever God wills. Jeremias XX.14–18. (Cursed be the day on which I was born . . . etc.) Lines I do not experience or understand. I hope to God I do not have to experience them. Reading them is enough."[15] The contrast he drew between the dreariest of truisms (Let sleeping dogs . . .) and the primal power of the prophet Jeremiah's words framed a mystery and challenge now detected. We can hope with Merton that there will be no cause to curse the day.

Meanwhile—of course!—so much else was going on. Merton was writing some of the best material he was destined to write. Read *Day of a Stranger* to confirm. "How I pray is breathe," he wrote there, abandoning grammar to embrace experience. It is a sustained poetic essay. For their sins (I suppose), Merton's superiors were bombarded in the course of 1965 with requests for him to travel, to speak, to participate far and wide. There was a splendid invitation in February to join an ecumenical meeting that included some of the most interesting Catholic and Protestant thinkers of the era—the Passionist Fr. Barnabas Ahern, a leading biblical scholar; Dom Jean Leclercq, Merton's trusted friend and a leading scholar of the history of monasticism; Douglas Steere, a

Quaker intellectual and professor, translator of Kierkegaard among many accomplishments; and others of equal weight. Merton belonged with them. Permission denied. "There was no discussion of why I should not go: just emotion on the part of the Abbot; that look compounded of suffering and stubbornness, interpretable in many ways, but which on this occasion made him look as if he thought I was stealing something from him—the key to his office for example. In a word a look of vulnerability and defiance: a man threatened in his belly or somewhere. . . . I have to learn to accept this without resentment. Certainly not easy to do! So far I have hardly tried and to tell the truth it angers and distracts me."[16]

In April Merton received a preliminary invitation, and later a formal one, from Fr. Charles Dumont, editor in chief of the order's journal, *Collectanea Cisterciensia,* to attend a meeting of the journal's board that fall at the Cistercian abbey in Chimay, Belgium—famed for its exceptionally good beer, not famed at the time for its journal ("The magazine is in crisis," Merton wrote. "Well might it be! It is awful.")[17] Merton had served for some time on the board. Fr. Dumont made the naive error of writing directly to Merton on the assumption that he needn't stand on ceremony with board members. He received a starchy letter from Dom Ignace. "I understand your idea," he wrote, "and assure you of my great gratitude for your zeal where *Collectanea* is concerned. But in all candor I must tell you that you have, I fear, made a false maneuver. If it is true, as Father Merton has told you, that Dom James is not disposed to allow him to travel to Europe, it may be that the Reverend Father Abbot of Gethsemani has excellent reasons for that. You may have put him in a difficult situation with regard to his religious, who already knows your intention. . . . I think that the legitimate concern to have much simplicity in our relations among monks should not make us forget the place of the abbot in our lives."[18] Duly communicated (if not by Dom James, then by Fr. Dumont himself), the refusal put Merton in mind of serial injustices: the injustice of the refusal itself, the injustice of the refusal when several other members of the community, including Merton's musical friend Fr. Chrysogonus, were in Europe at the time and at length.

Adding insult to injury that summer, a high Vatican official, no lesser a personage than the new cardinal prefect of the Sacred Congregation for Religious, had gotten in touch with the second in command of the Cistercian Order to suggest that Merton do an interview for Italian radio. The congregation had crushed Merton's 1959 request for an indult, but the new prefect had moved on. Merton may never have heard of this proposal. For once it was Dom Ignace who was upset. The interview would be a "*précédent fâcheux,*" he wrote to Dom James, a troublesome precedent, and "particularly unwelcome in the case of Fr Louis." If the cardinal insisted, then Merton should be interviewed at Gethsemani rather than in Rome, and the interview should be recorded for review before airing.[19] Dom James was relieved that the abbot general had dealt with the matter promptly, and he had himself written to the cardinal. He went on to remark that good Father Louis was preparing for the hermit life, though for some time to come he would say Mass daily in the novitiate and take the midday meal in the community. As well, he had agreed to give Sunday conferences, open to the entire community, for the foreseeable future. "I don't think," James added, "he could stand being an absolute hermit. But anyway, he is writing about it, and sending out articles right and left." He could not resist implying, for the *n*th time, that Merton was somewhat irresponsible, poorly self-governed. In view of Merton's impending status as a hermit, he concluded, "You see what a travesty—what a farce—it would be to have Father Louis, 'the hermit of 1965,' appearing on a national telecast!"[20] He wasn't concentrating—it was to have been a radio, not television, interview, but no matter.

The Gospel parable counsels against hiding one's light under a bushel basket but says nothing about extinguishing another's light.

There is excessiveness in Dom James's attitude, something from the night. Perhaps jealousy of the many calls for Merton from distinguished fellow religious? Merton couldn't help but think so, and he was not alone in that thought. "One would think an Abbot would have a little breadth of view in such matters as this," he wrote in his journal. "But there are all sorts of reasons why he has to be this way with me. . . . He is probably not aware of them all! Certainly one of them is a form of unconscious jealousy. I did not arrive at such a judgment myself—more than one other has expressed it to me. However, it is precisely for this kind of situation that I have a vow of obedience, and intend to keep it. But the irrationality remains."[21]

All things are bought at a price. Though Dom James and Merton had agreed that he would cease serving as master of novices at the end of the year and become a full-time hermit with very few duties in the community, James decided to make the change on August 20, auspiciously the Feast of Saint Bernard of Clairvaux. Merton was quite sure that the timing was determined by the invitation to Belgium: safely tucked into the hermitage, he would have little or no basis for travel requests, and James would have a mighty basis for refusing requests. James sent him off with a task—again, he was there for you when you needed him. "Before putting me away in my state of rest," Merton wrote to Naomi Burton Stone with bitter humor, "Fr. Abbot gave me a rush job to do for the monastery, a postulants' guide, you know, one of those things where the monks blushingly tell everyone how wonderful monks are. . . . Am settling down fine, actually I have stopped thinking about whether I am a hermit or what, and am simply living, with plenty to do, lots of reading, work, long meditations, and really this life makes an enormous amount of sense for me. . . . I am much less frustrated, spend less time mentally arguing against the ideas of the Abbot. . . . Thank God they finally got around to letting me live this kind of life."[22]

The hermitage hasn't changed much since Merton lived there;

it is still a sort of ménage, comfortable in its way. The fireplace stones are still streaked with soot, as in some photographs from his time. The bed is made, with a quilt; the hermitage remains in use as a retreat for Gethsemani's religious and for special friends of the community. I once met Msgr. Shannon there, standing on the porch, at home as well he might be. Some of Merton's knick-knacks and treasured objects remain where he put them. There are books, some surely from his time; furniture in part made at nearby Shakertown by traditional artisans. The view out over the long field has changed in a way that Merton would have found intolerable: a distant cell phone tower mars the view. Deer still pass across the field and pause. Merton used to like that. It is easy, and pleasant, to reinsert Merton into the hermitage by an act of imagination, as if the many photographs we still have could be reversed, life restored through them rather than snapped. The abbey has not permitted the hermitage to become a shrine, and yet it is one. A shrine and not a shrine: a Buddhist middle-way status that might have pleased him.

The early reviews of Merton's new living conditions were not uniformly positive. His friend Ed Rice had called on him in the cold season and reported to Naomi, who reported to Dom James, that Merton was freezing up there and had meager food. Dom James did his best by letter in early February 1966 to calm their anxieties. "[Ed Rice] happened to wander up to Father Louis's hermitage after supper . . . , and of course there was no sunshine. It was rather gloomy that day—and Father Louis pulled out a can of sardines and a few sandwiches, and they munched. But he didn't realize that Father Louis had a wonderful hot dinner at noontime with plenty of meat and vegetables." So much for the complaint about food, and meat *was* served in the infirmary where Merton typically took his meals. "Of course, he doesn't have running water, or New York City plumbing . . . , but he has a tremendous big fireplace, and he tells me that the logs are always still burning in the morning, with plenty of embers. . . . And even with zero outside, he tells me: 'Why, I had the window open all night—just put on more blankets. I couldn't sleep otherwise.' . . . Do you think that Ed Rice is going to write about this gloomy aspect in *Jubilee*? Lord, I'll shoot him if he does."[23] Rice was the founder of the Catholic magazine *Jubilee* and a most interesting, sympathetic biographer of Merton's.

From the beginning, as Dom James disclosed his personal interest, Merton was suspicious of the plan for a laura on the more distant acreage. He was well off where he was and had no wish to participate in what he thought would become "a little abbey" with Dom James running it, "everyone under his thumb not able to move or breathe."[24] That turned out not to be a worry; Merton stayed put and the laura never took shape as first envisioned. Through that fall and early winter in the hermitage, he had all the time he needed to feel his way as a hermit—it was at times far from easy—and to reflect on his long experience in the abbey community and as a "subject" of Dom James's. Where he himself was concerned, he was on the alert. "I find more and more the power—the dangerous power—of solitude working on me. The easiness of wide error. The power of one's own inner ambivalence, the pull of inner contradiction. How little I know myself really. . . . Everything has meaning, dire meaning, in solitude. . . . One has to start over and receive (in meekness) a new awareness of work, time, prayer, oneself. . . . And what I do not have I must pray for and wait for."[25] I cannot imagine a healthier, more active and searching response to his new life. On the other hand, Merton gave himself a year-end amateur physical and rejoiced to tally the result, as if he were a mildly demented character in a Samuel Beckett play. "What kind of a body!" he wrote.

> An arthritic hip; a case of chronic dermatitis on my hands for a year and a half (so that I have to wear gloves); sinusitis, chronic ever since I came to Kentucky; lungs always showing up some

funny shadow or other on x-rays (though not lately); perpetual diarrhea and a bleeding anus; most of my teeth gone; most of my hair gone; a chewed-up vertebra in my neck which causes my hands to go numb and my shoulder to ache—and for which I sometimes need traction; when you write it down it looks like something, and it is true, there is no moment any more when I am not aware that I have something wrong with me and have to be careful! What an existence! But I have grown used to it.[26]

He was ready for the New Year.

[20]

To Sleep Alone All of My Life

"BROTHER BASIL SAID DOM JAMES is like a man at a desk with wind blowing in through an open window, trying to hold down as many papers as possible with both hands."[1] This vivid remark is from spring 1964; it was equally true in the winter of 1966. They were winds of change originating in the Second Vatican Council, now concluded, and passing through successive levels of authority to the abbey, with its own authoritative abbot and council. The choir monks and lay brothers were now united, and their traditionally separate novitiates had been similarly united. The Mass and offices and all worship were increasingly conducted in English, and many elements of liturgy were changed or being considered for change. There was an authorized hermit out in the woods, soon to be followed by others. Plans were settled for a thoroughgoing renovation of the abbey church, which was frail and dangerous in some respects (the steeple was potentially unstable) and old-fashioned in ways that no longer felt right for the community. There was a very great deal to manage, and Dom James was at the center of it all.

Merton wasn't. In the early months of the year he suffered, more at some times than others, from his physical disabilities. He had his Trappist toughness, but still: "The curse is in the skin of my hands again—all broken up. Also I will need X-rays of the vertebra again soon, my hands easily get numb, and even hurt."[2] Despite such debilities, he was leading a rich life of meditation and prayer, study and writing, and spending limited time daily at the monastery. He would see the abbot privately from time to time and hear his letters home when he was traveling. The spiritual distance and mistrust between them remained. "I see aspects of his motives which he probably does not see. I do not agree with a sadomasochistic spirituality. I think he is simply wrong and even in some sense perverse. Yet I have to accept all this without evasion and without retaliation. Only the Grace of Christ can help me! . . . I have no confidence in the man, and am convinced his motives are much more 'natural' than he realizes, indeed somewhat neurotic. . . . To be a prisoner of such a man and helpless to do anything about it is a real problem to me, and can hardly see what to do but accept it."[3]

And so the word "neurotic," belonging to Dom James for so many years and applied to Merton, has changed ownership: Merton now applied it to James on more than one occasion, and Merton's psychiatrist, Dr. Wygal (like James's psychiatrist, Dr. Zilboorg, in the past), backed him up. In a letter to Dan Berrigan some months earlier, Merton had noted that Armand de Rancé, the original Trappist abbot, had an anniversary but no one seemed to be paying attention. Rancé was the "granddaddy of the willpower boys," he wrote, and drew a verbal portrait of him that suspiciously resembled Dom James.[4]

There was a minor conflict in early March that proved to be revealing. A brother who had been typing Merton's translation of a Spanish poem found the poem offensive and made his view known. In response Merton seems to have been short with him, and he later wrote a note to the abbey psychiatrist, Fr. John Eudes, in which he covered both that issue and his growing question as to whether it made sense for him to continue giving Sunday conferences. "I feel," Merton wrote, "that . . . these kids do not really understand what I am talking about, and that in any case it is perhaps a waste of time to tell them what I am telling them? . . . There is no point in my getting out the old monastic machine and grinding that again, and the new stuff is my business not theirs. If someone is really getting something out of it, . . . maybe it's ok. But I wonder if it would be simpler just to drop the whole thing."[5] Eudes responded at some length to say that Merton had exaggerated the brother's problem and likely hadn't approached him with sufficient understanding. He also reassured Merton that the conferences were "very useful. . . . I think everyone profits from hearing them."[6] And then he took up his own business in a most interesting way. "You are always going to be somewhat of an unsettling influence on people," he wrote, "perhaps even at times a thorn in people's side (sometimes I feel your sting myself). But that is your destiny, and most of us need somebody around to do the disturbing things you do. As mad as I could get at you, for example, about some of the things you say (or have said) about me, which I consider more of a distortion than a legitimate criticism, yet I have always felt that for me and for all of us you are a real help and a positive influence—even when you are wrong or unfair—since in the end you always come around. It is wonderful to have you with us, so do not make your retirement any more complete than it is now!" How welcome to see Merton not through his own eyes or through Dom James's, but through a third person, friend to them both and a trained observer of humanity.

It became evident in early March that Merton would need spinal surgery; it was scheduled for the 24th in Louisville. The few weeks before he left the hermitage had some taste of *kairos* again, a special time of sensitivity and insight. He was genuinely touched by the new liturgical music composed by Fr. Chrysogonus—"probably as good as any Church music being written now . . . may turn out to be the best."[7] Where the abbot was concerned, he was forgiving and generous: "Dom James himself, with all his limitations and idiosyncrasies, has done immense good to this community by stubbornly holding everything together. He too is an extraordinary man, many sided, baffling, often irritating, a man of enormous will, but who honestly and in his own way really seeks to be an instrument of God. And in the end that is what he has turned out to be. I am grateful to him. . . . The one thing for which I am most grateful: this hermitage."[8] For himself, as a promise to the future and thanks to the past, he wrote a few lines familiar to close readers of Merton. It is a demonstration, were one needed, that Merton's spiritual search had become universal in the sense that his insights, direction, and language are at home in all traditions. He hadn't engaged with Buddhism to become a Buddhist or with Taoism to become a Taoist—or with Islam to become a Muslim. He had engaged to find, with more clarity and breadth, his own ground and inner work and voice. That Meister Eckhart would understand these lines meant he hadn't left home.

> Beauty and *necessity* (for me) of solitary life—apparent in the sparks of truth, small, recurring flashes of a reality that is *beyond doubt,* momentarily appearing, leading me further on my way. Things that need no explanation and perhaps have none, but which say: "Here! This way!" And with final authority!
>
> It is for them that I will be held responsible. Nothing but immense gratitude! They cancel out all my mistakes, weaknesses, evasions, falsifications.
>
> They lead further and further in that direction that has been shown me, and to which I am called.[9]

I always pause over the firmness of the last lines. So mobile in his search for knowledge and awareness, Merton was nonetheless steady.

. . .

Merton resumed writing in his journal nearly three weeks after surgery, which went well. During his hospitalization he had been deeply stirred, more than he acknowledged at the time, by the care and person of a student nurse identified in much of the Merton literature simply as "M." "We were getting perhaps too friendly by the time she went off on her Easter vacation, but her affection—undisguised and frank—was an enormous help in bringing me back to life fast. In fact all the nurses were very interested and friendly and warm. . . . And I realized that though I am pretty indifferent to the society of my fellow monks . . . , I do feel a deep emotional need for feminine companionship and love, and seeing that I must irrevocably live without it ended by tearing me up more than the operation itself. The best thing of all was lying reading Eckhart, or sitting up. . . . It was this that saved me, and when I got back to the hermitage last evening to say the Easter offices everything else drained off and Eckhart remained as real. The rest was like something I had imagined."[10]

But it hadn't drained off, either in him or in her. "A letter came from M.," he recorded on April 19. "I was glad to hear from her. Have to think—my way around the problem of this tenderness."[11] He answered her letter, there were phone calls, chancy on his end because only one phone was available in a building where other community members had regular responsibilities, and they arranged to meet when he was next in Louisville for a medical checkup. He was living in the infirmary for a few weeks, though spending time at the hermitage. Thinking his way around the problem would not be an option; they had fallen in love.

The romance of Thomas Merton and M. has been written by a master: Merton himself. Volume six of his journal, published (as he wished, more than twenty-five years after his death) under the title *Learning to Love,* at nearly four hundred pages long, has scarcely any other theme. Its editor, Prof. Christine M. Bochen, points out in her introduction that we are hearing only from Merton; M.'s voice is largely missing and would remain so because she has meticulously maintained silence in the years since, and we know nothing of her later life. But Merton knew how to reflect her nature in his pages. After their first meeting, he wrote, "There is no question that I am in deep. Tuesday . . . M. met me at the doctor's. Appeared in the hall, small, shy, almost defiant, with her long black hair, her grey eyes, her white trench coat."[12] At the time he was fifty-one, she still a student. With Dr. Wygal's increasingly reluctant help as chauffeur and part-time table companion, they had lunch together, Wygal left them alone for a time, and "more than ever," Merton wrote, "I saw how much and instantly and how delicately we respond to each other on every level. Also I can see why she is scared. I am too. There is a sense of awful, awesome rather, sexual affinity—and of course there can be no hesitations about my position here. I have vows and must be faithful to them. . . . Apart from that, though, . . . it was clearer than ever that we are terribly in love, and it is the kind of love that can virtually tear you apart."[13] It seems inconceivable because so much had already occurred—wasn't he at last a settled hermit?—but in his instinctive search for growth and his openness to experience, Merton had upped the ante, pushed further "into the middle of all contradictions." He could have kept his eyes strictly on his readings in Eckhart, who makes such sense and poses such challenges, but he did not. He could have replied to M.'s first letter with warm thanks and farewell, but he did not. There is a wonderful line in the *Arabian Nights,* pronounced by a young merchant who has just met an enchanting, mysterious girl: "At last, O Abu al-Hasan, you have found an adventure and are carried into the mill of complication." A little later the young man reflects, "I was not used to such adventures and was taking my first step in complication."[14] Merton was not used to such adventures, either, and needless to say he had entered a mill of complication. "My response has been too total and too forthright," he wrote, "we have admitted too much, communicated all the fire to each other and now we are caught."[15]

Given that a master has already written the romance, it can't be our concern here to rewrite or follow its every joy and sorrow. There was much of both. They met when they could—frequent medical follow-up appointments were a convenience. They had some blissful private times, thanks in part to friends of them each—hers willing, his slightly appalled but doing their bit. Their relation sounded every note in the scale, from deep interest in the identity of the other to unashamed erotic attraction. That they couldn't see each other often and struggled by letter and phone to be in touch added to the intensity of their affair—let's call it that, as Merton did several times, although it seems that they refrained from consummating their love. In the solitude of the hermitage Merton was writing about her, about his dilemma and their dilemma, about love. This was his revolution. Whatever it was that he had detected in himself some months earlier ("There is something in the core of my being that needs to be revealed"), whatever prefigurations he had encountered in Proverb and the Chinese princess, it was all now gathered and revealed in himself, in M., and in the space of longing between them. It was his revolution and the deepest of contradictions because he entered into the relation as a vowed monk, never abandoned his religious mind and heart, and yet lived their love affair with passionate intensity.

Something quite like this had occurred before in Christendom. The fourteenth-century master poets, Dante and Petrarch, had each been stunned by a remote and unavailable young woman—Dante's Beatrice, Petrarch's Laura—and each wrote long cycles of love poetry that created the Italian lyric and influenced the course of European poetry. "Love found me altogether disarmed," Petrarch wrote—*Trovommi Amor del tutto disarmato;* "I know well I am pursuing what burns me."[16] Merton's poetry and journal from this year of years, 1966, are not unlike this. There is a place for this experience, if not in the calendar of saints, then in the calendar of poets. "Thank God for this blessed disturbance," Merton would write in early May.[17] But of course he was aware of all the rest. We should hear him:

> The question has obviously arisen: whether we should not just go off and live together "married." But the problems are appalling. Excommunication, *fuga cum muliere* [flight with a woman], apostasy, and all the hounds after me perpetually from Dom James to the Roman Curia! Yet strangely enough now I can see where this could be for some people the only answer. There comes a time

> when all this legal machinery for fulmination simply does not convince. It claims to be the voice of God, it pretends to damn in His name and by His authority. . . . Does it really? Is it a mark of faith to accept this in timid fear, so that one closes his mind in desperation to all other more intimate and more personal values? . . . One would always try to work it out with the Church, not against it. Yet with someone like Dom J. there are no possible solutions, no chances of reasonable communication. Especially where women are involved, everything has been long settled in advance and there are no questions even to be raised. . . . It is, however, now, to me, a really serious option: that if in the near future the way does open for a married clergy, I should take it.[18]

Merton was learning that he could love and that he was lovable. Such knowledge enters one's whole being; so it was for him. In other religious cultures—East Christian or Tibetan Buddhist—he would have had the possibility of marriage without loss of status and without disturbing long-established, highly valued relationships. The Roman Church could not offer him that possibility. Nor could it offer him for long what little peace he had.

Merton's calls from a community telephone controlled by the cellarer (the provisions manager) and accessible to a switchboard were, of course, utterly imprudent, but he had no other option if he were to speak with M. from the monastery. On June 13 he learned that a call had been overheard and reported to Dom James, who had just returned from a trip. "I don't know how much he knows," Merton recorded in his journal the next day,

> but I know he is mad and is waiting to give me the devil about it, which is only natural. I have to face the fact that I have been wrong and foolish in all this. Much as I loved M., I should never have let myself be carried away to become so utterly imprudent. But I suppose I knew that. . . . Well, it is clearly over now. I called

> her once more (she was desolate and so was I). She said, "I had the most terrible feeling something was wrong when I was waiting for you to call. . . . Will we ever see each other again? . . . What will I do without you? . . . How unfair it is, even inhuman. . . ." But we have both anticipated this. . . .
>
> Decided the best thing was to own up and face Dom James (about the phone calls *only*!) before he summoned me in. So I did. He was kind and tried to be understanding to some extent—his only solution was of course "a complete break." Wanted to write to M. himself but I refused—that would be disastrous—and he does not know who she is and I don't think he needs to know. He was hinting around about how lonely I have been in the hermitage, how I ought to come down and sleep in the infirmary, etc. But I refused. The only concrete solution we arrived at was that I should go back to ecumenical work in the retreat house—as a cure for loneliness!!—but I suppose some constructive contacts with others would be a good thing. Obviously though he thinks the hermitage has been too much for me and has made me too vulnerable.[19]

It is true that Dom James was quiet and patient. Merton felt that they were both frightened by the situation. After so many years and so many contests, they had reached the far edge of monastic authority. James angered Merton by visibly, seemingly with pleasure, withholding a letter from M., though written no doubt as conscience matter. No more letters would reach him—or her—except through the courtesy of friends; another round of samizdat. In response, Merton's private thoughts about James reached their nadir: he would never quite say or write such things again. "He is a providential affliction, a kind of skin disease that I have to live with in patience. I loathe everything he stands for. And yet I can see that basically he is a man of good desires: but they have been twisted and corroded and he is now, without knowing it, a most inhuman person: even though there is so much potential warmth and concern. Under it all is a deep contempt for man, for love, and for the persons of his monks."[20]

Notes jotted down by Dom James before and after his conversations with Merton have survived. They are written in a kind of shorthand, faintly, but they convey James's approach to their early encounters better than a finished account. By this time Merton had written at considerable length about the love affair, though of course privately, and there was much more to come. These notes in their brevity are muted, eloquent in their ineloquence.

God watches over us
Knows our weaknesses
Be on guard in future
1. Resist beginnings
2. Avoid occasions
Forewarned forearmed
Wygal—to call back
He comes *here*—next weekend

That was perhaps the first. By requiring Dr. Wygal to see Merton at the abbey, he was preventing at least some of Merton's trips to Louisville. This is another:

Some time ago
Long call
5 persons know about it
They know you called at night
They know you asked Clement how to operate

And another:

What do you think
Scandal?
1. Certainly—not to see the girl again.
Or else I'll have to see her.
2. Stay up in the infirmary nights for some time.[21]

Dom James insisted that Merton break all connection with his unnamed friend, and Merton agreed, with an unspoken reserve that he would do whatever was necessary to care for her well-being. In the coming months, summer and fall, he called her when he could, and they saw each other when they could, all of which somehow escaped the attention of Dom James. Under intense pressure, the couple's love for each other increased even as its tragic dimension—the near certainty of parting—became more evident. A seemingly stray detail speaks to this. They had chosen as their own a beautiful song of frustrated love; they both knew what lay ahead, though M. in an entirely uncomplicated way wanted to live with Thomas Merton as his wife. Fr. Chrysogonus—the learned, the traditional, the upward bound—had loaned Merton his copy of Joan Baez's first recording, and Merton temporarily possessed a phonograph, ironically enough Dom James's on loan. And so he heard the folk song "Silver Dagger," which in Baez's unforgettable performance has broken and soothed many hearts, including his.[22] It's a young woman's song; she has been warned by her mother about men's deceiving ways, and at the end sings to the one she loves that she would have "to sleep alone all of my life." That spring and summer the song belonged to Merton and his love. And because this was Merton, it wasn't too long before Joan Baez herself, with her mentor in the antiwar and social justice movements, Ira Sandperl, turned up for an afternoon and evening with him at the hermitage. Merton had the grace to invite Chrysogonus to hike up to the hermitage to meet her (he was "entranced"). Merton introduced Baez to Dom James at the gatehouse, and coolly observed that she "disliked him—saw through him at once and he was visibly upset at the way she looked through him."[23] Merton's observation may be disingenuous: they had been conversing for some time before this brief encounter, and it's more than likely that he had expressed a convincingly critical view of the abbot.

Merton would sleep alone all of what remained of his life. He belonged to his monastic world—belonged incomparably more to the future of monasticism than Dom James, who was rooted in its past. The solitude of the hermitage deeply suited him, and his mature vocation—the "direction that has been shown me, and to which I am called"—was his guiding star. He redefined his direction that summer as "the deepening and the exploration of consciousness," yet another sign of the universality and fertility for the future of his inner search in these late years.[24] He realized that his authorization to live as a hermit was at risk and did everything possible to reassure Dom James. At some point in these weeks he wrote to James, "I am not suffering that much from loneliness—certainly not as much as you think I am. On the contrary, solitude is the only real solace and help for me in the long run, and I have no alternative but to be faithful to this vocation. . . . Anything worthwhile is necessarily tested."[25] In midsummer he wrote again, "I do not think my failures are a reason for abandoning solitude but for continuing in it with renewed resolution and with greater understanding, prudence and reliance on prayer. Never think that I take the solitary life lightly. I cannot take it lightly. It is the most important thing in my existence and I have to cling to it with all my power."[26] Merton and Dom James found something to tinker at together: a new set of rules governing hermit life at Gethsemani. The result was solid. On September 8, Merton signed a solemn "Commitment to the Solitary Life" in the presence of James, a formal assurance that he could spend the rest of his life in solitude.[27]

M. and Merton were able to meet in mid-July when he sprained his ankle and needed medical care in Louisville. In his accounts of their rare meetings, and for the most part only there, we also meet her a little more directly. They went out to a park for a picnic. "She told me," he recorded, "that I am the 'only truly kind and gentle person' she has ever known." He could have said nearly the same. Her kindness and care at the hospital and later had changed him. "Whether she is right or not," he continued, "it means a lot to me to know . . . what my love means to her—that it is to her gentle, kind, warm, tender. I want to give her infinite tenderness. . . . She has said several times that this is the real love and no one accepts this kind of love. I have instinctively known that this, in any case, is what she loves in me, what is truest and most personal to me, whatever it is—something that no one else has ever fully accepted or believed in. . . . Here I am loving her more completely, more rooted in her love, than ever."[28]

As summer continued, he knew of course that a decision was needed, knew the decision, and knew something of what it would cost each of them. "Tonight—rain and frogs," he wrote at the end of July. "Can't sleep. Thinking of M.—and the two worlds, that of our love, which is not permitted to exist and yet is such an imperative *reality*—and the stupid, trite, artificial world of people who have their ways and standards which outlaw this reality. . . . I know that if we really let go I would be destroyed and so would she. And yet—would it not be worth it after all? I know she thinks so. . . . but I know I have something else to do."[29] At Dom James's request he was meeting with Fr. John Eudes as a psychological counselor. Eudes had told him, "You are no longer correct, as you used to be," and warned him that he was doing everything possible to ruin his life. In response to these reasonable assertions, Merton discovered something terrible and beautiful: "Strangely now I feel real, though wrong."[30] The following day he wrote to Eudes as if completing their conversation. "It is [an] error that you and Rev. Father both share that before I was in some measure whole and consistent and now I am not, and the thing for me to do is to recover my previous wholeness. Anyone that thinks that I was whole and consistent before simply does not know me. My fall into inconsistency was nothing but the revelation of what I am. . . . I am now in several disedifying pieces. . . . I am divided by having seen the despairing hope of wholeness with a partner of the other sex—which is of course totally out of the question—and a wholeness alone which

I do not have. . . . Meanwhile, up here I can live well enough with loneliness and division, and I will do my best not to let my inconsistencies frighten people down there. All I ask is the mercy of God and of the Order, and for my own part I will cultivate the honesty without which this life here would not be bearable at all. . . . I am almost capable of finally becoming a free man."[31]

At that moment in mid-summer all three were thinking not only of Merton's affair with M.; they were coming to terms with a chaotic incident that had occurred when Merton received the visit in late June of an interesting young woman, Linda Parsons, a Canadian for whom he had been serving for some time by correspondence as an informal spiritual director. She brought a picnic and beer, and they went out to one of the more distant ponds where they swam a little and drank too much. Merton made a pass at her, she accepted his kisses, they stopped there—but later he was so drunk he could scarcely stand. Mrs. Gannon, the monastic housekeeper who had clandestinely driven them from monastery to pond and fetched them later, told Parsons that she had "never seen him like this."[32] Lord knows how he made it back to the hermitage on his own. News of the incident reached Dom James a month later in an accusatory letter from a Canadian priest with whom Parsons had counseled, and James called Merton in on the very day Merton wrote the letter cited just above—"I am now in several disedifying pieces." Merton recorded little in his journal. "Momentous talk with Dom J. yesterday—repercussions from Linda P.'s visit end of last month," he wrote on July 29, and two days later reflected that everything he had been through that spring and summer had been "absolutely necessary. Well, not the Linda Parsons bit."[33] This too was Merton in the most difficult summer of his monastic life: not just a Petrarch-like lover but also a man in disarray. Fr. John Eudes recalls to this day with retrospective relief that Merton accepted his advice "to be more self-critical and self-disciplined."[34]

Not quite a week later Merton had what he called another

session with the abbot. "He lectured me again," Merton recorded in his journal, "—not unkindly, but of course with the great moral superiority he now enjoys. And he had engineered various small and humiliating 'solutions' to practical problems of monastic importance—too intricate to describe. I am mad at myself for being affected by all of it! . . . Then the Abbot started laughing at me. He said 'I am thinking of writing a book on how to get hermits into heaven!' And laughed heartily. He enjoys the whole thing very much. And I burned interiorly. And was mad at myself for feeling it! The man has to gloat. I have offended and disturbed him many times and now I should have the decency to let him enjoy his innocent satisfaction. However, on leaving I said: 'When the baby is born you can be its godfather!' A slight shadow crossed his face and he laughed with less enthusiasm. Was I really kidding? We are a pair of damned cats."[35] Merton's closing comment creates a strong echo to this day.

Gradually, as summer turned to fall and Merton had such difficulty communicating with or seeing M., the love between them seemed to cool. He could argue himself into belittling what had occurred, into thinking how foolish he had been. But a letter from M. that somehow got through forced him to see that it wasn't so simple. It was now early November. "M. Her little, clear, determined voice coming to me through all the cold and snow, in a letter, saying she has carefully considered it, and she really, powerfully loves me, and she is never going to stop. So definite. I read the letter out there in a field of snow, weeping, looking through hot tears at the icy hills, the frozen wood. . . . The fact of passion has to be faced, and I must not let it get too disruptive. The fact of my vocation to a deep mystical life has to be faced—though I am helpless to account for it or cope with it and am in danger of being terribly unfaithful. The fact of M.'s love has to be faced and met with my own most serious gift and trust. God alone can reconcile all that has to be reconciled. I have simply been torn by it."[36]

Perhaps it is time to leave these lovers to their lives. M. would distance herself and, it is believed, marry a Vietnam veteran. Among the older monks at Gethsemani she has left a legacy of admiration for her integrity in never making a sign after the affair was over, no kiss and tell, nothing at all. She left Merton wholly free. For Merton there was a months-long and sometimes awkward passage to inner freedom, surely altered forever by his experience of the love of a man for a woman, a woman for a man. At times what he had understood took shape in words, never more powerfully than in a journal note of mid-November 1966. If I were asked, "Who was Thomas Merton?" I might well respond, he was the human being who lived deeply and hard enough to understand this, and had such love of God's gift of language that he could say this:

> Actually one decides one's life by responding to a word that is not well defined, easily explicable, safely accounted for. One decides to love in the face of an unaccountable void, and from the void comes an unaccountable truth. By this truth one's existence is sustained in peace—until the truth is too firmly grasped and too clearly accounted for. Then one is relying on words—i.e. on his own understanding and his own ingenuity in interpreting existence and its "signs." Then one is lost—has to be found once again in the patient Void.[37]

There is very much more in that year—not least, difficulties with Dom James, and James with good Father Louis. Merton didn't hesitate to put his gift for language to work on the matter. "The real difficulty with Dom James is his mentality, his character, his prejudices, his background. He is the very incarnation of New England middle-class, efficiency-loving, thrifty, crafty, operating, sanctimonious religiosity. He is at once calculating and sentimental, comfort loving and disciplined, a mystically inclined businessman, secretive, suspicious, solitary, yet in many ways self-sacrificing and dedicated."[38] That takes care of that. But what Merton seems not to have known is that Dom James refrained from informing the abbot general that there was a grave and novel difficulty in the life of Father Louis. I may have missed something, but the sole letter I've seen between them that summer is a dull report on Merton's surgery and recovery and a bit about the other hermit, Fr. Flavian Burns, now established in the woods. It's the least colorful letter James ever wrote. This was perhaps self-protective; he may have found the situation embarrassing. But it was an unmistakable kindness, as well.

Thinking about Dom James toward the end of the year, Merton admonished himself, "Don't make the Abbot too big a question," and asked himself for patience not only about Dom James but about all else. "Everything is still uncertain," he wrote, "hidden in hearts, the end not known, we do not see, we cannot see until God Himself throws His light into those depths."[39]

[21]

It Seems So Absurd

THEY BUILT A BEAUTIFUL white church. In the fall of 1962, two of the abbey's most practical members visited the Ohio studio of William Schickel, architect and designer, to explore how he could help. Educated at the University of Notre Dame and quite specialized in designing spaces and furnishings for religious communities, Schickel had been recommended by the editors of *Liturgical Arts,* a magazine devoted to the arts of the Catholic Church. The visiting monks apparently asked Schickel a leading question: did he appreciate the Shaker aesthetic? As they knew, the Shaker buildings at nearby Pleasant Hill, Kentucky, set a high standard for simple beauty. Schickel understood. Through the earlier 1960s, he designed furnishings for the abbey church that could be fabricated by the monks in their workshops, and by 1966 he was hired to take in hand a complete renovation of the abbey church and cloister. Where the church was concerned, if the original motive was to remove the shaky steeple and shore up century-old roofing, what Schickel successfully proposed was to create a new church from the bones of the old. It was a thrilling project, which Dom James understood, appreciated, and funded through his circle of loyal donors. Gradually, if not at first, he also realized that the project was likely to be his last hurrah. To Merton's surprise, James's occasional references to retiring—and retiring to the life of a hermit on the abbey property—were not a deception intended to build support for him to stay on. Much was absurd and troubled in his last year as abbot, 1967; we'll hear of that. But they built a beautiful white church.

The first generation of Trappists at Gethsemani, refugees from

FIG. 13. The abbey church prior to the renovation of 1966–67.

the anticlerical turmoil of mid-nineteenth-century France, raised in effect two churches, one inside the other. The outer structure was bare-bones simple and grand: high, thick brick walls, no architectural detail of significance, arched openings for stained glass windows. That generation of monks must have thought of this vast, airy box with its semicircular apse at the north end as a neutral armature for what they wanted, which was a church as traditionally Gothic as possible—a quote in central Kentucky from medieval France (fig. 13). The Gothic interior was plaster and lath, less solid than it looked but visually convincing, and the space was filled with dark choir stalls and screens, numerous altars, and

FIG. 14. The renovated abbey church as it is today.

sentimental sculpture, bathed in the light of stained glass windows on traditional themes.

Schickel had a powerful mind. He was able to see past the Gothic scrim to the austere beauty—or the potential for austere beauty—concealed in the original structure. In a project description submitted to the abbot and a building committee (which included Merton) as work was getting under way, he wrote, "We are tearing out the plaster replica of a neo-Gothic church from the

FIG. 15. Holy water font, the abbey church.

inside of the building. . . . The space that we hope to have will be simple, uncluttered, forthright, bright and cheerful, one of basic values and without frivolity. . . . The Abbey church . . . should have a . . . joyful austerity. It should be simple and honest. It should be respectful of the past and yearning for the future."[1] In April 1966, perhaps even from as far off as the hermitage, Merton could "hear the demolishers shouting from the top of the steeple. They are now stripping it. A momentous change."[2] The church that appeared out of an effort exceeding a year, which left the walls and hand-hewn timber roof supports in place but little else, was a modest masterpiece (fig. 14). Its kinship was no longer the spiny Gothic of medieval France but rather the austere and luminous architecture of the first Cistercian centuries. It brings to mind monastic churches in France—Le Thoronet, Senanque, Fontenay—which to this day envelop the visitor and speak without words. Schickel even managed to include a reference to the Shaker aesthetic in small, wall-mounted holy water fonts (fig. 15), that bear some resemblance to classic Shaker bentwood boxes. He has been said to have been working in a contemporary Brutalist idiom, rooted in the work of Le Corbusier, but even the industrial I beams in the apse deliver a different message: simplicity and elegance, Brutalism tamed and in prayer. New stained glass windows, abstract and geometric in design and set in deep rectangular openings, wash the space with changing hues as the day progresses. Their design isn't captivating, but the light and color they throw is quite perfect; that may well have been the point (fig. 16). What a brilliant exercise at all levels. Some of the younger monks participated. Br. Paul Quenon recalls being part of the wrecking crew. "You know, there is something about having a sledge hammer and knocking plaster off the wall. It is very therapeutic, especially if you were part of that anti-institutional generation."[3]

During construction, Merton prowled and observed. In early May, for example, he heard Dom James in evening chapter read aloud written suggestions about the renovation that had been solicited from community members. Merton was not pleased: "The notes were well meant and often tried to make good points, but in every case he read each note in such a way as to make it sound idiotic, and in each case the community accepted this distortion. In this way the community . . . consented to its own . . . humiliation. . . . What a burlesque of 'family life' and of community!"[4] But he continued prowling and by summer found much to content him. A letter to Schickel, August 10, could not be more positive. "I just wanted to tell you what a splendid job I think you have done on our Abbey Church & cloister. I particularly like the interior of the Church—bright, simple, clear-cut, no nonsense, and perfectly in accord with the spirit of our life."[5] Merton wasn't enchanted by the massiveness of certain key furnishings—the main altar, the presiding officiant's throne—but he didn't insist. In a note about the renovation and much else to several community members studying in Rome, he added: "I think that there is absolutely only one

FIG. 16. The abbey church: I beams and light.

hope for Gethsemani: for those of us who have some brains to hang together . . . and try to salvage the reality of what we came here for. . . . The most Dom James can and will ever do will be to hold things together as they are and implicitly prevent any real change."[6] His tone is arrogant in part, but turning to trusted peers at a difficult time is sensible.

The community's day, and Dom James's, fell on September 3 of that year: the reconsecration of the church. James's subsequent letter "to the diaspora"—community members temporarily elsewhere—is the best account we have.[7] He began with praise. "The rehabilitated church . . . is definitely what we all had in mind when we submitted ourselves to the ordeal of a renovation. It is definitely more pure—and more chaste—more austere and severe in its utter naked simplicity—much more unornate—and therefore much more prayerful." He was just as delighted by the music—"Father Chrysogonus had captured a few hymns from somewhere or other, and they were terrific." The archbishop was on hand, and together with many other participants they entered into the exacting process of consecration, first of the high altar and then many others. James remembered and recounted it all as if reliving it. Only the liturgists among us would find the full description rewarding, but we should all have a taste: "The Archbishop . . . incenses the altar . . . as for a Solemn Mass. Then he traces with grains of incense five crosses on . . . the altar. . . . Then a small taper in the form of a cross is put on each of these five crosses of incense. The tapers are made in the form of a cross with four ends of the cross turned upwards. . . . The Archbishop kneels and the whole community kneels as he intones the Antiphon: 'Come Holy Spirit.'" There were many new altars, each to be seeded with relics of saints and martyrs, of which the abbey in its century had accumulated an extraordinary number. It may be difficult to keep in mind even for the monastic community, but the church itself is vowed to seriousness and striving by the presence of relics of great men and women—Saint Paul, Saint Basil, Thomas

Aquinas, Teresa of Avila, John of the Cross . . . Even if some of the relics are inauthentic, others may well be authentic, and they raise something like a voice: remember what you are about. The choreography of the multiple consecration services that day must have deeply delighted Dom James; he was in his element. "Brother John . . . lit . . . thirty-five tapers. It made a very beautiful sight. . . . We all pray that we will be worthy of the great new gift God has given us."

Merton's own benediction was published nearly a year later in *Liturgical Arts*. "A monastic church," he wrote, "ought first of all to be an *uncluttered* place where everything is simple, clean, clear, light, plain, evident. . . . The new Church at Gethsemani has providentially come at the best possible time to help in the renewal, the new self-definition of the monastic community here."[8]

I have a sense of shame for both Merton and Dom James as they continued their broken dialogue through much of 1967—shame because nothing had changed for or in either of them. They were fixed in place, as if some dance had long since ended but they had nowhere to go. "It seems so absurd," Merton wrote.[9] James continued to confine Merton, to fend off even the most sensible invitations to him, even from a cardinal; he stopped reading Merton's mail and that of all others for a time, owing to a collective demand to cease and desist, but then resumed doing so. On his side, Merton couldn't back far enough away even at the hermitage to be thoroughly free of the abbot's hold. He was writing, corresponding, praying, meditating, meeting friends from time to time, all of this freely and creatively. But his thoughts and resentment returned often to Dom James. "By God's mercy there is a truth here in spite of all that is done against it in His Name. But the distortions, the evasions, the perversion of love into power and resentment . . . All of these slowly strangling hope until in the end a final despair has to be embraced as the ultimate hope. True, one is driven to Jesus in desperation. The place imposes a dark night of inhumanity in which one is forced to cling to something beyond all this—or perish."[10] Was this also to go on and on? Would neither man release the other? A wise friend has spoken of their obsession with each other. Would their circumstances open in some way to release them, to let them fall through into lives with no further focus on each other?

There was just one possibility: Dom James's retirement and apparent wish to be a hermit. In mid-July he called on Merton. "Yesterday afternoon Dom James came up to the hermitage on an 'official' visit. Don't quite know what he was at—you never do. We conversed for about ½ hour without really communicating anything except the fact that we don't use the same language. Yet I decided to talk to him about his own desire (?) to retire and be a hermit, encouraging him to do this, and saying I did not think he had a 'duty' to remain in command of this monastery."[11] A few days after the September consecration of the church, James reopened the conversation. "Suddenly today," Merton recorded, "Dom James told me he had reached his decision about what he wanted to do: he is planning to *resign* and live in a hermitage over in Edelin's place. I was surprised, and respect him for the decision! In fact I envy him the little place . . . planned for him, out on a high spur—and it will be much more solitary there than here. . . . After supper, . . . I walked on the brow of my hill and looked out over the valley and mused on everything. Certainly it is better for Dom J. to retire. He has been abbot there for nineteen years. It will be a relief to get someone younger. But who?"[12] Edelin's place was the new acreage, five miles distant from the monastic property, reached by jeep in twenty-five or thirty minutes, in part over a steep, rough track. Of all things, Dom James invited Merton to move to a hermitage out there, not far from him. You can imagine Merton's reaction: "One other absurdity was that Dom James proposed I take up a hermitage on the next ridge to him over at Edelin's. I can think of nothing worse! Having him watching everything I do, or just being in the same acreage. It would drive me crazy."[13]

Members of the community who kept their eyes on things weren't that surprised by Dom James's decision to retire. Fr. Michael Casagram had felt that James couldn't adapt to the changing atmosphere of monastic life after the Second Vatican Council. "I remember having a sense in the last years," he told me, "that things were happening much more rapidly, were evolving in a way he could no longer deal with, post–Vatican II. I just sensed that he knew his time had come—he knew he could no longer give the community what it needed. Part of it was the tension with Merton. Merton was reviving that rich spiritual tradition, and Dom James just couldn't."[14] The small circle of Gethsemani priests studying in Rome in 1967 also read the tea leaves from afar. Midyear, the directive came down that sign language would no longer be necessary at work time, and soon it became obvious that if the monks could talk about cheese and fruitcake, why couldn't they speak of things spiritual—of the concerns at the center of the community's life?[15] The retirement of sign language was consequential. "I was in Rome when they changed that law," Fr. Timothy Kelly recalled. "We were four from the abbey, and one of us said, 'James is going to retire.' I said, 'Never.' He said, 'James will retire. He has lost control of communication, and if he loses that, he cannot continue.' A few months later James retired. It was spring when they dropped sign language, and in December he retired. It was a big thing for him, a control factor; silence was a means of control. The brothers were good—they were really quite observant of the silence."[16] Of course, the abandonment of sign was only one factor among many. James's age and long service, the cumulative change in monastic practice, and the call of the hermit life must have been larger factors. But who would have imagined, without this insight from a member of the community, that freedom of conversation was a factor?

In late November Merton caught a ride with some other monks to visit the construction site where James's hermitage was rising. The view was spectacular—"out on a rocky spur, high over the valley"—and the hermitage itself, to be completed with a window wall and thoughtful interior planning, reflected the design sense of a brother who had worked in Frank Lloyd Wright's office.[17] "It will be a real pretty place," Merton decided. "The only thing is I have trouble imagining him in it. I guess he will make himself think he likes it—but is that what he wants? I wonder. But you don't really know people here. The fact that he was able to choose such a place and get the whole thing going is a very sobering thought! It is one of the only things I have ever found in the man to admire. He has my respect at least for this: he has got himself one very fine hermitage going!" The day after his visit, Merton put a note in the mail to Dan Berrigan and expressed an intuitive reservation. The new hermitage was "out in moonshine country," he wrote. "Place where the local boys have orgies, and you find all the bushes full of beer cans with bullet holes through them. . . . Anything can happen."[18]

You may recall, many pages ago, a reluctantly autobiographical letter written by Dom James to his superior, Dom Ignace. We learned much from it. His larger purpose in the letter was to justify his retirement into the hermit life, to ensure that the abbot general was with him, and to tender his resignation as abbot, effective December 30. He reported that there were rumors going around the abbey, "but from all that I have been able to gather, everyone is very sorry from a natural point of view—but everyone as far as I know seems to be happy from a supernatural point of view. I leave the entire matter now in your hands—before God—as to your decision."[19] He hadn't neglected to cite Father Louis's approval. "In speaking to Father Louis . . . about my case, he said: 'Why do you wait any longer? God indeed will enlighten you but you yourself must do something. You must correspond.'" Dom Ignace thought well of the plan.

Dom James gave his last sermon as abbot on Christmas night. "Simple and quite loving," Merton felt.[20] The election of the new abbot was to take place on January 15. Merton had taken a vow never to serve as abbot or superior, but not everyone in the community knew of it; he was considered a candidate by some, in a small pool of possibles that included Fr. Flavian Burns, the other hermit. Merton posted a notice to the community—"My Campaign Platform"—in late December to make clear his position and, through its rather nasty humor mixed with sincere confession, managed to upset a good many people. "I would be completely incapable of assuming the duties of a superior," he wrote, "since I am in no sense an administrator still less a business man. Nor am I equipped to spend the rest of my life arguing about complete trivialities with one hundred and twenty-five slightly confused and anxiety ridden monks. The responsibility of presiding over anything larger than a small chicken coop is beyond my mental, moral and physical capacities. . . . Since I have been a constant and unfailing disedification to the community for twenty-six years, it is obvious that anyone voting for me would have to be in a dubious condition spiritually. . . . In all seriousness, I feel obligated in conscience to do everything in my power to prevent this happening and to refuse it if it happens."[21]

No worries. On the third round of voting, Fr. Flavian was elected to the satisfaction of many, decisively including Merton, who knew the younger man well, respected him, and could hope to work with him as a colleague. "New abbot is a very good man," he wrote to a friend. "Young, but willing, definite, open, with solid monastic ideas not crackpot ones. Old Abbot still in no hurry to rush off into the freezing woods. Is around getting his 'papers together' for a few weeks."[22] To Dan Berrigan he wrote reassuringly: "As to getting around. [Fr. Flavian] will certainly let me have any freedom of movement that is normally recognized in the Order."[23] In his journal on election day he recorded his joy: "A real sense of liberation. Almost a shock to realize that the secrecy, the suppression and manipulation exercised by Dom James no longer dominate us. That we have a man we can talk to, work with frankly, exchange ideas with."[24]

On the day Merton had expected Dom James to retire to his hermitage, he wrote to him with great simplicity.

> To Fr James: My prayers go with you into the desert this Feb. 2 – and I hope you will find there all that you seek.
> In Him
> brm Louis[25]

A few months before, Merton had written a comparable note to himself: "There is still something I have not said: but what it is I don't know, and maybe I have to say it by not saying."[26] The year remaining to him would uncover what it was.

[22]

Make Peace Before the Sun Goes Down

AT MASS ON ELECTION DAY, with new music composed by Chrysogonus as a farewell to Dom James, Merton noted down later that "Dom J. seemed suddenly remote from all this, . . . the farewell really meant *farewell*."[1] It was true for Merton. Dom James all but disappears from his journal and correspondence. Of course, they would hear of each other. In April Merton learned from Fr. Flavian (who had refused the lordly title "Dom") that "Dom James in *his* hermitage is writing many voluminous letters. . . . This made me laugh like crazy since Dom James was always preaching so furiously against letter-writing."[2] "We are entitled to smile—without malice,"[3] he wrote to a friend. But that was the past, and Merton was deeply appreciative of the present and of new possibilities under discussion with Fr. Flavian. Because we have accompanied Merton through many hard years, we should know a little more of how he felt now. It was August; he would soon leave on an extended voyage of discovery in Asia.

> It is so utterly new to have an abbot here who is completely open to new possibilities! And it is certainly much more stimulating for the spiritual life! Here I am suddenly on the edge of something totally new, completely unplanned and unforeseen, something that has simply dropped out of the sky. The sense that one can move with this new swing and explore it is very inspiring and does much to lift the burden of depression, suspicion, doubt that has become almost second nature with me after years of the other kind of policy! Now I find I have to shake myself, wake up, pray, think

> for myself, estimate risks and possibilities, make halfway wise decisions. But this is what we have all been needing.[4]

In January both Merton and Flavian had received invitations from Dom Jean Leclercq to attend a meeting in Bangkok in the fall of 1968 under Benedictine auspices, the AIM conference (Aide à l'Implantation Monastique), with speakers and guests from many parts of the world. Flavian himself would not attend, and he was wary of dispatching Merton. He asked for letters from distinguished religious—Merton helped with that—who would advocate Merton's participation; they did arrive. Dom Jean was especially sure and lucid in his letter of invitation to Merton himself. "Looking at the general situation of monasticism and inter-religion relations today," he wrote, "I think you've been cut off long enough and the Church needs you to go out and share with others, not only in writing. Your personality . . . is a witness of the liberty in Christ, and that has to be *shown*."[5] Eventually Flavian approved Merton's participation and, perhaps as a trial run, authorized him in May to visit two small monasteries in New Mexico and California. Flavian obviously felt secure in granting Merton a six-month leave for travel in Asia—Bangkok, major Indian cities, Dharamsala in the north Indian mountains to speak with the Dalai Lama, Sri Lanka, and eventually returning to Bangkok again in early December for the AIM gathering. He would visit Buddhist and Christian monasteries and practitioners, lecture at several religious gatherings, see remarkable works of art and landscapes, and possibly go on to explore Zen in Japanese monasteries.

We are once again on famous ground: Merton's experience in Asia, deep and wide-ranging, became nearly the template for religious and spiritual developments in America from his time to ours. Some magnetism or Providence drew him to individuals and religious cultures that would influence many Americans in later years: preeminently the Dalai Lama, also Trungpa Rinpoche (then a young abbot), and the Burmese form of Buddhist practice, known in the English-speaking world as Insight Meditation. A year earlier he had intuited that "there is still something I have not said: but what it is I don't know." Could it have been to explore needed links between Western religion and Eastern meditative practice? He was meeting Asian religious elders, the abbots and hermits of their world. He looked toward home—and saw such possibilities for the deepening of religious experience, Catholic and other. "You are a Catholic *geshe,*" the Dalai Lama said to him as their conversations concluded.[6] The compliment could not be more striking; a *geshe* is a deeply learned lama, the product of long schooling and personal effort.

Merton left Gethsemani on September 9 after celebrating Mass at the hermitage with monks to whom he felt close. Very few knew of his departure—he was afraid that James, if informed, might interfere. On this famous Asian ground, for which Merton's journal and correspondence and other sources provide a vivid sense of what he saw and thought and how he lived, we should concern ourselves abstemiously with just two documents: an exchange of letters between Dom James and Merton. James took the initiative in a letter dated October 6, which Merton received in Calcutta.[7] His response carries the date October 20. We need to read nearly the entire text of each.

> My dear Fr Louis
> Perhaps you are not expecting a note from me—at least so soon.
>
> But I do want you to know—that right from the beginning of your trip, both my heart, and my poor prayers and sacrifices, go with you.
>
> As you so well know, the point of view, or attitude towards many of the fundamental features of cloistered, contemplative life are changing rapidly and radically, during these very last few years.
>
> For example, the question of Silence, which had been always so sacrosanct, and almost "sine qua non" of a Trappist Community.

First, it was allowed to speak at work. Now, almost anyone can speak to anyone else—almost any time or place. This includes novices.

Or, the question of hermits. Only a few years ago, as you may recall, I myself could not reconcile the place of a hermit in our Cistercian life.

Yet, ironically enough, evaluations had changed, and so rapidly, that it was myself, in the arrangements of Divine Providence, who, at the General Chapter, defended the vocation of hermits in our Order.

Then—"mirabile dictu," it was only a little while later that Jesus called me to follow Him, in the very vocation of a hermit, within the Order.

Or the question of trips outside the enclosure for cloistered monks. This also is rapidly becoming more and more, an accepted thing. Some excess perhaps—as one Community, where one-third were absent on trips this summer. . . .

The entire "climate" or "atmosphere" in regard to trips has gone thru a kaleidoscopic change. Your present trip takes place in a "milieu" entirely different, and also with less astonishment, than it would have, even a few years ago. . . .

In your own regard, dear Fr Louis, I would not be the least surprised, if I have indeed appeared as your "Bête noire"—"number one"—your "Nemesis."

But really, no. Such is not the case.

You never had, nor will you have—one, who has been a more faithful and loyal friend and brother—than myself. I never had any other motive in your regard than your best eternal interests. . . .

I often admired your basic Faith and ultimate humility in the face of crosses, and the pressures of trials, and frustrations of past years—whether on the part of myself or of others.

I was only an instrument in God's hands—for example, in regard to your trip to the Orient. Previously God's time for it had not come.

Now—it has. You will see that the fruits you will reap from it—for yourself—and for others, will be far more abundant and lasting—because you waited for God!!

It is Jesus' way of rewarding your Faith.

I look forward to hearing your accounts of possible retreats in Zen Buddhist Monasteries, to which you used to look forward, so much. Drop us a card, once in a while, if convenient.

Be assured, that my poor prayers and sacrifices in Calvary Hermitage will follow you, every inch of the trip, until you return to us again.

Your brother and friend
Love—in Him, Thru Her
Fr. M. James

Merton must have responded quite promptly. His handwritten letter survives, its words clear and pitched slightly forward as if to the future. I'll transcribe directly from the letter, although it is published; there is latent magic in the written word.

Dear Fr James
I have been waiting for a chance to thank you for your warm and gracious letter, which reached me after some delay, due to a mix-up. Anyway I certainly want you to know I appreciated it and certainly you must not feel that I failed to understand the situation. I never personally resented any of your decisions because I knew you were following your conscience and the policies that seemed necessary then. It is also true that the new "openness" might lead to abuses and deviations. I am not responsible for what *others* do but I certainly want to make sure that whatever *I* do is really for a spiritual goal and for the good of the Church and of the monastic life.

This trip is a hard one—Asia is very different from America and Europe—I have already had a slight case of dysentery from bad water (at Mass!—¼ cruet of it was enough!). But on the whole the journey is a real grace. I have been in contact with Buddhist monks who are really meditating and have learned of meditation centers that have never been made known in the West. This information is invaluable and very helpful to me personally and may have important results for all. Today I am having a long talk with a young Tibetan Buddhist abbot who made a heroic escape from the Communists a few years ago, and he is a very fine person indeed. These contacts seem to be really blessed by God. I feel it is my duty to make the most of every chance and perhaps eventually the experience will be profitable and will help the contemplative life in America—unfortunately it has to be admitted that Americans don't really meditate, or don't go deep enough and *never really know themselves*. Perhaps I can bring back some ideas that will change this. So many look to us for depth, and finding that it is not there, turn elsewhere!

So far every move here has been very quiet. I have avoided people who might make a fuss over me and frequent mostly Asians and non-Catholics to which I am not "famous." That is a blessing. . . .

I trust in your good prayers. Be sure that I have never changed in my respect for you as Abbot and affection as Father: our different views certainly did not affect our deep agreement on the real point of life and of our vocation. I hope you are enjoying a beautiful quiet fall out in the wild knobs!

With all my warmest regards in the Lord
brm Louis[8]

There were truths in both letters, and lies—of such things is reconciliation often made. Dom James had noticeably set out to justify his conduct toward Merton by situating it in an earlier, more restrictive era and invoking the Will of God as his guide, but he did so with warmth toward Merton, and that matters. It is surprising that God's Will immediately took a different course with the change of abbot, surprising also that James viewed himself as Merton's loyal friend and brother, none better. But the letter must have given him comfort, as it was intended to give Merton comfort.

"Drop us a card, once in a while, if convenient": curiously moving words, as if James feared that he would no longer be noticed. Did their long, somewhat tragic relation come down to this: drop us a card once in a while? Not at all—each of them knew what it had been, however differently interpreted. It was more than a postcard.

On Merton's side, he offered James the assurances that any person of common decency and a live heart would offer. He must have been sincerely touched that James had bothered to write; he saw the letter for what it was, a movement toward reconciliation. For that reason he was willing to lie. "I never personally resented any of your decisions." But his closing paragraph is not a lie: members of the community prayed for one another in good faith, and the two men did agree on the real point of life and their shared vocation. As well, Merton told truth by expressing his towering sense of adventure and happiness as he met Buddhist practitioners from whom so much could be learned and eventually returned to America—not least to Gethsemani. He was giving James the opportunity to accept what he was, what he valued, what he loved. Good letters! They made peace before the sun went down.

As you know, the sun set too quickly on one of these lives. In Singapore on December 8, soon to depart for the Bangkok conference, Merton was in perfect tune with himself. Listen to what he wrote that day:

> Suddenly there is a point where religion becomes laughable. Then you decide you are nonetheless religious.[9]

He was still "in the middle of all contradictions," but with joy. Two days later, he was dead, electrocuted by a faulty fan in his bedroom at the Bangkok conference. He died precisely twenty-seven years to the day after he entered Gethsemani. That day, December 10, was also Dom James's birthday.

His body was interred in the abbey graveyard under a simple white cross, like all of his brothers. Dom James, now Fr. James, lived on for many years, a far more solitary hermit than Merton. On Sundays he came to the abbey for Mass and dinner and gave occasional homilies to the community. Some brothers delivered food and news—and gossip—to his hermitage frequently enough to keep him interested. Nine years passed in this way. Until two toughs, as Merton had somehow intuited, broke into the hermitage, terrorized its elderly resident, took a few things, and left without physically harming him apart from a mysterious bruise on his face that a brother noticed when James came down to the abbey. He never returned to the hermitage. He spent a few days in Merton's hermitage—think of that—and soon chose to live in the abbey infirmary where other elderly monks made their home. It was convenient not least because there was a little chapel nearby where he would often offer a private Mass well into the night; he was always a man of prayer. James had recognized one of his assailants—a man for whom the abbey had done charitable works, helped him build a simple house. Neighbors in the nearby town of New Haven were beside themselves. No doubt proceeding methodically, the police department received a message from town: if you don't arrest those fellows in twenty-four hours, you'll find them hanging from a tree. That was old-fashioned Kentucky justice. They were found, arrested, no tree needed. James never pressed charges, saw one of the men from time to time, and prayed for them both.

James died on Good Friday, 1987, in his ninety-first year. His mortal remains were interred alongside Merton's grave: another white cross, another name inscribed on it. The only difference is that retreatants and visitors at the abbey often leave whatever homage they can at Merton's grave—flowers, a rosary, a miniature cairn of stones—while Dom James's grave is bare (fig. 17); he is scarcely noticed. That they are buried side by side has seemed to me and many others the last contradiction: who decided, and why? Couldn't there be a little distance between them? Hadn't they seen enough of each other in their lifetimes? I approached this question

FIG. 17. Adjoining graves of Thomas Merton and Dom James Fox at the Abbey of Gethsemani.

with my informants in the Gethsemani community as if a great truth might be revealed, a transcendent thought that has escaped most of us who care for Merton's example and writings. But no one seemed really to know: it just was that way and not some other way. Finally, in conversation with Fr. Timothy Kelly, abbot of Gethsemani at that time, I heard the simple facts. "I don't think there was any great decision made on it. I recall that Br. Gerlac, who arranged things in the cemetery, said to me, 'Let's bury Dom James beside Fr. Louis,' and I agreed. I think he saw it as a sign of reconciliation and of the brotherhood of our relations in eternity. I wouldn't look for any more profound reason than that. That is the depth of the matter—unless it also had something to do with Br. Gerlac's Irish sense of humor."[10]

[23]
Compline

COMPLINE IS THE LAST office of the day, a gentle time of prayer and psalm and chant. In winter, the sun has long since set at the appointed hour, 7:30; in summer it will be some time before it sets. Apart from a short reading, the sequence never changes. Afterward, the Great Silence until vigils early the next day. Compline concludes with bells—the Angelus, three rounds of bells—and a lovely custom: one or two lines form, monks first, then retreatants and visitors, to pass and bow before the abbot, who sprinkles drops of holy water on each one's head from a pierced vessel.

Lord have mercy, Christ have mercy, Lord have mercy.

Ancient words from compline. We have been speaking of an abbot who belonged to the past and a monk who gave his all for renewal. It is time to return them to the largest world we can conceive, be it a world where God reigns and gives peace to souls or a world without divinity where things nonetheless fall into place, vibrating or pulsing until harmony and peace sift out and make things right again. Their encounter here on earth had terrible aspects, that can no longer be doubted: coercion over many years, resentment over many years, such grave misunderstandings. Yet they were bound by religious obligation and perhaps even by Providence to live it, and they learned from and through each other. Dom James, the monastic entrepreneur and world traveler, became in the end a hermit with nowhere to go except within himself. Father Louis, the contemplative and writer and man of conscience, became in the end a world traveler who drew East and West together. His vision is still unfolding.

Lord, save us, save us while we are awake, protect us while we are asleep.

They did their best to forgive each other. How well did they succeed? Let us say: well, very well. Their judgments of each other could have lasted forever; they did not.

Lord, now let your servant go in peace, your word has been fulfilled.

In that spirit, can we let these two passionate servants of the Lord go their ways? Sound the Angelus. Merton and Dom James must equally have loved to hear it. A little holy water may get in your eye, like a tear. No matter. It's to be expected.

Chapter 42 of the Rule of Saint Benedict: After compline, no one may speak.

Completed at some distance from the Abbey of Gethsemani during compline, May 22, 2014

NOTES

Abbreviations Used in the Endnotes

General Abbreviations

Abbey Archive	Archive of the Abbey of Gethsemani (Trappist, Ky.)
DJ	Dom James Fox
n.d.	no date
TM	Thomas Merton
TMC	The Thomas Merton Center, Bellarmine University (Louisville, Ky.)

Volume Numbers of the Relevant Merton Journals

II Thomas Merton, *Entering the Silence,* ed. Jonathan Montaldo, vol. 2, *The Journals of Thomas Merton,* 1941–1952 (San Francisco: HarperSanFrancisco, 1997)

III Thomas Merton, *A Search for Solitude,* ed. Lawrence S. Cunningham, vol. 3, *The Journals of Thomas Merton,* 1952–1960 (San Francisco: HarperSanFrancisco, 1997)

IV Thomas Merton, *Turning toward the World,* ed. Victor A. Kramer, vol. 4, *The Journals of Thomas Merton,* 1960–1963 (San Francisco: HarperSanFrancisco, 1996)

V Thomas Merton, *Dancing in the Water of Life,* ed. Robert E. Daggy, vol. 5, *The Journals of Thomas Merton,* 1963–1965 (San Francisco: HarperSanFrancisco, 1997)

VI Thomas Merton, *Learning to Love,* ed. Christine M. Bochen, vol. 6, *The Journals of Thomas Merton,* 1966–1967 (San Francisco: HarperSanFrancisco, 1997)

VII Thomas Merton, *The Other Side of the Mountain,* ed. Patrick Hart, vol. 7, *The Journals of Thomas Merton,* 1967–1968 (San Francisco: HarperSanFrancisco, 1998)

Abbreviations of Specific Merton Books

CT Thomas Merton, *The Courage for Truth: The Letters of Thomas Merton to Writers,* ed. Christine M. Bochen (New York: Farrar, Straus and Giroux, 1993)

HGL Thomas Merton, *The Hidden Ground of Love: The Letters of Thomas Merton on Religious Experience and Social Concerns,* ed. William H. Shannon (New York: Farrar, Straus and Giroux, 1985)

RJ Thomas Merton, *The Road to Joy: The Letters of Thomas Merton to New and Old Friends,* ed. Robert E. Daggy (New York: Farrar, Straus and Giroux, 1989)

SC Thomas Merton, *The School of Charity: The Letters of Thomas Merton on Religious Renewal and Spiritual Direction,* ed. Patrick Hart (New York: Farrar, Straus and Giroux, 1990)

WF Thomas Merton, *Witness to Freedom: Letters in Times of Crisis,* ed. William H. Shannon (San Diego: Harcourt Brace, 1994)

Chapter 1. Nuance

1. For example, DJ letter to Dom Gabriel Sortais, Abbot General of the Cistercian Order, 5 August 1956, Abbey Archive.
2. Armand Jean le Bouthillier de Rancé, *De la sainteté et des devoirs de la vie monastique,* vol. 1 (Paris: François Muguet, 1683; facsimile ed., n.p.: ReInk Books, 2013), 389, 392–93.
3. For perspective on this issue, see Chrysogonus Waddell, "The Abbé de Rancé and Monastic Revival," in *The Roots of the Modern Christian Tradition,* ed. E. Rozanne Elder (Kalamazoo, Mich.: Cistercian Publications, 1984), 145–81. See also the comprehensive and sympathetic account in David N. Bell, *Understanding Rancé: The Spirituality of the Abbot of La Trappe in Context* (Kalamazoo, Mich.: Cistercian Publications, 2005), which includes an annotated bibliography.
4. Author interview with Fr. John Eudes Bamberger, September 2013.
5. DJ letter to Dom Gabriel Sortais, 17 May 1955, TMC.
6. TM letter to James Laughlin, 19 September 1967, in *Thomas Merton and James Laughlin: Selected Letters,* ed. David D. Cooper (New York: W. W. Norton, 1997), 332–33.
7. Saint John of the Cross, cited in a letter to DJ, 1955, source otherwise unidentified.
8. Among those from whom we shall hear, the Kentucky scholar Dean Lucas will soon publish the first biography of Dom James. I have not had the opportunity to see it.

Chapter 2. With Great Reluctance, an Autobiography

1. DJ letter to Dom Ignace Gillet, 6 November 1967, Abbey Archive.
2. Author interview with Fr. Timothy Kelly, March 2014.
3. For guidance to Passionist information online, see the Passionist Congregation Web site at www.cptryon.org/passionist/.
4. DJ, "Conference given in Chapter Room to our Community, on the occasion of the 50th Anniversary of Solemn Vows at Gethsemani," 3 June 1979 (Pentecost), Abbey Archive.
5. *III,* 30 March 1958, 187.
6. Author interview with Fr. James Conner, January 2014.

7. Morgan Atkinson interview with Fr. John Eudes Bamberger, April 2006 (private collection).
8. *Gethsemani Magnificat: Centenary of Gethsemani Abbey* (Trappist, Ky.: Gethsemani Abbey, 1949), unpaginated.
9. *II,* 22 August 1948, 227.
10. *II,* 25 August 1948, 227–28.

Chapter 3. All for Jesus thru Mary with a Smile

1. Author interview with Fr. Alan Gilmore, August 2013.
2. See Robert Barakat, *Cistercian Sign Language* (Kalamazoo, Mich.: Cistercian Publications, 1975).
3. *II,* 8 May 1949, 310.
4. Author interview with Br. Paul Quenon, August 2013.
5. Author interview with Br. Patrick Hart, January 2014.
6. Account based on interviews with the monks of Gethsemani, notably Fr. Timothy Kelly, a former abbot at Gethsemani, now procurator general of the order (second in authority to the abbot general).
7. Author interview with Br. Giuseppe Nazionale, January 2014.
8. TM refers to his work on the volume in *II,* 9 February 1949, 278.
9. Dom James, preface, *Gethsemani Magnificat,* unpaginated.
10. *II,* 3 October 1948, 235.
11. DJ, "The Contemplative Life in the United States," typescript of 1952, Abbey Archive.

Chapter 4. The Wall Street Journal *in a Cubbyhole*

1. Author interview with Br. Paul Quenon, August 2013.
2. Author interview with Br. Frederic Collins, January 2014.
3. Author interview with Fr. John Eudes Bamberger, September 2013.
4. Video of uncertain date (early 1980s), private collection. DJ's entrepreneurial skill survives to this day at Gethsemani's daughter house in Georgia. See August Turak, *Business Secrets of the Trappist Monks: One CEO's Quest for Meaning and Authenticity* (New York: Columbia University Press, 2013).
5. Author interview with Fr. James Conner, January 2014. The char-

acterization "shrewd" was used by nearly all interviewed members of the community.

6. Author interview with Fr. Timothy Kelly, March 2014.

Chapter 5. His Mind Is So Electrical

1. Fr. Raymond Flanagan, like Merton an author and monk of Gethsemani, published a biography of Dom Frederic a few years after the abbot's death: Rev. M. Raymond, *The Less Traveled Road: A Memoir of Dom Mary Frederic Dunne, OCSO, First American Trappist Abbot* (Milwaukee: Bruce Publishing, 1953).
2. TM, *The Sign of Jonas* (New York: Harcourt, Brace, 1953), 90–91, 113.
3. *II,* 3 October 1948, 235.
4. TM handwritten note to DJ, June 1950, TMC.
5. TM letter to DJ, *SC,* 11.
6. *Into Great Silence,* directed by Philip Gröning (Zeitgeist Films, 2005); available as a DVD.
7. *II,* 16 October 1948, 237.
8. *II,* summer 1949, 12.
9. Dom Gabriel Sortais letter to TM, 11 November 1952, TMC: "Ce qui m'intéresse, c'est vous, mon cher petit Père. Le bon Dieu vous éprouve par la sécheresse persistante" (What interests me is you yourself, my dear little Father. The good Lord is testing you through persistent dryness).
10. TM letter to DJ, n.d., but likely year-end 1949, TMC.
11. *II,* 1 December 1948, 247.
12. TM letter to DJ, spring 1949, *SC,* 11.
13. TM letter to DJ, summer 1949, *SC,* 12.
14. Ibid.
15. TM letter to Jacques Maritain, 9 July 1949, *CT.*
16. *II,* 7 January 1949, 262.
17. *II,* 12 June 1949, 323–24.
18. TM letter to DJ, 10 September 1949, *SC,* 15–16.
19. Ibid.
20. TM letter to DJ, 27 September 1950, *SC,* 22.

21. DJ letter to Dom Dominique Nogues, 4 January 1950, TMC.
22. *II,* 11 February 1950, 409.
23. DJ letter to Dom Dominique Nogues, 27 March 1950, TMC.
24. *II,* 25 March 1950, 425.

Chapter 6. Saint Anne's, a Toolshed

1. Cited in an editor's note, *RJ,* 208–9.
2. DJ letter to Dom Dominique Nogues, 6 April 1951, TMC.
3. *II,* 7 May 1951, 457.
4. DJ letter to Dom Louis de Gonzague Le Pennuen, 20 June 1951, TMC.
5. TM letter to DJ, 7 October 1951, *SC,* 27.
6. DJ letter to Dom Louis de Gonzague Le Pennuen, 5 February 1952, TMC.
7. DJ letter to Dom Louis de Gonzague Le Pennuen, 11 April 1952, TMC.
8. TM handwritten note to DJ, n.d., TMC.
9. *III,* 3 September 1952, 14; and 13 September 1952, 15.
10. *III,* 10 October 1952, 19–20.
11. "Private Vow," 8 October 1952, signed by TM and DJ, TMC.
12. TM letter to Dom Gabriel Sortais, 3 September 1952, TMC (trans. from French by the author).
13. TM letter to DJ, 5 November 1952, TMC.
14. TM letter to DJ, end of December 1952, TMC.
15. TM letter to Dom Gabriel Sortais, 4 November 1952, TMC.
16. Dom Gabriel Sortais letter to TM, 11 November 1952, Abbey Archive (trans. from French by the author).
17. TM letter to DJ, day of recollection, January 1953, TMC.
18. TM letter to DJ, 9 August 1953, TMC.
19. TM letter to DJ, 15 September 1953, TMC.
20. TM letter to DJ, 20 January 1953, *SC,* 49–50.
21. *III,* 16 February 1953, 32. The quiet at Saint Anne's didn't last. In summer 1955, TM wrote to Jean Leclercq that "machines are always working near it, and there is a perpetual noise. Nobody uses it very much." TM letter to Jean Leclercq, 11 August 1955, in *Survival or*

Prophecy? The Correspondence of Jean Leclercq and Thomas Merton, ed. Patrick Hart (New York: Farrar, Straus, and Giroux, 2002), 68.

22. TM letter to Fr. Barnabas M. Ahern, 22 January 1953, *SC,* 51.
23. DJ letter to Dom Louis de Gonzague Le Pennuen, 9 April 1953, TMC.

Chapter 7. The Journaling Seminar

1. DJ letter to Dom Louis de Gonzague Le Pennuen, 17 June 1953, TMC.
2. DJ letter to Dom Gabriel Sortais, 16 February 1963, TMC.
3. TM letter to DJ, Quinquagesima 1953 (15 February), TMC.
4. Dom Gabriel Sortais letter to TM, 9 March 1953, TMC (trans. from French by the author).
5. DJ letter to Dom Gabriel Sortais, 16 March 1953, TMC.
6. Dom Gabriel Sortais letter to TM, 11 April 1953, TMC (trans. from French by the author).
7. *III,* 17 July 1956, 45.

Chapter 8. Piety and Thunder

1. TM letter to DJ, Passion Sunday, April 1954, TMC.
2. Jean Leclercq letter to TM, 7 April 1954, in Hart, *Survival or Prophecy?,* 49.
3. DJ letter to Dom Louis de Gonzague Le Pennuen, 14 June 1954, TMC.
4. TM letter to DJ, 22 September 1954, TMC.
5. "Fr M Louis" or "fr m Louis" was Merton's standard signature in monastic correspondence, the "M" referring to "Mary," which figured in all Cistercian names in religion at the time.
6. TM letter to DJ, day of recollection, November 1954, TMC.

Chapter 9. Vincolata la Sua Libertà

1. TM letter to DJ, 29 November 1954, *SC,* 80–81, with an addition from the original document in TMC.
2. Dom Gabriel Sortais letter to DJ, 15 April 1955, TMC (trans. from French by the author).

3. DJ to Dom Gabriel Sortais, 16 March 1955, TMC.
4. DJ to Dom Gabriel Sortais, 28 March 1955, TMC.
5. Terrence G. Kardong, *Benedict's Rule: A Translation and Commentary* (Collegeville, Minn.: Liturgical Press, 1996), 34–35. This is the most comprehensive edition of the Rule, with Latin, English, and extensive commentary.
6. DJ letter to Dom Gabriel Sortais, 2 April 1955, TMC.
7. DJ letter to Dom Louis de Gonzague Le Pennuen, 28 March 1955, TMC.
8. James Fox, "The Spiritual Son," in *Thomas Merton, Monk: A Monastic Tribute,* ed. Patrick Hart (New York: Sheed and Ward, 1974), 141–59, esp. 152, concerning TM's role as confessor.
9. DJ letter to Dom Gabriel Sortais, 17 May 1955, TMC.
10. TM letter to Dom Jean Leclercq, 27 April 1955, in Hart, *Survival or Prophecy?,* 59–60.
11. Ibid., 61.
12. TM letter to Giovanni Battista Montini, archbishop of Milan, 25 April 1955, TMC.
13. DJ letter to Dom Gabriel Sortais, 17 May 1955, TMC.
14. Ibid.
15. Dom Gabriel Sortais letter to TM, 5 May 1955, TMC (trans. from French by the author).
16. DJ letter to Dom Gabriel Sortais, 17 May 1955, TMC.
17. Ibid.
18. TM letter to Jean Leclercq, 11 August 1955, in Hart, *Survival or Prophecy?,* 67.
19. Ibid.
20. DJ letter to Dom Gabriel Sortais, 18 May 1955, TMC.
21. DJ letter to Dom Gabriel Sortais, 25 May 1955, TMC.
22. For an excellent example of the practice, see Mark Scott, *At Home with Saint Benedict: Monastery Talks* (Trappist, Ky.: Cistercian Publications, 2011).
23. Dom Gabriel Sortais letter to DJ, 28 May 1955, TMC (trans. from French by the author).
24. Ibid.

25. Dom Louis de Gonzague Le Pennuen letter to DJ, 5 June 1955, TMC (trans. from French by the author).
26. DJ letter to Dom Gabriel Sortais, 18 October 1955, TMC.
27. TM letter to DJ, 15 August 1955, TMC.
28. Giovanni Battista Montini letter to TM, 20 August 1955, TMC.
29. Giovanni Battista Montini letter to DJ, 20 August 1955, TMC.
30. TM letter to Giovanni Battista Montini, 1 October 1955, TMC.
31. DJ letter to Giovanni Battista Montini, 20 October 1955, TMC.
32. Br. Alfred McCartney e-mail to Paul Pearson, director of the Thomas Merton Center, 15 January 2010.
33. TM letter to Jean Leclercq, 3 December 1955, in Hart, *Survival or Prophecy?,* 71–72.
34. DJ letter to Dom Gabriel Sortais, 18 October 1955, TMC.
35. DJ letter to Dom Gabriel Sortais, 29 November 1955, TMC.
36. TM letter to DJ, n.d. (by internal evidence, late 1955), TMC.

Chapter 10. The Shadow Abbot

1. DJ letter to Dom Gabriel Sortais, 9 January 1956, TMC.
2. TM letter to DJ, February 1956, *SC,* 95.
3. DJ letter to Dom Gabriel Sortais, 17 March 1956, TMC.
4. Ibid.
5. Quoted in Dom Gabriel Sortais letter to the canon E. Berrar, 16 June 1956, attached to Dom Gabriel Sortais letter to TM, 16 June 1956, TMC.
6. TM letter to Dom José Surchamp (Dom Angelico), 24 September 1956, TMC.
7. Dom Gabriel Sortais letter to the Canon E. Berrar, 16 June 1956, copy included in the letter cited in the following note (trans. by the author).
8. Dom Gabriel Sortais letter to DJ, 16 June 1956, TMC (trans. by the author).
9. DJ letter to Dom Louis de Gonzague Le Pennuen, 18 June 1956, TMC.
10. Michael Mott, *The Seven Mountains of Thomas Merton* (Boston: Houghton Mifflin, 1984), esp. 290–98.

11. TM, "The Neurotic Personality in the Monastic Life," first published in *The Merton Annual,* vol. 4 (New York: AMS Press, 1991), 3–19. Br. Patrick Hart notes in his introduction (3–4) that "Zilboorg had read Merton's manuscript about the neurotic personality and advised against its publication at that time, encouraging Merton rather to deepen his understanding of psychology and its relationship to the monastic life. He thought Merton was rushing into print in a seizure of enthusiasm without really mastering the subject adequately." Hart provides no source for this information.
12. *III,* 22 July 1956 through 4 August 1956, 49–63.
13. See Rob Marchesani, "Introduction—a Hermit in Times Square: Setting the Stage," *Psychotherapy Patient* 11, nos. 3/4 (2001), 1–9; Alexander Smith, "Burnt Offerings to Prometheus: The Consultation Meetings between Thomas Merton and Gregory Zilboorg," *Psychotherapy Patient* 11, nos. 3/4 (2001), 37–54; and Fiona Gardner, "Thomas Merton and Dr. Gregory Zilboorg: Understanding the Dynamics," *Merton Journal* 11, no. 1 (Easter 2004), 6–12.
14. *III,* 29 July 1956, 59–60.
15. Mott, *Seven Mountains,* 297.
16. *III,* 2 August 1956, 61.
17. Author interview with Fr. John Eudes Bamberger, September 2013.
18. *III,* 1 September 1956, 77.
19. DJ letter to Gregory Zilboorg, 13 August 1956, Abbey Archive.
20. DJ letter to Gregory Zilboorg, 3 September 1956, Abbey Archive.
21. Gregory Zilboorg letter to DJ, 10 September 1956, Abbey Archive.
22. DJ letter to Gregory Zilboorg, 14 September 1956, Abbey Archive.
23. DJ letter to Dom Gabriel Sortais, 4 September 1956, TMC.
24. TM letter to Gregory Zilboorg, 14 September 1956, TMC.
25. TM letter to Gregory Zilboorg, 20 September 1956, TMC.
26. TM letter to Gregory Zilboorg, 9 October 1956, TMC.
27. DJ letter to Gregory Zilboorg, 11 June 1957, Abbey Archive.
28. TM letter to Sr. Thérèse Lentfoehr, 25 September 1956, TMC; an abridged version of this letter is published in *RJ,* 225.
29. DJ letter to Naomi Burton Stone, 26 November 1956, Abbey Archive.
30. DJ letter to Gregory Zilboorg, 19 December 1956, Abbey Archive.

31. Gregory Zilboorg letter to DJ, 3 January 1957, Abbey Archive: "I hope prayerfully that I was of some use, or [a] little help while your guest. I learned to know Fr Louis better. Quite naturally I was able to come a little closer to the purely human side of Fr Louis. I like him a great deal. I have not changed my mind about him being analyzed. He should not be. His should be the path of spiritual development."
32. DJ letter to Gregory Zilboorg, 28 January 1957, Abbey Archive.
33. *IV,* 10 March 1963, 302.

Chapter 11. Out of a Chrysalis

1. DJ letter to Dom Gabriel Sortais, 4 February 1957, TMC.
2. *III,* 28 February 1958, 175–76.
3. *III,* 25 March 1958, 184–85.
4. DJ letter to Jean Leclercq, 30 December 1957, TMC.
5. *III,* 15 November 1957, 137–38.
6. *III,* 5 May 1958, 200. With thanks to Mark Meade at the Thomas Merton Center for verifying in the original Merton journal that the text reads "out of a chrysalis"; the published version omits the "a."
7. For Cardenal's account of TM and Gethsemani, see Ernesto Cardenal, *Vida Perdida: Memorias I* (Madrid: Trotta, 2005), s.v. index.
8. TM letter to DJ, 15 July 1957, *SC,* 105.
9. *III,* 24 December 1957, 148.
10. *III,* 23 January 1958, 159.
11. *III,* 15 February 1958, 167.
12. *III,* 28 February 1958, 176.
13. *III,* 4 March 1958, 176.
14. *III,* 19 March 1958, 181–82.
15. TM letter to Boris Pasternak, 23 October 1958, *CT,* 90.
16. *III,* 236–38, 11 December 1958.
17. Martin Buber, *I and Thou,* trans. Ronald Gregor Smith (New York: Scribner's, 1958), 115–16.
18. *III,* 24 April 1958, 195–96.

Chapter 12. The Moon, Venus, or Mars!

1. Dom Gabriel Sortais letter to DJ, 20 March 1958, TMC (trans. from French by the author).
2. TM letter to Fr. Riccardo Lombardi, 16 June 1958, TMC.
3. DJ letter to Fr. Riccardo Lombardi, 4 August 1958, with 5 August 1958 postscript, TMC.
4. *III,* 25 July 1958, 209–10.
5. *III,* 22 July 1958, 208.
6. DJ letter to the community, 21 April 1956, Abbey Archive.
7. DJ letter to Dom Gabriel Sortais, 5 August 1958, TMC.
8. DJ letter to Dom Gabriel Sortais, 12 August 1958, TMC.
9. Dom Gabriel Sortais letter to DJ, 18 August 1958, TMC (trans. from French by the author).
10. DJ to Dom Gabriel Sortais, 21 October 1958, TMC.
11. *III,* 23 October 1958, 225.
12. *III,* 27 December 1958, 240.
13. *III,* 7 December 1958, 234–35.
14. *III,* 27 December 1958, 241.
15. Fr. Amédée Hallier letter to Dom Colomban Bissey, 25 November 1958, TMC (trans. from French by the author with the exception of "with smiling," in English in the original).
16. Amédée Hallier, *The Monastic Theology of Aelred of Rievaulx,* trans. C. Heaney, with a preface by Thomas Merton (Dublin: Irish University Press, 1969).

Chapter 13. When Will We Become Christians?

1. Karl Adam, *The Christ of Faith* (New York: Pantheon, 1957), 3.
2. The most convenient place to find their essays is in Thomas Merton, *Zen and the Birds of Appetite* (New York: New Directions, 1968), 99–141.
3. DJ letter to Dom Gabriel Sortais, 31 August 1959, TMC.
4. TM, *Wisdom of the Desert* (New York: New Directions, 1960), 23.
5. Ibid., 24.
6. *III,* 25 January 1959, 251.
7. *III,* 26 January 1959, 253.

8. *III,* 15 March 1959, 268.
9. *III,* 28 May 1959, 285.
10. *III,* 9 June 1959, 289.
11. *III,* 16 June 1959, 294.
12. *III,* 5 July 1959, 302–3.
13. *III,* 12 July 1959, 304.
14. *III,* 26 July 1959, 310.
15. Concerning this incident, Br. Paul Quenon (a choir novice at the time) told the author that TM's "tears" may have been sardonic: "Most of us choir novices considered a spiritual bouquet corny." E-mail correspondence.
16. DJ letter to the diaspora incorporating a chapter homily, 29 July 1973 (italics substituted for DJ's underlining), Abbey Archive.
17. *III,* 25 July 1959, 309–10.
18. *III,* 8 December 1959, 355–56.

Chapter 14. Fuge, Tace, Quiesce

1. Richard Lombardi, *Towards a New World* (New York: Philosophical Publishing House, 1958).
2. DJ letter to Fr. Riccardo Lombardi, 12 January 1959, TMC.
3. *III,* 1 February 1959, 254.
4. DJ letter to Dom Gabriel Sortais, 20 March 1959, TMC.
5. *III,* 16 June 1959, 295.
6. *III,* 22 August 1959, 319.
7. James Thurber, *The Years with Ross* (Boston: Little, Brown, 1959).
8. *III,* 22 August 1959, 320.
9. TM letter to Pablo Antonio Cuadra, 22 August 1959, *CT,* 187.
10. *III,* 30 August 1959, 325.
11. *III,* 21 September 1959, 330–31.
12. *III,* 26 September 1959, 332.
13. TM letter to DJ, 23 September 1959, TMC.
14. *III,* 24 April 1960, 385.
15. DJ letter to Dom Gabriel Sortais, 25 May 1959, TMC.
16. *III,* 6 September 1959, 325–26.
17. Ibid., 326.
18. Dom Gabriel Sortais letter to DJ, 28 September 1959, TMC.

19. DJ letter to Fr. Jean Daniélou, 6 July 1959, Abbey Archive.
20. Fr. Jean Daniélou letter to DJ, 17 July 1959, Abbey Archive (trans. from French by the author).
21. Fr. Jean Daniélou letter to DJ, 12 August 1959, Abbey Archive (trans. from French by the author).
22. DJ letter to Fr. Jean Daniélou, 25 August 1959, Abbey Archive.
23. DJ letter to Dom Jean Leclercq, 9 November 1959, TMC.
24. TM letter to Ernesto Cardenal, 8 October 1959, *WF,* 207.
25. TM letter to Fr. Jean Daniélou, 5 December 1959, recounting news Merton had received considerably earlier, *WF,* 209.
26. *III,* 15 November 1959, 342–43.
27. DJ, "Memorandum re: Fr. L.," 9 December 1959 (internal evidence shows that its addressee was Dom Gabriel Sortais), TMC.
28. *III,* 28 November 1959, 349.
29. Dom Gabriel Sortais letter to DJ, 8 November 1959, TMC (trans. from French by the author).
30. DJ, "Rapport relatif au Père M. Louis (Thomas Merton) du Monastère de N. D. de Gethsemani, Etats-Unis d'Amérique (Ordre des Cisterciens, S. O.)," 19 November 1959, TMC.
31. DJ letter to a monsignor, presumably Paul-Pierre Philippe, newly elected secretary of the Sacred Congregation for Religious, October 1960, TMC.
32. DJ, "Rapport," 1, TMC (trans. from French by the author). TMC has recently acquired DJ's English-language original. Here it is preferable to translate from the French version actually delivered to the congregation; the differences are small but telling.
33. TM letter to Dom Gregorio Lemercier, 17 December 1959, *WF,* 212–13.
34. Author interview with Fr. James Conner, January 2014.
35. TM letter to Fr. John Eudes Bamberger, n.d. (not after 1965), TMC.
36. *III,* 5 December 1959, 350–51.
37. TM letter to Fr. Jean Daniélou, 5 December 1959, *WF,* 210–11.
38. *III,* 17 December 1959, 358–59.
39. TM letter to Ernesto Cardenal, 17 December 1959, *WF,* 121–22.
40. TM letter to DJ, 17 December 1959, *WF,* 214–15.

41. *III,* 18 December 1959, 360.
42. TM letter to DJ, ca. 17 December 1959, *WF,* 215–16.
43. DJ letter to Dom Gabriel Sortais, 23 December 1959, Abbey Archive.
44. *III,* 29 December 1959, 363.
45. TM letter to Pablo Antonio Cuadra, 4 January 1959, *WF,* 187.

Chapter 15. Solidity and Ashes

1. TM letter to Pope John XXIII, 11 February 1960, *HGL,* 484.
2. TM letter to Pope John XXIII, 11 April 1960, *HGL,* 485.
3. Dom Gabriel Sortais letter to DJ, 25 April 1960, TMC (trans. from French by the author).
4. DJ letter to Dom Gabriel Sortais, 2 May 1960, TMC.
5. Dom Gabriel Sortais letter to DJ, 27 July 1960, TMC (trans. from French by the author).
6. TM letter to DJ, 23 May 1960, TMC.
7. Ibid.
8. *IV,* 26 June 1960, 16–17.
9. *IV,* 2 October 1960, 55.
10. TM letter to Fr. Jean Daniélou, 2 January 1960, *WF,* 220.
11. TM letter to Valerio Cardinal Valeri, 2 January 1960, *WF,* 218.
12. DJ letter to Arcadio Cardinal Larraona, 14 January 1960, TMC.
13. *IV,* 16 October 1960, 58.
14. TM letter to Dom Jean Leclercq, 24 December 1960, *Survival or Prophecy?,* 89.
15. *IV,* 1 December 1960, 71.
16. *IV,* 20 February 1961, 96.
17. *IV,* 3 March 1961, 97.
18. Dom Gabriel Sortais letter to DJ, 1 March 1960, TMC (trans. from French by the author).
19. *IV,* 28 November 1960, 70.
20. *IV,* 15 November 1960, 67.
21. *III,* 10 January 1960, 367–68.
22. *IV,* 5 June 1960, 7–8.
23. *IV,* 11 September 1960, 46.

24. *IV,* 15 November 1960, 67.
25. *III,* 24 March 1960, 381.
26. See Dag Hammarskjöld, *Markings,* trans. Leif Sjöberg and W. H. Auden (New York: Knopf, 1964); and Roger Lipsey, *Hammarskjöld: A Life* (Ann Arbor: University of Michigan Press, 2013).
27. *IV,* 7 August 1960, 28.
28. DJ letter to Dom Gabriel Sortais, 13 October 1960, TMC.
29. *IV,* 13 December 1960, 73.

Chapter 16. A Deeper Kind of Dedication

1. TM letter to Robert Lax, 4 June 1962, in *The Letters of Thomas Merton and Robert Lax: When Prophecy Still Had a Voice,* ed. Arthur W. Biddle (Lexington: University Press of Kentucky, 2001), 237.
2. Very belatedly published as *Peace in the Post-Christian Era,* ed. and with an introduction by Patricia Burton, foreword by Jim Forest (Maryknoll, N.Y.: Orbis, 2004).
3. TM letter to Boris Pasternak, 22 August 1958, *CT,* 88.
4. *IV,* 6 June 1960, 9.
5. *IV,* 5 June 1960, 9.
6. *IV,* 22 November 1960, 69.
7. Thomas Merton, ed., *Gandhi on Non-Violence: A Selection from the Writings of Mahatma Gandhi* (New York: New Directions, 1965).
8. *IV,* 8 April 1961, 106–7.
9. *IV,* 20 May 1961, 121.
10. Thomas Merton letter to Etta Gullick, October 1961, *HGL,* 347.
11. Morgan Atkinson interview with Fr. Daniel Berrigan, 14 December 2005 (private collection).
12. TM letter to Fr. Daniel Berrigan, 10 November 1961, *HGL,* 71.
13. TM letter to Dorothy Day, 23 August 1961, *HGL,* 139.
14. *IV,* 23 October 1961, 172.
15. *IV,* 10 May 1963, 318.
16. *IV,* 8 September 1961, 158–59.
17. *IV,* 17 February 1962, 203–4.
18. TM letter to Fr. Daniel Berrigan, 25 June 1963, *HGL,* 78–79.
19. TM letter to Fr. Daniel Berrigan, 14 February 1966, *HGL,* 90.

20. Dom Gabriel Sortais letter to TM, 12 May 1962, TMC (trans. from French by the author).
21. See *Passion for Peace: The Social Essays,* ed. William H. Shannon (New York: Crossroad, 1995).
22. TM letter to Fr. Daniel Berrigan, 23 February 1964, *HGL,* 80–81.
23. *Cold War Letters,* ed. Christine M. Bochen and William H. Shannon (Maryknoll, N.Y.: Orbis, 2006).
24. TM letter to James Forest, 29 October 1961, *HGL,* 257.
25. TM letter to W. H. "Ping" Ferry, 18 January 1962, *HGL,* 204–5.
26. TM letter to James Forest, 17 January 1963, *HGL,* 273.
27. Morgan Atkinson interview with Fr. Daniel Berrigan, 14 December 2005 (private collection).
28. TM letter to Dorothy Day, 17 August 1960, *HGL,* 138.
29. TM letter to Fr. Daniel Berrigan, 10 March 1962, *HGL,* 73.
30. TM letter to Fr. Daniel Berrigan, 25 June 1963, *HGL,* 77.
31. Dom Gabriel Sortais letter to TM, 12 May 1962, TMC (trans. from French by the author).
32. TM letter to James Forest, 29 April 1962, *HGL,* 266–67.
33. TM letter to James Forest, 22 September 1962, *HGL,* 270–71.
34. TM letter to James Forest, 8 December 1962, *HGL,* 272.
35. TM letter to Pope John XXIII, 11 November 1961, *HGL,* 486
36. TM letter to Dom Gabriel Sortais, Easter Day 1963 (April 14), *SC,* 166 (published translation slightly altered by the author on the basis of the TMC original).
37. *IV,* 27 April 1962, 216.

Chapter 17. Who Can Say?

1. TM note to Fr. John Eudes Bamberger, n.d., TMC.
2. Ibid.
3. *V,* 1965, 334, in undated section entitled "Some Personal Notes: End of 1965."
4. *V,* 16 August 1964, 136.
5. *V,* 12 May 1964, 104.
6. *IV,* 16 April 1963, 313.
7. *V,* 20 August 1963, 11.

8. Paul Pearson communication to the author, June 2014, relaying an observation by Fr. Matthew Kelty.
9. Fr. Alan Gilmore, letter to the author, 30 June 2014.
10. TM letter to Etta Gullick, 28 July 1963, *HGL,* 362.
11. On TM's ink drawings and prints in this period, see Roger Lipsey, *Angelic Mistakes: The Art of Thomas Merton* (Boston: New Seeds, 2006).
12. For DJ's willingness, see TM letter to James Laughlin, 13 December 1964, in Cooper, *Thomas Merton and James Laughlin,* 252.
13. TM letter to Dan Walsh, November 1963, *RJ,* 306–7 (date not further specified).
14. *IV,* 10 May 1963, 318.
15. DJ letter to the Gethsemani diaspora, 1965, Abbey Archive.
16. *IV,* 22 July 1963, 344.
17. *IV,* 30 July 1963, 349.
18. *IV,* 20–21 May, 1963, 320–21.
19. *IV,* 21 May, 1963, 321.
20. *IV,* 14 November 1963, 34–35.

Chapter 18. The Tea, the Joy

1. *V,* 10 January 1964, 58–59.
2. *V,* 23 January 1964, 66.
3. *V,* 10 July 1964, 125.
4. For details see *V,* 13 January 1964, 60–61; DJ, "The Spiritual Son," in Hart, *Thomas Merton, Monk,* 155–56; and Christine M. Bochen, "Merton's 'Absurd Enterprise': A Brief Foray into Script-Writing," *Merton Seasonal* 38, no. 1 (Spring 2013), 3–14. A surprisingly informative online source about the Vatican Pavilion of so many years ago may be found at nywf64.com/vatican04.shtml.
5. *V,* 18 January 1964, 64.
6. See Roger Lipsey, "In the Zen Garden of the Lord: Thomas Merton's Stone Garden," *The Merton Annual,* vol. 21 (2008), 91–105.
7. TM letter to Paul Sih, 2 January 1962, *HGL,* 551.
8. On DJ's scant knowledge of Zen, see TM letter to Fr. Heinrich Dumoulin, 24 September 1964, *HGL,* 172.
9. *V,* 2 June 1964, 107–8.

10. *V,* 12 June 1964, 108–9.
11. TM letter to D. T. Suzuki, 11 June 1964, *HGL,* 569; for the complete correspondence, see *Encounter: Thomas Merton and D. T. Suzuki,* ed. Robert E. Daggy (Monterey, Ky.: Larkspur Press, 1988).
12. See Roger Lipsey, "Merton, Suzuki, Zen, Ink: Thomas Merton's Calligraphy in Context," in *Merton and Buddhism: Wisdom, Emptiness, and Everyday Mind,* ed. Bonnie Bowman Thurston (Louisville, Ky.: Fons Vitae, 2007), 125–58; also relevant pages in Lipsey, *Angelic Mistakes.*
13. TM, "D. T. Suzuki: The Man and His Work," in *Zen and the Birds of Appetite,* 60–62.
14. *V,* 16 and 20 June, 1964, 113–16.
15. Ibid., 117.
16. Fr. Heinrich Dumoulin letter to TM, 16 September 1964, TMC.
17. TM letter to Fr. Heinrich Dumoulin, 24 September 1964, *HGL,* 172.
18. TM petition to DJ, 24 September 1964, TMC.
19. DJ letter to Dom Ignace Gillet, 17 October 1964, TMC.
20. DJ letter to Dom Ignace Gillet, 9 November 1964, TMC.
21. Dom Ignace Gillet letter to DJ, 18 November 1964, TMC (trans. from French by the author).
22. John C. H. Wu letter to TM, 27 December 1964, TMC.

Chapter 19. A Hermit Now

1. *V,* 25 September 1964, 148.
2. *V,* 2 October 1964, 151.
3. See *VII,* 28 November 1967, 17.
4. DJ letter to Fr. Heinrich Dumoulin, 17 October 1964, TMC.
5. TM letter to DJ, dated by internal evidence to September 1964, attached to DJ letter to Dom Ignace Gillet, 29 September 1964, *SC,* 239.
6. Dom Ignace Gillet letter to DJ, 18 November 1964, TMC (trans. from French by the author).
7. DJ letter to Dom Ignace Gillet, 27 November 1964, TMC (trans. from French by the author).

8. DJ, "Call to Greater Solitude in Our Order," presumed to be 1965, TMC.
9. *V,* 19 November 1964, 167–68.
10. *V,* 30 January 1965, 198.
11. *V,* 26 June 1965, 259.
12. *V,* May 1965, 240.
13. *V,* 17 August 1965, 281.
14. *V,* 6 October 1965, 301.
15. *V,* 11 October 1965, 302.
16. *V,* 14–16 February 1965, 205–6.
17. *V,* 29 June 1965, 262.
18. Dom Ignace Gillet letter to Fr. Charles Dumont, 9 July 1965, TMC (trans. from French by the author).
19. Dom Ignace Gillet letter to DJ, 16 July 1965 (trans. from French by the author).
20. DJ letter to Dom Ignace, 22 July 1965, TMC.
21. *V,* 1 September 1965, 288.
22. TM letter to Naomi Burton Stone, 31 August 1965, *WF,* 147.
23. DJ letter to Naomi Burton Stone, 2 February 1966, TMC.
24. TM letter to Dom Jean Leclercq, 11 May 1965, *Survival or Prophecy?,* 127–28.
25. *V,* 30 October 1965, 310.
26. *V,* 21 December 1965, 326.

Chapter 20. To Sleep Alone All of My Life

1. *V,* 12 May 1964, 104.
2. *VI,* 23 February 1966, 20.
3. *VI,* 24 February 1966, 364, and 25 February 1966, 21.
4. TM letter to Fr. Tarcisius (James Conner), 23 June 1963, *SC,* 174.
5. TM letter to Fr. John Eudes Bamberger, 11 March [1966?], TMC.
6. Fr. John Eudes Bamberger letter to TM, n.d., TMC.
7. *VI,* 23 March 1966, 33.
8. Ibid.
9. *VI,* 6 March 1966, 367.
10. *VI,* 10 April 1966, 38.
11. *VI,* 19 April 1966, 41.

12. *VI,* 27 April 1966, 45.
13. Ibid., 45–46.
14. "The Tale of Pearl-Harvest," in *The Book of the Thousand Nights and One Night,* trans. Powys Mathers from the French edition by J. C. Mardrus (St. Martin's Press: New York, 1972), vol. 4, pp. 7, 10.
15. *VI,* 27 April 1966, 46.
16. Robert M. Durling, trans. and ed., *Petrarch's Lyric Poems: The* Rime sparse *and Other Lyrics* (Cambridge, Mass.: Harvard University Press, 1976), 39, 54.
17. *VI,* 4 May 1966, 51.
18. *VI,* 9 May 1966, 55.
19. *VI,* 14 June 1966, 82–83.
20. *VI,* 22 June 1966, 329–30.
21. DJ notes, June 1966, TMC.
22. Joan Baez's performance of "Silver Dagger" may be available online at youtube.com/watch?v=4Xlmb8gG7HU.
23. *VI,* 10 December 1966, 167.
24. *VI,* 23 June 1966, 344.
25. TM note to DJ, n.d., summer 1966, TMC.
26. TM letter to DJ, 28 July 1966, *WF,* 238.
27. TM, Commitment to the Solitary Life (1966), *SC,* Appendix 2: Two Private Vows, 419.
28. *VI,* 16 July 1966, 96–97.
29. *VI,* 29 July 1966, 104.
30. *VI,* 31 July 1966, 105.
31. *VI,* 31 July 1966, 106 (full text of TM letter to Fr. John Eudes Bamberger of that date).
32. Linda Miroslava Sabbath [Linda Parsons], *The Unveiling of God,* 2010, no further publication data, chapters 2 and 3.
33. *VI,* 29 and 31 July, 103 and 105.
34. Author interview with Fr. John Eudes, August 2014, and *VI,* 31 July 1966, 107.
35. *VI,* 5 August 1966, 108.
36. *VI,* 4 November 1966, 157.
37. *VI,* 13 November 1966, 160–61.

38. *VI,* 5–8 August 1966, 110–13.
39. *VI,* 16–20 December 1966, 171–72.

Chapter 21. It Seems So Absurd

1. William Schickel, "A Point of View for the Renovation of the Abbey Church at Gethsemani," 27 April 1966, Abbey Archive. For Schickel's career and major works, see Gregory Wolfe, *The Art of William Schickel: Sacred Passion,* 2nd ed. (Notre Dame, In.: University of Notre Dame Press, 2010); for Schickel's further commentary on the Gethsemani project, see "Unifying the Old and the New," *Liturgical Arts* 36, no. 4 (August 1968), 99–100. The issue includes articles on the renovation by Fr. Matthew Kelty and TM (see note 8 below).
2. *VI,* 20 April 1966, 42.
3. Author interview with Br. Paul Quenon, August 2013.
4. *VI,* 2 May 1966, 50.
5. TM letter to William J. Schickel, 10 August 1967, *WF,* 241.
6. TM letter to Br. Patrick Hart and Fr. Timothy Kelly, 23 August 1967, *SC,* 344.
7. DJ letter "to the diaspora," n.d., but soon after 3 September 1967, Abbey Archive.
8. TM, "Note on the New Church at Gethsemani," *Liturgical Arts* 36, no. 4 (August 1968), 100–101.
9. *VI,* 18 November 1967, 12.
10. *VI,* 7 February 1967, 194–95.
11. *VI,* 14 July 1967, 256.
12. *VI,* 7 September 1967, 286.
13. *VI,* 11 September 1967, 289.
14. Author interview with Fr. Michael Casagram, January 2014.
15. Author interview with Br. Paul Quenon, August 2013.
16. Author interview with Fr. Timothy Kelly, March 2014.
17. *VII,* 28 November 1967, 17.
18. TM letter to Fr. Daniel Berrigan, 27 November 1967, *HGL,* 99.
19. DJ letter to Dom Ignace Gillet, 6 November 1967, Abbey Archive.
20. *VII,* 24–25 December 1967, 30.
21. TM, "My Campaign Platform," mid-December 1967, *SC,* 356–57.

22. TM letter to W. H. "Ping" Ferry, 21 February 1968, *HGL,* 237.
23. TM letter to Fr. Daniel Berrigan, 8 February 1968, *HGL,* 99.
24. *VII,* 15 January 1968, 40–41.
25. TM letter to DJ, 2 February 1967, TMC
26. *VI,* 30 September 1967, 297.

Chapter 22. Make Peace Before the Sun Goes Down

1. *VII,* 15 January 1968, 42.
2. *VII,* 6 April 1968, 77.
3. TM letter to Fr. Charles Dumont, 13 April 1968, *SC,* 376.
4. *VII,* 13 August 1968, 153.
5. Jean Leclercq letter to TM, 21 January 1968, *Survival or Prophecy?,* 167.
6. *VII,* 8 November 1968, 266. TM writes there that the Dalai Lama "remarked that I was a 'Catholic geshe,' . . . the highest possible praise from a Gelugpa, like an honorary doctorate!" In his autobiography of 1990, the Dalai Lama also recalled their exchange and his remark to Merton that he was a "Catholic geshe." "It was Merton," he wrote, "who introduced me to the real meaning of the word 'Christian.'" See Tenzin Gyatso, *Freedom in Exile: The Autobiography of the Dalai Lama* (New York: HarperCollins, 1990), 189.
7. DJ letter to TM, 6 October 1968, TMC.
8. TM letter to DJ, 20 October 1968, transcribed from the original in TMC, with small differences from its place of publication, *SC,* 405–6.
9. *VII,* 6 December 1968, 325.
10. Author interview with Fr. Timothy Kelly, March 2014.

SELECT BIBLIOGRAPHY

The works listed here are directly germane to topics explored in this book. Merton bibliography is an ongoing project. Current works by and about him are cited in the quarterly *Merton Seasonal,* available by subscription through the International Thomas Merton Society. The standard bibliography is *More Than Silence: A Bibliography of Thomas Merton,* edited by Patricia A. Burton (Lanham, Md.: Scarecrow Press / American Theological Library Association, 2008).

I. Works by Thomas Merton

1. Journals

The Asian Journal of Thomas Merton. Edited by Naomi Burton, Patrick Hart, and James Laughlin. New York: New Directions, 1973.

Dancing in the Water of Life. Edited by Robert E. Daggy. Vol. 5 of *The Journals of Thomas Merton* (1963–1965). San Francisco: HarperSanFrancisco, 1997.

Entering the Silence. Edited by Jonathan Montaldo. Vol. 2 of *The Journals of Thomas Merton* (1941–1952). San Francisco: HarperSanFrancisco, 1997.

Learning to Love. Edited by Christine M. Bochen. Vol. 6 of *The Journals of Thomas Merton* (1966–1967). San Francisco: HarperSanFrancisco, 1997.

The Other Side of the Mountain. Edited by Patrick Hart. Vol. 7 of *The Journals of Thomas Merton* (1967–1968). San Francisco: HarperSanFrancisco, 1998.

A Search for Solitude. Edited by Lawrence S. Cunningham. Vol. 3 of *The Journals of Thomas Merton* (1952–1960). San Francisco: HarperSanFrancisco, 1997.

Thomas Merton in Alaska: The Alaskan Conferences, Journals, and Letters. Edited by Robert E. Daggy et al. New York: New Directions, 1989.

Turning toward the World. Edited by Victor A. Kramer. Vol. 4 of *The Journals of Thomas Merton* (1960–1963). San Francisco: HarperSanFrancisco, 1996.

A Vow of Conversation: Journals 1964–1965. Edited by Naomi Burton Stone. New York: Farrar, Straus Giroux, 1988.

2. Correspondence

At Home in the World: The Letters of Thomas Merton and Rosemary Radford Ruether. Edited by Mary Tardiff. Maryknoll, N.Y.: Orbis, 1995.

Cold War Letters. Edited by Christine M. Bochen and William H. Shannon. Maryknoll, N.Y.: Orbis, 2006.

The Courage for Truth: The Letters of Thomas Merton to Writers. Edited by Christine M. Bochen. New York: Farrar, Straus and Giroux, 1993.

Encounter: Thomas Merton and D. T. Suzuki. Edited by Robert E. Daggy. Monterey, Ky.: Larkspur Press, 1988.

The Hidden Ground of Love: The Letters of Thomas Merton on Religious Experience and Social Concerns. Edited by William H. Shannon. New York: Farrar, Straus and Giroux, 1985.

The Road to Joy: The Letters of Thomas Merton to New and Old Friends. Edited by Robert E. Daggy. New York: Farrar, Straus and Giroux, 1989.

The School of Charity: The Letters of Thomas Merton on Religious Renewal and Spiritual Direction. Edited by Patrick Hart. New York: Farrar, Straus and Giroux, 1990.

Survival or Prophecy? The Correspondence of Jean Leclercq and Thomas Merton. Edited by Patrick Hart. New York: Farrar, Straus and Giroux, 2002.

Thomas Merton and James Laughlin: Selected Letters. Edited by David D. Cooper. New York: W. W. Norton, 1997.

When Prophecy Still Had a Voice: The Letters of Thomas Merton and Robert Lax. Edited by Arthur W. Biddle. Lexington: University Press of Kentucky, 2001.

Witness to Freedom: Letters in Times of Crisis. Edited by William H. Shannon. San Diego: Harcourt Brace, 1994.

3. Books and Articles by Merton

"A Christian Looks at Zen." Introduction to *The Golden Age of Zen: Zen Masters of the Tang Dynasty*, by John C. H. Wu, 1–23. 1967. Reprint, Bloomington, Ind.: World Wisdom, 2003.

The Climate of Monastic Prayer. Kalamazoo, Mich.: Cistercian Publications, 1969.

Conjectures of a Guilty Bystander. Garden City, N.Y.: Doubleday, 1966.

Contemplation in a World of Action. Garden City, N.Y.: Doubleday, 1971.

Day of a Stranger. Salt Lake City, Utah: Gibbs M. Smith, 1981.

Gandhi on Non-Violence: A Selection from the Writings of Mahatma Gandhi. Edited with an introduction by Thomas Merton. New York: New Directions, 1965.

Gethsemani: A Life of Praise. A book of photographs with text by Thomas Merton. Trappist, Ky: Gethsemani Abbey, 1966.

Gethsemani Magnificat: Centenary of Gethsemani Abbey. Trappist, Ky.: Gethsemani Abbey, 1949.

Hagia Sophia. Lexington, Ky.: Stamperia del Santuccio, 1962.

Introductions East and West: The Foreign Prefaces of Thomas Merton. Edited by Robert E. Daggy. Greensboro, N.C.: Unicorn Press, 1981.

Introduction to *God Is My Life: The Story of Our Lady of Gethsemani.* Photographs by Shirley Burden. New York: Reynal, 1960.

Mystics and Zen Masters. New York: Farrar, Straus and Giroux, 1967.

"The Neurotic Personality in the Monastic Life." First published in *The Merton Annual,* vol. 4, 3–19. New York: AMS Press, 1991.

New Seeds of Contemplation. New York: New Directions, 1961.

Passion for Peace: The Social Essays. Edited by William H. Shannon. New York: Crossroad, 1995.

Peace in the Post-Christian Era. Edited and with an introduction by Patricia Burton. Foreword by Jim Forest. Maryknoll, N.Y.: Orbis, 2004.

Raids on the Unspeakable. New York: New Directions, 1966.
The Sign of Jonas. New York: Harcourt, Brace, 1953.
The Way of Chuang Tzu. New York: New Directions, 1965.
The Wisdom of the Desert: Sayings from the Desert Fathers of the Fourth Century. New York: New Directions, 1960.
Zen and the Birds of Appetite. New York: New Directions, 1968.

II. Books and Articles about Merton and his Context

Abe, Masao. *A Zen Life: D. T. Suzuki Remembered*. New York: Weatherhill, 1986.
Adam, Karl. *The Christ of Faith*. New York: Pantheon, 1957.
Aprile, Dianne. *The Abbey of Gethsemani: Place of Peace and Paradox*. Louisville, Ky.: Trout Lily Press, 1998.
Bamberger, John Eudes. "Merton's Vocation as Monastic and Writer." Interview by Victor A. Kramer. Edited by Dewey Weiss Kramer. In *The Merton Annual* 4:21–38. New York: AMS Press, 1991.
———. *Thomas Merton: Prophet of Renewal*. With a foreword by Jonathan Montaldo. Collegeville, Minn.: Liturgical Press, 2008.
Barakat, Robert. *Cistercian Sign Language*. Kalamazoo, Mich.: Cistercian Publications, 1975.
Bell, David N. *Understanding Rancé: The Spirituality of the Abbot of La Trappe in Context*. Kalamazoo, Mich: Cistercian Publications, 2005.
Berrigan, Daniel. *Portraits of Those I Love*. New York: Crossroad, 1982.
Bochen, Christine M. "Merton's 'Absurd Enterprise': A Brief Foray into Script-Writing." *Merton Seasonal* 38, no. 1 (Spring 2013): 3–14.
Buber, Martin. *I and Thou*. Translated by Ronald Gregor Smith. New York: Scribner's, 1958.
Burton, Patricia A. *More Than Silence: A Bibliography of Thomas Merton*. Lanham, Md.: American Theological Library Association, 2008.
Cardenal, Ernesto. *Vida Perdida: Memorias I*. Madrid: Trotta, 2005.
Conner, James. "'A Dedication to Prayer and a Dedication to Humanity': An Interview about Thomas Merton with James Conner,

OCSO." Conducted and edited by Paul M. Pearson. *The Merton Annual,* Vol. 23. Louisville, Ky.: Fons Vitae, 2010.

The Decree on Ecumenism of the Second Vatican Council: A New Translation by the Secretariat for Promoting Christian Unity. With a commentary by Thomas F. Stransky. New York: Paulist Press, 1965.

Elder, E. Rozanne. *The Joy of Learning and the Love of God: Studies in Honor of Jean Leclercq.* Kalamazoo, Mich.: Cistercian Publications, 1995.

———. *Praise No Less Than Charity: Studies in Honor of M. Chrysogonus Waddell, Monk of Gethsemani Abbey.* Kalamazoo, Mich.: Cistercian Publications, 2002.

Forest, Jim. *Living with Wisdom: A Life of Thomas Merton.* Revised edition. Maryknoll, N.Y.: Orbis, 1991.

Furlong, Monica. *Merton: A Biography.* New York: Harper and Row, 1980.

Gardner, Fiona. "Thomas Merton and Dr. Gregory Zilboorg: Understanding the Dynamics." *The Merton Journal* 11, no. 1 (Easter 2004), 6–12.

Greeley, Andrew. *The Catholic Revolution: New Wine, Old Wineskins, and the Second Vatican Council.* Berkeley: University of California Press, 2004.

Griffin, John Howard. *Follow the Ecstasy: Thomas Merton, the Hermitage Years, 1965–1968.* Fort Worth: Editions / Latitude Press, 1983.

———. *A Hidden Wholeness: The Visual World of Thomas Merton.* Boston: Houghton Mifflin, 1979.

Gyatso, Tenzin. *Freedom in Exile: The Autobiography of the Dalai Lama.* New York: HarperCollins, 1990.

Hart, Patrick, ed. *The Legacy of Thomas Merton.* Kalamazoo, Mich.: Cistercian Publications, 1986.

———. *The Monastic Journey.* Garden City, N.Y.: Doubleday, 1978.

———. *Thomas Merton, Monk: A Monastic Tribute.* New York: Sheed and Ward, 1974.

Kardong, Terrence G. *Benedict's Rule: A Translation and Commentary.* Collegeville, Minn.: Liturgical Press, 1996.

Lipsey, Roger. *Angelic Mistakes: The Art of Thomas Merton.* Boston: New Seeds, 2006.

———. "In the Zen Garden of the Lord: Thomas Merton's Stone Garden." In *The Merton Annual,* vol. 21, 91–105. Louisville: Fons Vitae, 2008.

———. "Merton, Suzuki, Zen, Ink: Thomas Merton's Calligraphy in Context." In *Merton and Buddhism: Wisdom, Emptiness, and Everyday Mind,* edited by Bonnie Bowman Thurston. Louisville, Ky.: Fons Vitae, 2007.

Liturgical Arts 36, no. 4 (August 1968). Articles by architect William Schickel, Thomas Merton, and Fr. Matthew Kelty on the renovated church at Gethsemani, with photographs.

Lombardi, Richard. *Towards a New World.* New York: Philosophical Publishing House, 1958.

Marchesani, Rob. "Introduction—a Hermit in Times Square: Setting the Stage." *Psychotherapy Patient* 11, nos. 3/4 (2001), 1–9.

Merton Annual, The. Multivolume annual publication. First volume was published in 1988.

Moses, John. *Divine Discontent: The Prophetic Voice of Thomas Merton.* Foreword by Rowan Williams. London: Bloomsbury, 2014.

Mott, Michael. *The Seven Mountains of Thomas Merton.* Boston: Houghton Mifflin, 1984.

Oury, Guy. *Dom Gabriel Sortais: An Amazing Abbot in Turbulent Times.* Kalamazoo, Mich.: Cistercian Publications, 2006.

Oyer, Gordon. *Pursuing the Spiritual Roots of Protest: Merton, Berrigan, Yoder, and Muste at the Gethsemani Abbey Peacemakers Retreat.* Eugene, Ore.: Cascade Books, 2014.

Rice, Edward. *The Man in the Sycamore Tree: The Good Times and Hard Life of Thomas Merton.* Garden City, N.Y.: Doubleday, 1970.

Sabbath, Linda Miroslava (aka Linda Parsons). *The Unveiling of God.* Self-published, 2010.

Scott, Mark. *At Home with Saint Benedict: Monastery Talks.* Trappist, Ky.: Cistercian Publications, 2011.

Second Vatican Council. *Decree on the Adaptation and Renewal of the Religious Life.* Vatican City, 1965.

Shannon, William H. *Silent Lamp: The Thomas Merton Story.* New York: Crossroad, 1996.

Shannon, William H., Christine M. Bochen, and Patrick F. O'Connell, eds. *The Thomas Merton Encyclopedia.* Maryknoll, N.Y.: Orbis, 2002.

Smith, Alexander. "Burnt Offerings to Prometheus: The Consultation Meetings between Thomas Merton and Gregory Zilboorg." *Psychotherapy Patient* 11, nos. 3/4 (2001), 37–54.

Talbott, Harold. "'We Don't Want the Watcher': Thomas Merton in India." *Vajradhatu Sun,* October–November 1984.

Waddell, Chrysogonus. "The Abbé de Rancé and Monastic Revival." In *The Roots of the Modern Christian Tradition,* edited by E. Rozanne Elder. Cistercian Studies Series 55, 145–81. Kalamazoo, Mich.: Cistercian Publications, 1984.

———. "The Cistercian Dimension of the Reform of La Trappe (1662–1700): Preliminary Notes and Reflections." In *Cistercians in the Late Middle Ages: Studies in Medieval Cistercian History VI,* edited by E. Rozanne Elder. Cistercian Studies Series 64. Kalamazoo, Mich.: Cistercian Publications, 1981.

Wolfe, Gregory. *The Art of William Schickel: Sacred Passion.* 2nd ed. Notre Dame, In.: University of Notre Dame Press, 2010.

Zilboorg, Gregory. *Psychoanalysis and Religion.* Edited and with an introduction by Margaret Stone Zilboorg. New York: Farrar, Straus and Cudahy, 1962.

CREDITS

Every effort has been made to contact rights holders. Sincere thanks to the Abbey of Gethsemani (Trappist, KY) and to the Thomas Merton Center, Bellarmine University (Louisville, KY), for access to their unique archival resources.

Publishers' permission has been granted to excerpt from the following volumes:

The Courage for Truth: The Letters of Thomas Merton to Writers, ed. Christine M. Bochen (New York: Farrar, Straus and Giroux, 1993).

Dancing in the Water of Life, ed. Robert E. Daggy, *The Journals of Thomas Merton*, vol. 5, *1963–1965* (San Francisco: HarperSanFrancisco, 1997).

Entering the Silence, ed. Jonathan Montaldo, *The Journals of Thomas Merton*, vol. 2, 1941–1952 (San Francisco: HarperSanFrancisco, 1997).

The Hidden Ground of Love: The Letters of Thomas Merton on Religious Experience and Social Concerns, ed. William H. Shannon (New York: Farrar, Straus and Giroux, 1985).

Learning to Love, ed. Christine M. Bochen, *The Journals of Thomas Merton*, vol. 6, *1966–1967* (San Francisco: HarperSanFrancisco, 1997).

The Other Side of the Mountain, ed. Patrick Hart, *The Journals of Thomas Merton*, vol. 7, *1967–1968* (San Francisco: HarperSanFrancisco, 1998).

The Road to Joy: The Letters of Thomas Merton to New and Old Friends, ed. Robert E. Daggy (New York: Farrar, Straus and Giroux, 1989).

The School of Charity: The Letters of Thomas Merton on Religious Renewal and Spiritual Direction, ed. Patrick Hart (New York: Farrar, Straus and Giroux, 1990).

A Search for Solitude, ed. Lawrence S. Cunningham, *The Journals of*

Thomas Merton, vol. 3, *1952–1960* (San Francisco: HarperSanFrancisco, 1997).

Turning Toward the World, ed. Victor A. Kramer, *The Journals of Thomas Merton*, vol. 4, *1960–1963* (San Francisco: HarperSanFrancisco, 1996).

Witness to Freedom: Letters in Times of Crisis, ed. William H. Shannon (San Diego: Harcourt Brace, 1994).

INDEX

Note: page numbers in **bold** indicate photographs.